PSYCHOLOGY RESEARCH PROGRESS

PSYCHOLOGY OF NEGLECT

PSYCHOLOGY RESEARCH PROGRESS

Additional books in this series can be found on Nova's website
under the Series tab.

Additional E-books in this series can be found on Nova's website
under the E-book tab.

PSYCHOLOGY RESEARCH PROGRESS

PSYCHOLOGY OF NEGLECT

YLENIA SPITERI AND
ELIZABETH M. GALEA
EDITORS

Nova Science Publishers, Inc.
New York

Copyright © 2012 by Nova Science Publishers, Inc.

NOTICE TO THE READER

The Publisher has taken reasonable care in the preparation of this book, but makes no expressed or implied warranty of any kind and assumes no responsibility for any errors or omissions. No liability is assumed for incidental or consequential damages in connection with or arising out of information contained in this book. The Publisher shall not be liable for any special, consequential, or exemplary damages resulting, in whole or in part, from the readers' use of, or reliance upon, this material. Any parts of this book based on government reports are so indicated and copyright is claimed for those parts to the extent applicable to compilations of such works.

Independent verification should be sought for any data, advice or recommendations contained in this book. In addition, no responsibility is assumed by the publisher for any injury and/or damage to persons or property arising from any methods, products, instructions, ideas or otherwise contained in this publication.

This publication is designed to provide accurate and authoritative information with regard to the subject matter covered herein. It is sold with the clear understanding that the Publisher is not engaged in rendering legal or any other professional services. If legal or any other expert assistance is required, the services of a competent person should be sought. FROM A DECLARATION OF PARTICIPANTS JOINTLY ADOPTED BY A COMMITTEE OF THE AMERICAN BAR ASSOCIATION AND A COMMITTEE OF PUBLISHERS.

Additional color graphics may be available in the e-book version of this book.

LIBRARY OF CONGRESS CATALOGING-IN-PUBLICATION DATA

Psychology of neglect / editors, Ylenia Spiteri and Elizabeth M. Galea.
p. cm.
Includes index.
ISBN 978-1-62100-180-5 (hardcover)
1. Child abuse. 2. Abused children. 3. Families. I. Spiteri, Ylenia. II. Galea, Elizabeth M.
HV6626.5.P79 2012
361.7601'9--dc23
    2011032369

Published by Nova Science Publishers, Inc. + New York

CONTENTS

PREFACE

Neglect is a syndrome in which patients fail to attend to or respond to contralesional stimuli or events. Neglect has traditionally been considered a disorder of spatial attention. This book discusses various topics on neglect including neglect as a disorder of representational updating; trauma of sexual abuse and the family; the relationship between neglect and other childhood adversities; dietary neglect and its influence on feeding; landmark recognition and mental route navigation disorders in patients with imagery neglect and perceptual neglect; the exploration of unilateral spatial neglect through the phenomenon of mirror agnosia and the psychobiological consequences of emotional neglect.

Chapter 1 - Neglect – a syndrome in which patients fail to attend to or respond to contralesional stimuli or events – has traditionally been considered a disorder of spatial attention. Spatial attention is disproportionately focused on ipsilesional stimuli and patients struggle to efficiently reorient attention to contralesional space. More recent models of neglect have broadened the scope to suggest that problems in remapping space may better characterise the observed deficits. In addition, work over the past twenty years has broadened the authors' understanding of neglect by bringing to light many non-spatial deficits including poor sustained attention, impaired allocation of attention over time and disrupted perception of time. However, these latter deficits are generally considered to merely exacerbate the cardinal symptoms of the syndrome – i.e., the impairments of spatial attention. The authors propose the novel hypothesis that the core component of the neglect syndrome is a deficit of representational updating. That is, a disorder of the ability to develop, use, maintain and update the mental models of the external world that all humans use to guide their behaviour and expectations. After introducing the basic clinical features of the neglect syndrome the authors will show how deficits in motor imagery, spatial reorienting and remapping, spatial working memory, temporal perception and decision making can be unified by reference to an inability of patients with neglect to efficiently update mental models of the external world. The authors hypothesise that the neglect syndrome results from a combination of disturbed representational updating and pathological ipsilesional attentional biases. This combination results in an inability to consciously represent contralesional space or to overcome this inability through practice and experience.

Chapter 2 – The authors research investigated the difference in functioning within families of sexually abused children and families with no sexual abuse experience. The authors did not focus, however, on the fact whether the person was sexually abused within the family or outside of it. The authors used FOS (Family-of-Origin) scale by Hovestadt, Anderson, Piercy, Cochran and Fine (1985) to measure the degree of healthy functioning in the family. 339 people completed the questionnaire (M = 22.5 years, SD = 3.5), 202 girls and 137 boys. 17 % of participants have experienced sexual abuse, which is approximately one in five girls (5.2) and one in seven boys (6.8). 78 % of all sexually abused participants in the authors survey were girls and 22 % were boys. The families of sexually abused participants show statistically significant differences in the way of functioning when compared to families with no experience in sexual child abuse.

Chapter 3 - Experiences of neglect typically create a threat to a child's health and well-being. On the one hand, neglectful parents show a lack of interest in relation to material care (e.g. feeding, clothing, cleanliness, hunger), friendships, school work and career prospects of their children; on the other hand, they fail to meet the emotional needs of their children, being unsuccessful in providing a secure base for the development of competent social behaviours. For these reasons, neglect can play a critical role in the origins of psychological maladjustment and in the early onset of psychiatric disorders. In the present study, the Childhood Experience of Care and Abuse interview (CECA; Bifulco, Brown, & Harris, 1994) was administered to 100 Italian non-clinical respondents, aged from 19 to 50, in order to assess how neglect combines with other childhood adversities in generating a fertile ground where psychological risk grows and produces poisoned fruits. Results of the study show that severe experiences of neglect were always associated with other types of maltreatment and failures of care. Adults who were neglected during their childhood were exposed to a number of other adversities, including prolonged separation from mother, financial problems, parental discord and violence, and less involvement with peers. Neglected individuals also experienced more hostility and coldness from their parents, were more likely to be physically abused, were more often left alone without supervision, and had responsibilities of running the household and caring for the emotional and material needs of parents and siblings. A discriminant analysis showed that severe experiences of neglect (those rated at 'marked' or 'moderate' levels in the CECA) were predicted by family discord, role reversal/parentification by mother, and a prolonged separation (more than 12 months) from her, leading to 95% of cases correctly classified. The present findings are consistent with the research literature, underlining that childhood neglect merges with other parental abuses and failures of care, leading to a condition of psychological risk in the child. Results also show the possibility for early detection –and, in the most fortunate cases, even a prevention– of such a risk. This is crucial for avoiding the negative effects of neglect on the development of personality and behaviour.

Chapter 4 - Both humans and other mammals possess an innate ability to detect dietary deficiencies that operates at a subconscious level. This is accomplished by alterations in specific sensitivities of the taste bud. Thus, the sensitivity of the mammalian taste system displays a degree of plasticity based on short term nutritional requirements. Deficiency in a particular substance may lead to a perceived increase in palatability of this substance, providing an additional drive to redress this nutritional imbalance through modification of intake. This alteration occurs not only in the brain, but before any higher level processing has occurred, in the taste buds themselves. Many studies, both psychophysical and physiological have detailed this phenomenon. This becomes particularly relevant in cases of neglect, where systemized patterns stereotypical of dietary deficiency are ingrained. The same phenomenon can present itself in something as mundane as the reduced desire of diabetics to consume salty foods, which would exacerbate problems caused by water retention in diabetes mellitus, or as extreme as geophagy, where subjects, particularly small children, will seek the nutrients denied them by eating dirt or clay. Subjects suffering from eating disorders, or denied nutrients due to neglect will experience an alteration in the hedonics of particular taste qualities, symptoms of their neglect, but often holding clues to the source of this neglect. Even a subject's mood, of course drastically altered in cases of neglect, can affect psychophysical taste sensitivity. A review of recent thinking is offered, along with some original results.

Chapter 5 - The complex relationship between perceptual neglect and imagery neglect is still not completely understand because, at least in part, these disorders depend on are associated with, different neural systems and can be dissociated even in the same patient (Beschin, Basso, & Della Sala, 2000).

Recent studies show that imagery neglect affects specific mechanisms underlying human orientation. In particular, it impairs the ability to manipulate mental representations of the environment and thus prevents the use of previous navigational experience (see for instance Guariglia et al., 2005; Piccardi, 2009; Guariglia & Piccardi, 2010).

In this study, the authors compared the route learning and delayed recall task performance of imagery neglect patients with pure perceptual neglect patients, patients with no neglect and healthy participants.

They had to learn a circular pathway in an unexplored area of the hospital; it included 13 landmarks and five turning points (three on the right and two on the left). During the learning phase, the participants explored the pathway three times with the examiner, who pointed out the landmarks. At the end of this phase, the participants performed two different tasks: a) Landmark Recognition Task and b) Navigational Questions. The first task included 26 pictures of landmarks (13 target pictures and 13 fillers) located along the pathway that the participants had to recognize. Fillers were the same type of stimuli as the target, but with different characteristics (e.g., two different doors). The second, delayed recall task consisted of 30 questions investigating the participants' ability to recall a learned pathway and the landmarks encountered along the way.

The authors assessed 23 right brain-damaged patients (4 patients with pure perceptual neglect, 8 patients with imagery neglect and 11 patients without neglect) and 17 healthy participants matched for age and education.

Our results showed that only patients with imagery neglect had a pervasive disorder in recognizing landmarks met along the route and in mentally navigating the previously learned pathway. Specifically, they were unable to answer navigational questions investigating their mental representation of the pathway. Differently, perceptual neglect patients were able to recognize landmarks as well as answer navigational questions in spite of their exploration disorder. Right brain-damaged patients without neglect showed no deficit on the tasks.

In summary, only the imagery neglect patients were unable to build or retrieve a mental representation of the new environment and, thus, failed in performing these tasks. In fact, results showed they were deficient in using a cognitive map of the environment. It is still unknown whether the deficit observed in imagery neglect patients is due to difficulty in building a mental map, recalling it from memory or using it during navigation, leaving unknown the exact point in which the navigational process is compromised.

Chapter 6 - Unilateral spatial neglect (USN) is a syndrome that manifests differently in every patient. One of the symptoms of neglect is mirror agnosia, where patients who are asked to grasp an object placed in their neglected field but viewed through a mirror placed on their ipsilesional side cannot grasp it and instead try to grasp the mirror image, despite knowing they are using a mirror. To examine how patients with USN neglect space, by researching mirror agnosia specifically, this study investigated the presence of mirror agnosia in patients with USN and the associated clinical characteristics, as well as the effectiveness of a single-session intervention using a mirror for mirror agnosia and neglect. The results indicated that 6 of 13 patients with USN had mirror agnosia. These 6 patients were characterized by more widespread brain damage and the complication of anosognosia. In 4 of the 6 patients, treatment using a mirror immediately improved the symptom of mirror agnosia as well as their results on the line cancellation test. Patient responses to the mirror suggest the possibility that the difference between USN with and without mirror agnosia is associated with a deficit of distinguishing between mirror space and real space. The findings suggest that the appearance of USN is influenced by multiple factors, namely, ipsilesional spatial attentional bias, a representational deficit, and illusion.

Chapter 7 - Emotional neglect (EN) can be understood as a failure to give children an emotional environment that allows adequate psychological and physical development. EN is known to affect psychobiological states via a complex matrix of behavioral, emotional, and cognitive factors. It also elevates the risk of psychiatric and medical diseases in the future. There is a growing evidence of its short-term and long lasting effects in the developing brain of children and adolescents. However, psychobiological variations observed in individuals exposed to EN may be explained through complex interactions between genetic, epigenetic, and environmental factors. In this review, the authors comprehensively outline the topics currently involved in the psychobiological research of EN. Results of recent neurobiological studies of subjects that have been exposed to EN are reviewed and provide a basis for a better comprehension of the putative immediate and enduring psychobiological consequences of EN.

Chapter 8 - *Background.* The consequences of child neglect are still too often played down. It is important to intervene at an early stage, approaching families at home through means adapted to community-level action.

Interventions by health and social professionals face several hurdles: (1) the difficulty for front-line health and social professionals to make a diagnosis; (2) the difficulty of entering into a dialog with possible beneficiaries of the interventions owing to distrust; and (3) the difficulty of assessing the outcome of the interventions.

In order to answer the need for the medium-term assessment of the authors intervention programs in the field of neglect and attachment disorders, the authors multidisciplinary team (psychologists, a general practitioner, an anthropologist and an educationalist) designed a tool aimed at supporting the observation of challenging indicators by parents and intervening parties in a given educational situation.

Method. The MASPIN tool (Method for Analysis of Situations and Project on Individual cases of Neglect) was designed on the basis of a review of existing literature on assessment tools for actions in the field concerning parental disorders, focusing on children up to three years old. Field professionals were involved in the design process in order to make sure that the tool matched their daily practice.

Results. The tool allows a six-fold assessment of: interactions between parents and child, parental skills, acknowledgement by parents of their difficulties or responsibilities, environmental factors, how the family experienced the intervention, and the intervening party's experience.

Discussion and Conclusion. The MASPIN tool could foster the development of a common knowledge and culture regarding intervention on neglect. The authors' limited use unveiled unexpected potential. It makes for interesting prospects in structuring the dialog between front-line professionals (medics, nurses and social workers) and experts. Moreover, it helps to ease the dialog between intervening parties and parents, clearly identifying existing parental skills and specific issues that might call for educational assistance.

Chapter 9 - According to Sir Francis Bacon (1620), insensitivity to missing information is the single most important source of bias and error in human judgment and choice. Recently, extensive research on omission neglect has supported Bacon's keen observation. Omission neglect refers to insensitivity to missing or unknown attributes, features, properties, qualities, alternatives, options, cues, stimuli, or possibilities. Insensitivity to omissions occurs for several reasons: Omissions are typically not salient, singular judgment tasks frequently mask omissions, presented information can inhibit consideration of omissions, and people often anchor on the implications of presented information and adjust insufficiently for the implications of omissions.

Omission neglect influences all stages of information processing -- including perception (change blindness, errors of omission and self-assessment, attributions for inactions), learning (feature-positive effect, insensitivity to cause-absent and effect-absent cells in covariation estimation), evaluation (absence of between-subjects set-size effects, presence of within-subject set-size effects, overweighing presented attributes), persuasion (cross-category set-size effect, tip-of-the-iceberg effect, insensitivity to non-gains, non-losses, and hidden fees), and decision making (omission neglect contributes to overconfidence, intransitive preference, the Ellsberg paradox, and subadditivity). Increasing sensitivity to omissions is often a useful debiasing technique for improving a wide variety of judgments and decisions.

In everyday life, people typically receive limited information about just about everything -- including political candidates, public policies, job applicants, defendants, potential dating partners, business deals, consumer goods and services, healthcare products, medical procedures, and other important topics. News reports, advertisements, group meetings, conversations, and other sources of information typically provide only limited information. When people overlook important missing information, even a little presented information can seem like a lot. Ideally, people should form stronger beliefs when a large amount of relevant information is available than when only a small amount is available. However, when people are insensitive to omissions, they form strong beliefs regardless of how little is known about a topic. Furthermore, in rare instances in which a large amount of information is available, forgetting occurs over time and insensitivity to information loss from memory, another type of omission, leads people to form beliefs that increase in strength over time.

Chapter 10 - Evidence from the studies available regarding to the nature of neglect dyslexia and neglect dysgraphia remains contradictory. The authors asked the Japanese left neglect dyslexics to read kana (phonograms) words and kanji (ideograms) words. The results showed that neglect errors typically involved omission. Some patients with enough errors had a tendency that longer words were more susceptible to errors than short words. And the patients continued to misread the letters on the left end when asked to read words written from right to left. The authors also describe a 73-year-old woman who experienced a writing deficit in the right-sided component of kanji letters. The authors concluded that unilaterally disrupted processing of internal representations affected the writing of Kanji letters in this patient.

In: Psychology of Neglect
Editors: Y. Spiteri, E. Galea, 1-28
ISBN 978-1-62100-180-5
© 2012 Nova Science Publishers, Inc.

Chapter 1

NEGLECT AS A DISORDER OF REPRESENTATIONAL UPDATING

James Danckert[a,b]*, Elisabeth Stöttinger[a] and Britt Anderson[a,b]
[a]Department of Psychology
[b]Centre for Theoretical Neuroscience

ABSTRACT

Neglect – a syndrome in which patients fail to attend to or respond to contralesional stimuli or events – has traditionally been considered a disorder of spatial attention. Spatial attention is disproportionately focused on ipsilesional stimuli and patients struggle to efficiently reorient attention to contralesional space. More recent models of neglect have broadened the scope to suggest that problems in remapping space may better characterise the observed deficits. In addition, work over the past twenty years has broadened our understanding of neglect by bringing to

*
Correspondence should be addressed to:
Dr. James Danckert
Department of Psychology
University of Waterloo
200 University Avenue West
Waterloo, Ontario, CANADA, N2L 3G1
Ph: 1 519 888 4567 ext. 37014
Fax: 1 519 746 8631
Email: jdancker@uwaterloo.ca

light many non-spatial deficits including poor sustained attention, impaired allocation of attention over time and disrupted perception of time. However, these latter deficits are generally considered to merely exacerbate the cardinal symptoms of the syndrome – i.e., the impairments of spatial attention. We propose the novel hypothesis that the core component of the neglect syndrome is a deficit of representational updating. That is, a disorder of the ability to develop, use, maintain and update the mental models of the external world that all humans use to guide their behaviour and expectations. After introducing the basic clinical features of the neglect syndrome we will show how deficits in motor imagery, spatial reorienting and remapping, spatial working memory, temporal perception and decision making can be unified by reference to an inability of patients with neglect to efficiently update mental models of the external world. We hypothesise that the neglect syndrome results from a combination of disturbed representational updating and pathological ipsilesional attentional biases. This combination results in an inability to consciously represent contralesional space or to overcome this inability through practice and experience.

Keywords: Neglect, Mental Models, Spatial Attention

1. SPATIAL DEFICITS – THE CARDINAL SYMPTOM OF THE NEGLECT SYNDROME

Lesions affecting the right inferior parietal or superior temporal cortex often lead to the syndrome of neglect in which the patient behaves as if the left side of space has ceased to exist (Halligan et al., 2003; Heilman et al., 1993; Mesulam, 1981). The patient may fail to dress or groom the left side of their body, fail to eat food on the left side of their plate and generally fail to respond or attend to events occurring on the left side of space. The syndrome is also evident for neglect of right space following left parietal lesions, however this presentation is far less common, the symptoms are less severe and tend to resolve more completely than they do following right cortical lesions (Albert, 1973; Bowen et al., 1999; Ogden, 1985; Ringman et al., 2004). On bedside clinical tests neglect patients will fail to cancel targets on the left half of a page, will omit left-sided details of figures they are asked to copy and when asked to bisect a horizontal line will place their mark to the right of true centre (Danckert & Ferber, 2006; Halligan et al., 2003; Figure 1).

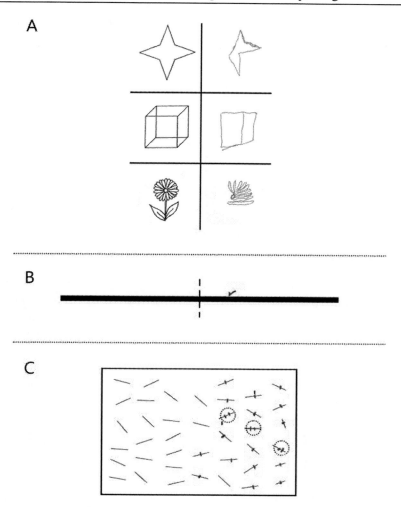

Figure 1. Representative behaviours of neglect patients on clinical tests of the disorder.
Panel A. Figure copying task – the patient is asked to copy the model shapes presented
on the left. In this case clear neglect of the left half of each object is seen. Panel B.
Line bisection – the patient must place a mark (indicated here by the red mark) where
they think the centre of a horizontal line is (true centre is indicated by the dashed line).
Here the patient marks the line well to the right of true centre. Panel C. Albert's Lines –
a typical cancellation task in which the patient must place a mark through all the lines
on the page. The patient in this instance fails to cancel many of the targets on the left
of the page. The dotted circles indicate revisiting behaviour in which the patient
cancels a target more than once, treating an 'old' target as if it were 'new'.

Although the syndrome was initially described more than 60 years ago (Brain, 1941; Patterson & Zangwill, 1944; see Mattingley, 1996 for review), conclusive neurological models of the disorder have yet to be developed. This may in part be due to the vast heterogeneity of symptom profiles that are in turn a consequence of the size and variability of naturally occurring lesions in humans (see Adair & Barret, 2008; Danckert & Ferber, 2006; Kerkhoff, 2001 for recent reviews).

Early models of the neglect syndrome, and many since, emphasised the spatial nature of the disorder (e.g., Posner et al., 1984, 1987; Driver & Mattingley, 1998). Furthermore, the predominance of neglect following right hemisphere lesions suggests that the right hemisphere is specialised for controlling spatial attention (Corbetta & Shulman, 2002; Corbetta et al., 2002; Kinsbourne, 1970, 1993; Mesulam, 1981). The notion is that the right hemisphere directs attention towards both left and right hemispace, whereas the left hemisphere only directs attention contralaterally towards right space (Corbetta & Shulman, 2002; Kinsbourne, 1993). Within this framework, a lesion to the left hemisphere is less consequential for mechanisms of spatial attention as the right hemisphere is able to compensate for any loss of attentional control in right space. In contrast, lesions of the right hemisphere dramatically impair the ability to control spatial attention as the unaffected left hemisphere orients attention to only right space. Models of the neglect syndrome that focus solely on the deficits of spatially directed attention suggest that there are two main components to the disorder: first, a bias towards orienting to stimuli and events in right space and second, a difficulty in shifting or reorienting attention towards events in left space – the so-called 'disengage deficit' (Posner et al., 1984).

In keeping with a rightward orientation bias, neglect patients demonstrate strong perceptual biases such that they preferentially respond to or report stimuli and events occurring in right space. For example, Mattingley and colleagues (1994) showed neglect patients two horizontally arranged rectangles that gradually changed in intensity from light-to-dark (the so-called 'greyscales' images). One of the rectangles was darkest at the left end and the other was darkest at the right. When patients were then asked to indicate which of two greyscales appeared to be 'darkest', they consistently choose the rectangle with the dark end in right space (healthy controls show the opposite bias; Mattingley, et al., 1994). Similarly, when presented with two chimaeric faces (faces smiling on one half and showing a neutral emotion on the other) one above the other and asked which appears to be 'happier', neglect patients will choose the face shown to be smiling on the right, whereas healthy controls consistently choose the face that is smiling on the left (Mattingley et al., 1994; Heller & Levy, 1981; Levy et al., 1983). Such biases are not restricted to faces. For example, research has demonstrated that numbers can be represented in a spatial manner with smaller numbers occupying left space and larger numbers occupying right space – the so-called mental number line (Dehaene, 2003; Umiltà et al., 2009). Neglect patients demonstrate spatial biases in their mental number line such that they misjudge the midpoint of a numerical interval to be to the right (e.g., indicating that 5 is the midpoint of an interval between 2 and 6; Zorzi et al., 2002, 2006). In some circumstances, the rightward attentional biases of neglect patients can even lead to absolutely faster responses compared with healthy controls, such that manual and saccadic reaction time benefits are observed for neglect patients for targets appearing in restricted regions of right space (Behrmann et al., 2002; De Renzi et al., 1989; Natale et al., 2007). These and other orienting biases, that are consistently in opposition to those seen in healthy individuals, indicate an attentional bias towards right space.

The second attentional deficit traditionally invoked to explain the neglect syndrome involves a difficulty in *reorienting* attention to events in contralesional space, particularly after attention has first been attracted to ipsilesional space. Posner and colleagues (1984) used a covert orienting task in which individuals fixate centrally while detecting targets that appear in the periphery. Targets can be preceded by a cue at the same location (i.e., a valid trial) or they may appear at a location opposite that of the cue (i.e., an invalid target). Typically, reaction times are faster to validly cued vs. invalidly cued targets. In healthy individuals this reaction time advantage for validly cued targets is generally equivalent for targets appearing in left or right space (Posner, 1980). In contrast, following parietal injury patients are slower to respond to targets presented in contralesional space when they are preceded by a cue in ipsilesional space – the so-called disengage deficit (Posner et al., 1984; Figure 2).

Disengage Deficit in Neglect

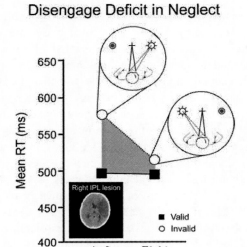

Data adapted from one of the patients tested in Striemer & Danckert, 2007.

Figure 2. Schematic representation of the disengage deficit shown here in one neglect patient. In the covert orienting task the patient is cued to the left or right landmark with a target (indicated in the schematic by a filled red circle) appearing either at the cue (valid trials indicated by filled squares) or at the opposite location (invalid trials indicated by open circles). Reaction time advantages are typically seen for valid over invalid trials. When a patient with neglect arising from a right parietal lesion is first cued to ipsilesional, right space, he is disproportionately slower to disengage attention from the cue and reorient to left space (i.e., on invalid trials).

For example, for a patient with right parietal damage, when attention is first drawn to a stimulus in right space the patient will be disproportionately slow to respond to a subsequent target appearing in left space relative to the opposite circumstance (i.e., a cue in left space followed by a target in right space; Figure 2). This disengage deficit is evident following either left or right parietal lesions, however, the deficit is more pronounced following right parietal injury (Bartolomeo & Chokron, 2002; Losier & Klein, 2001; Posner et al., 1984; Figure 2). When coupled with the strong rightward orienting bias discussed above, this deficit in *reorienting* attention towards left space makes it difficult for neglect patients to attend to and consciously represent stimuli or events in left space.

2. NON-SPATIAL DEFICITS IN NEGLECT

Research of the past two decades has substantially broadened our understanding of the full spectrum of impairments evident in neglect, which has led to the suggestion that deficits in non-spatial domains also form a core feature of the syndrome. For example, sustained, non-spatial attention is impaired in neglect (Barrett et al., 2006; Robertson, 2001; Robertson et al., 1995, 1997; see also O'Connell et al., 2008). These deficits correlate with neglect severity and may reflect impaired tonic arousal levels due to disruption of the reticular activating system and its connections with right fronto-parietal attention systems (Robertson, et al., 1995). This has led to the suggestion that poor sustained attention in neglect acts to exacerbate the spatial symptoms of the disorder (Husain & Nachev, 2007; Husain & Rorden, 2003; Robertson, 2001). In other words, there is a positive relationship between the spatial deficits in neglect and concomitant deficits in sustained attention. In addition, providing patients with brief *phasic* alerting cues – for example, loud auditory tones or even barking loud commands at the patient to 'look left' – temporarily improves some of the spatial symptoms of the disorder (Robertson et al., 1995, 1997; Robertson, 2001).

Neglects patients also demonstrate deficits in the allocation of attention over time (Husain et al., 1997). When presented with a rapid stream of alphanumeric stimuli (i.e., rapid serial visual presentation; RSVP) in which two targets are embedded for discrimination, performance for identifying the second target diminishes when it is presented close in time to the first target – the so-called 'attentional blink' (Chun & Potter, 1995; Raymond et al., 1992). Husain and colleagues (1997) showed that the attentional blink was almost three times longer in neglect patients when contrasted with healthy controls. That is, once attentional resources had been allocated to target one it took the neglect patients around 1200 msec before they were able to accurately identify target two. The same refractory period in controls was closer to 400 msec (Husain et al., 1997). However, an increased attentional blink has been demonstrated in patients with lesions of the left or right superior temporal gyrus (Shapiro et al., 2002), frontal cortex (Rizzo et al., 2001) and even the cerebellum (Schweizer et al., 2007) in patients not demonstrating neglect. Since impaired allocation of attention over time is not unique to the neglect syndrome and may reflect long-term changes to tonic arousal levels as a consequence of any neural insult, this deficit is usually considered to exacerbate the cardinal spatial symptoms of neglect (Husain & Rorden, 2003).

Table 1. Summary of studies exploring the anatomical basis of neglect

Reference	# Patients	Method	Critical region associated with neglect
Buxbaum et al., 2004	166 (80 neglect, 42 acute, 38 chronic)	CT/MRI	Acute = BG, inf/mesial temp Chronic = cingulate, OFC, IPL, IT, inf/mesial temp, occ, sup/mid temp
Chechlacz et al., 2010	41 (21 RH patients; 19 left neglect, 4 right neglect)	DTI, VLSM	IPS, TPJ, SLF, ILF, SFOF, IFOF, thalamic radiation, corona radiata Allocentric neglect = pSTS, AG, mid temp, mid occ Egocentric neglect = mid front, PCG, STG, SMG
Karnath et al., 2001	33 neglect patients (25 w/o field cuts)	MRI, VLSM	STG, ventral PCG, parietal operculum
Karnath et al., 2004, 2009	140 RH (78 neglect)	MRI, VLSM	STG, insula, putamen, caudate, SLF, IFOF, SFOF,
Karnath et al., 2011	54 (24 neglect; 8 chronic, 16 recovered)	MRI, VLSM	STG, MTG, BG, IFOF, extreme capsule + uncinate fasiculus in chronic patients
Mort et al., 2003	35 (24 MCA/14 neglect; 11 PCA/5 neglect)	MRI	MCA = AG, STG in 50% PCA = Parahippocampal
Urbanski et al., 2008	4 (2 neglect)	DTI	IPL, IFOF

Urbanski et al., 2011	12 (6 neglect)	DTI	Perisylvian w.m., ant. limb of IC, w.m. underlying IFG (ant. segment of arcuate fasciculus)
Vallar & Perani, 1986	110 (47 neglect, 29 severe neglect)	CT	IPL, thalamus, BG
Verdon et al., 2010	80 (55 neglect, 16 severe neglect)	MRI, VLSM	Visuospatial neglect = IPL Motor neglect = DLPFC Allocentric neglect = parahippocampal gyrus

CT=computerised tomography; MRI=magnetic resonance imaging; DTI=diffusion tensor imaging; VLSM=voxel-wise lesion symptom mapping; BG=basal ganglia; OFC=orbitofrontal cortex; IPL=inferior parietal lobule; IT=inferotemporal; IPS=intraparietal sulcus; TPJ=temporo-parietal junction; SLF=superior longitudinal fasiculus; ILF=inferior longitudinal fasiculus; SFOF=superior frontal-occipital fasiculus; IFOF=inferior frontal-occipital fasiculus; STS=superior temporal sulcus; AG=angula gyrus; PCG=precentral gyrus; STG=superior temporal gyrus; SMG=supramarginal gyrus; MCA=middle cerebral artery; PCA=posterior cerebral artery territory; IFG=inferior frontal gyrus; MFG=middle frontal gyrus; IC=internal capsule; DLPFC=dorsolateral prefrontal cortex; inf=inferior; sup=superior; occ=occipital; temp=temporal; front=frontal; par=parietal; mid=middle; ant=anterior; w.m.=white matter.

3. ANATOMY OF NEGLECT – EXPLAINING THE HETEROGENEITY OF SYMPTOM PROFILES

There has been some controversy over the past decade regarding the critical lesion site for demonstrating the neglect syndrome (Karnath et al., 2001; Mort et al., 2003). Vallar and Perani (1986), using CT scans, initially claimed that the inferior parietal cortex was the most commonly lesioned region of cortex in the patients they tested, with white matter pathways playing little to no role in the presentation of the syndrome. More recently, studies making use of more detailed MRI scans and more sophisticated statistical techniques have variously claimed that the superior temporal gyrus (STG) or the angular gyrus of the inferior parietal lobule (IPL) represent the critical cortical lesion site for neglect (Karnath et al., 2001; Mort et al., 2003; Table 1).

The differences evident in these studies may in part be due to different selection criteria for inclusion in the neglect group, including differences in the tests used to demonstrate neglect and the presence or absence of concomitant hemianopias. In addition, further studies have highlighted distinct regions of cortical involvement depending on specific symptom profiles (Buxbaum et al., 2004; Chechlacz et al., 2010; Verdon et al., 2010; Table). Despite this heterogeneity, the regions most commonly highlighted as being involved in neglect (i.e., portions of the IPL, the temporo-parietal junction (TPJ) or the STG) represent association cortices that are heavily connected with the rest of the brain.

Many of the studies exploring the anatomical basis of neglect also highlight the involvement of subcortical structures including the thalamus, caudate and putamen, or deep cortical structures such as the insula (Table 1). In addition, the consistent involvement of white matter pathways in neglect has led some to suggest that neglect is best characterised as a disconnection syndrome (Bartolomeo et al., 2007; Doricchi et al., 2008). In other words, deficits arising from loss of function in any one single cortical region may not be sufficient to explain the syndrome. What may be more critical, both in terms of the presence or absence of neglect and the particular symptom profile presented, are the involvement of long range white matter fibre pathways connecting frontal and parietal cortices (Bird et al., 2006; Doricchi et al., 2003; Thiebaut de Schotten et al., 2005; Urbanski et al., 2008, 2011). The picture may be even more complicated as pathways connecting frontal and parietal regions with the subcortical structures shown to be commonly involved in neglect are also likely to be critical in determining the nature and severity of the syndrome. The challenge ahead for developing a more comprehensive model of the neglect syndrome lies in associating specific symptoms (or functions in the healthy brain) with particular brain regions/pathways injured in neglect. This work has begun in earnest over the past decade (Table 1) and may hold the key to explaining what is a heterogeneous disorder.

4. IMPAIRED MENTAL MODEL BUILDING: NEGLECT AS A DISORDER OF REPRESENTATIONAL UPDATING

The symptoms described above are commonly observed in neglect, but they do not give a complete picture of the functional impairments that neglect patients demonstrate. Also, disorders of spatial and sustained attention (Sections 1 and 2) are inadequate for explaining the resistance of some neglect patients to improve with attentional training or attentional manipulations (see Striemer & Danckert, 2010).

Mental models of the environment serve a multitude of functions including inferring the intentions of others (i.e., theory of mind; Aboulafia-Brakha, et al., 2011), predicting the sensory consequences of our own actions (Wolpert et al., 1998a, b), and the learning of new skills based on prior experiences (Tenenbaum et al., 2011). Below we review a range of deficits demonstrated in patients with neglect that can be characterised as deficits in the generation or use of mental models.

4.1. Neglect as an Internal Representational Deficit

Neglect has, in at least some subgroup of patients, been considered a representational disorder (e.g., Bisiach & Luzatti, 1978). That is, rather than representing a deficit in primary sensory or motor processes, neglect has been characterised as an inability to generate or make use of mental models of the external environment. Perhaps the most famous demonstration of a representational deficit comes from two patients examined by Bisiach and Luzatti (1978). They asked their patients to imagine standing in a famous square in Milan and to describe what they 'saw' in their mind's eye. The patients were first asked to imagine standing in the south end of the square facing north. In this instance they reported many details from the right (east) side of the square and neglected details from the left (west) side. When asked to imagine standing at the north end facing south, the patients now reported details from the previously neglected west side of the square and failed to mention details from the previously reported east side (Bisiach & Luzatti, 1978). What this demonstrates is that these patients did not have a deficit in recalling the details of the square, nor did they have any difficulty in generating an adequate image of particular details in their mind's eye. Instead, at any given point in time the patients' internal representation of the external world was impoverished and contained only the right half of space relative to an egocentric position. Subsequent research has demonstrated that the representational and perceptual components of neglect can be dissociated (Anderson, 1993).

4.2. Motor Imagery and Saccadic Remapping

The ability to imagine a motor action is constrained by the same laws that influence the execution of those actions (e.g., Fitts, 1954). That is, when asked to imagine walking different distances people take longer to imagine walking longer distances, just as they would if they were to *actually* walk those distances (Decety, et al., 1989). Imagined motor actions can be used to contrast intended actions with actual sensory outcomes; any mismatch between the two can be used to modify behaviour on-line (Blakemore et al., 1998, 2001; Jeannerod, 1997; Wolpert et al., 1998b). As such, imagined actions represent a mental model of our intended actions, sometimes referred to as an efference copy. Patients with parietal lesions (an area commonly damaged in neglect) demonstrate impaired motor imagery such that imagined movements fail to demonstrate the same speed-accuracy trade-offs that would be expected from actual movements (Sirigu et al., 1996; Danckert et al., 2002a; Figure 3).

Whereas patients with left parietal lesions demonstrate impaired motor imagery on praxic motor tasks (e.g., alternate finger-thumb touches; Sirigu et al., 1996), in one right parietal patient with neglect, we showed that *spatial* motor imagery (i.e., reciprocal pointing to targets of different sizes) was impaired. This was true when the patient imagined performing the reciprocal pointing task with either his left or right hand and when he imagined moving to the left or right (Figure 3; Danckert et al., 2002a). In other words, his deficit in spatial motor imagery was independent of which hand he imagined using, which direction he imagined moving in and whether he imagined moving in left or right space (Danckert et al., 2002). Functional neuroimaging studies of healthy individuals generally show bilateral activation of the superior parietal cortices when individuals imagine performing an action (e.g., Gerardin et al., 2000). In one such study additional activation for imagined movements was seen in the inferior parietal lobule (IPL) of the right hemisphere only (Gerardin et al., 2000; but see also Fleming et al., 2010 for bilateral IPL activations). In addition, for patients with left hemisphere lesions, imagined movements are still capable of eliciting readiness potentials in primary motor cortex (M1) in the contralesional hemisphere (Stinear et al., 2007). In contrast, patients with right hemisphere lesions show no readiness potentials in either hemisphere when imagining motor actions (Stinear et al., 2007). Taken together, this research suggests that the right parietal cortex plays a vital role in generating and making use of mental models of intended actions.

Another striking demonstration of the role played by the right parietal cortex in creating and using mental models of space comes from the double-step saccade task (Colby & Goldberg, 1999; Colby et al., 1996; Duhamel et al., 1992). In this task two successive targets for saccadic eye movements are presented and extinguished in under 200 msec. Planning saccades on the basis of retinal locations alone leads to an erroneous saccade to target two. Instead, participants must anticipate the sensory consequences of their first saccade to target one and remap a mental model of space in order to accurately acquire target two – so-called saccadic remapping (Duhamel et al., 1992). Patients with parietal lesions, and in many cases neglect, fail to acquire the second target when it appears in ipsilesional space following an initial saccade made to contralesional space (Figure 3; Duhamel et al., 1992; Heide et al., 1995). Although this deficit is evident following left or right parietal lesions it tends to be more severe for right parietal patients (Heide, et al., 1995).

The deficits in motor imagery and saccadic remapping discussed above suggest that patients with neglect fail to either generate or appropriately make use of mental models of the spatial layout of the environment. This has prompted recent suggestions that the neglect syndrome could be considered to be due to a combination of the classic deficits in spatial attention (i.e., a rightward attentional bias and a leftward disengage deficit) and impaired spatial remapping (i.e., either overtly or covertly; Pisella & Mattingley, 2004). A range of other deficits evident in neglect might suggest that the right inferior parietal cortex plays a more general role in generating or updating mental models – a role not restricted to *spatial* remapping.

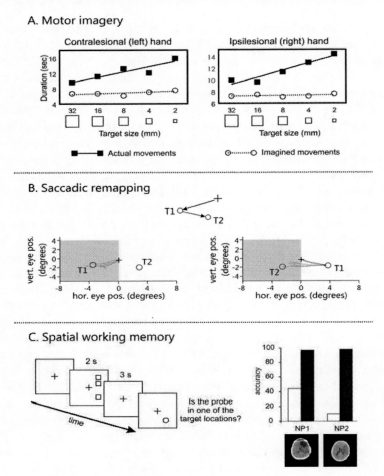

Figure 3. Data from three tasks suggestive of deficits in mental model generation or use. Panel A. Impaired motor imagery in a neglect patient. Actual movements (filled squares) show a speed-accuracy trade-off with movement time increasing as target size decreases. Imagined movements in contrast show no such relationship for either hand and for movements imagined in left or right space (not shown: data adapted from Danckert et al., 2002). Panel B. Saccadic remapping deficit in a right fronto-parietal patient with neglect adapted from Duhamel et al., 1992. When the target for the first saccade (T1) is in contralesional space the patient is unable to remap a mental model of space to accurately acquire target 2 (T2). Panel C. Performance of two of the four neglect patients tested by Ferber & Danckert (2006) on a spatial working memory task (open bars; schematic to the right) and a verbal working memory task (black bars). Note, the other two patients showed the same level of impairment.

4.3. Spatial Working Memory

Patients with neglect often demonstrate poor performance on a range of clinical tasks even for stimuli presented in central or right, presumably non-neglected space (Figure 1C). For example, patients often fail to cancel targets presented in right space indicative of a difficulty in accurately representing or acting upon the external environment even on their 'good' side. In addition, patients will often place multiple cancellation marks on a single target essentially treating an 'old' item as if it were 'new' (Figure 1C). This is especially true if the patient's cancellation marks are hidden from view, and is improved when cancelled targets are removed from the display (Parton et al., 2006; Wojciulik et al., 2001, 2004). Increased revisiting of targets when cancellation marks are invisible (Wojciulik et al., 2004) suggests that patients are unable to accurately keep track of their own behaviours in space. The same revisiting behaviour has also been observed in eye movement studies, even when patients are explicitly instructed to avoid looking at targets that they have already found (Husain et al., 2001).

These deficits are consistent with impaired spatial working memory (SWM). The clinical and experimental tasks described above that essentially examine visual search performance, are complex and multifactorial in that they typically include a large number of targets (i.e., placing a load on attentional resources), involve multiple distractor items (i.e., requiring perceptual discrimination) and span a large region of space, at least in the horizontal extent (i.e., requiring covert and overt shifts of attention and remapping processes). We and others have explored SWM in neglect patients using stimuli that avoid many of these confounds (Figure 3; Ferber & Danckert, 2006; Malhotra et al., 2004). We presented patients with three vertically aligned targets in right space, the locations of which were to be held in SWM over a short delay. Following the delay a probe was presented with the patient judging whether the probe was in one of the locations previously occupied by a target (Figure 3). In a group of four neglect patients, all performed below chance on this task, whereas their ability to maintain alphanumeric stimuli over an identical delay period was at ceiling (Figure 3; Ferber & Danckert, 2006). Similar deficits in SWM have been shown for stimuli presented in central space (Malhotra et al., 2004). Given the fact that these deficits are evident in central and right space, for relatively simple displays that involve no distractors, it is difficult to explain the impaired performance in terms of spatial attention or remapping deficits alone.

4.4. Temporal Perception

Motor imagery, saccadic remapping and SWM invoke spatiotemporal processing over distinct time scales and for different purposes. Recent research has demonstrated a range of deficits in temporal processing in patients with damage to brain regions that commonly cause neglect including the right parietal cortex (Basso et al., 1996; Battelli et al., 2003; Danckert et al., 2007; Harrington et al., 1998; see Becchio & Bertone, 2006 for review). In one neglect patient, sub-second durations were overestimated when presented in the *leftmost* positions of a display (in which targets all appeared entirely within right space) and were underestimated for the *rightmost* positions (Basso et al., 1996). Similarly, patients with right hemisphere lesions were impaired at sub-second temporal discrimination tasks, with lesion overlay analyses demonstrating two foci, one in inferior parietal cortex and the other in frontal cortex (Harrington et al., 1998). In addition, TMS of right but not left parietal cortex impairs sub-second temporal discrimination processes (Alexander et al., 2005). We recently demonstrated massive underestimation of multisecond durations in neglect patients, such that for a 60 second duration none of the eight neglect patients made estimates greater than ten seconds (Danckert et al., 2007). In another neglect patient, we found an identical magnitude of underestimation for visual, verbal and non-verbal auditory stimuli suggesting the deficit is multimodal in nature (Merrifield et al., 2010). Finally, Battelli and colleagues (2003) have shown that patients with right parietal damage fail to detect sudden onsets and offsets of visual stimuli regardless of their position in space. They posit the existence of a third visual pathway specialised for temporal processing that runs from primary visual cortex (V1) to the motion processing complex (MT+) and the temporo-parietal junction and is lateralised to the right hemisphere (Battelli et al., 2007).

Temporal deficits of the kind described above cannot explain, nor be explained by, the spatial nature of neglect. However, time represents a key component of any mental model of the environment given that the world is in a constant state of flux. If one of the primary functions of a mental model is to detect any mismatches between what the model would predict and incoming sensory data, an inability to accurately time stamp events will severely hamper the functioning of that model.

5. A GENERALISED UPDATING IMPAIRMENT IN NEGLECT

The principle challenge in developing a comprehensive theoretical model of the neglect syndrome lies in explaining the full gamut of deficits observed in neglect patients, only a handful of which have been discussed thus far (for more comprehensive reviews see Adair & Barrett, 2008; Danckert & Ferber, 2006). It is more likely to be the case that the full neglect syndrome arises as a consequence of a combination of several key impairments (Danckert & Ferber, 2006). Problems with motor imagery, spatial updating, SWM, time perception and to some extent even the cardinal deficits of spatial attention (see Druker & Anderson, 2010), could be construed to be difficulties in generating or making use of mental models of the environment and our own actions within it (Craik, 1943; Johnson-Laird, 2010).

Humans construct mental models of the world that represent learned rules and expectations regarding the manner in which the world should operate. Such models can greatly simplify the calculations needed to flexibly control our behaviour in optimal ways. Of necessity, these mental models should be updated as new information indicates a change in environmental state. This requires some kind of comparative process that can determine whether new information matches the rules and expectations of the current mental model and, when there is a mismatch, to determine whether the mental model needs to be updated or abandoned altogether. Such a comparator model has previously been invoked to describe the role of the parietal cortex in motor control and motor imagery (Wolpert et al., 1998b). For example, an efference copy of an intended action represents, in our terms, a mental model of that action. Parietal cortex compares the actual outcomes of an action with the expected outcomes generated by the efference copy (or mental model) and corrects movements when any mismatch between the actual outcomes and the model occur (Blakemore et al., 1998; Desmurget et al., 1999; Frith et al., 2000; Wolpert et al., 1998b).

Many of the deficits evident in neglect could be construed as problems in generating or making use of mental models of space and time. If the regions typically damaged in neglect patients – the inferior parietal and superior temporal cortex (Table 1) – are found to be responsible for generating and updating mental models, one would also expect to see generalised, non-spatial deficits in model creation and updating in neglect. That is, injury to these regions may be expected to impair not only updating spatial (i.e., poor motor imagery, deficits in saccadic remapping) and temporal (e.g., temporal underestimation, impaired detection of temporal changes) components of mental models.

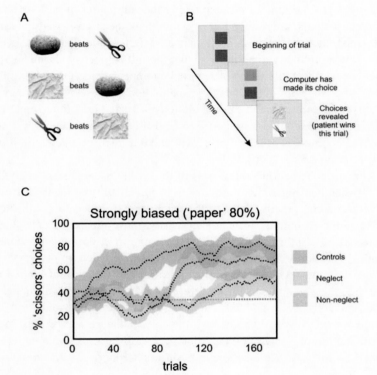

Figure 4. Panel A. Schematic representation of the rules that govern the classic children's game 'rock, paper, scissors'. Panel B. Schematic representation of a trial sequence in Danckert et al (under consideration). Two red squares are presented one above the other with the top square representing the computer's choice and the bottom representing the patient's choice. The top square turns green to indicate the computer has made its choice and once the patient makes their choice the two are revealed to indicate the result. Panel C. A moving average (n=20 trials) of 'scissors' choices under the condition in which the computer chose 'paper' on 80% of trials. Controls (grey shaded area represents SE) quickly adopt an optimal strategy to maximise their wins. Right hemisphere damaged patients without neglect (blue shaded area represents SE; n=6) take far longer to adopt an optimal strategy. Neglect patients (pink shaded area represents SE; n=7) perform worst, with 5 of the 7 patients never fully adopting an optimal strategy to maximise wins suggesting they have a poor mental model of their opponent's play strategy.

5.1. Updating Strategies within a Competitive Game

We recently investigated whether right hemisphere brain damaged patients would show a non-spatial deficit in mental model updating by having them play the classic children's game 'rock, paper, scissors' against a computer opponent (Figure 4; Danckert et al., under consideration).

In this game opponents face one another and on the count of three reveal hand gestures to indicate one of three choices. Each choice can beat and be beaten by one other (e.g., rock beats scissors, scissors beats paper and paper beats rock; Figure 4). In our version the computer first indicated that it had made a choice (a square representing the computer player changed from red to green; Figure 4) before the patient made their choice. In one condition the computer chose each of the three options on an equal number of trials. In this instance no strategy can earn a player more than 33% wins. In another condition, the computer played a biased strategy in which one of the three options was chosen on 80% of trials. The logic here was that if the patients detected the change in the opponent's play they would alter their own play strategy to maximise wins. Five of the seven neglect patients never altered their play strategy from uniform random choices (i.e., choosing each option around a third of the time), even when the computer played a strongly biased strategy (Figure 4). Two patients did eventually alter their play, but only after more than 100 trials, a history that far outstripped the controls, and they never reached the level of performance achieved by healthy controls (Figure 4).

Some brain damaged patients without neglect also failed to update their play strategy when the computer's play was strongly biased, indicating that they too had a deficit in representational updating (Danckert et al., under consideration). This is a common refrain for the deficits found in neglect. For example, disengage deficits are evident following left and right parietal lesions in patients with and without clinical signs of neglect (Posner et al., 1984). Deficits in saccadic remapping, motor imagery and the temporal allocation of attention are also evident following left or right parietal damage (Heide et al., 1995; Sirigu et al., 1996; Shapiro et al., 2002). Underestimation of time itself is also evident, although to a much less severe degree, in right hemisphere patients without neglect (Danckert et al., 2007). None of these deficits alone is sufficient for producing neglect, a conclusion that applies to deficits in updating mental models. Neglect is therefore best characterised as a constellation of impairments, and one crucial impairment is the inability to generate or update mental models of the environment across a range of different modalities and behaviours.

The precise constellation of deficits evident in any given neglect patient will vary with the lesion (see Section 3 above), but what we emphasise is that a patient already biased towards responding to events from a restricted region of space will be unlikely to explore beyond that region if her internal mental model of the environment is poorly constructed in the first place and second, is never accurately updated based on new information.

6. CONCLUSION

Neglect is a common consequence of right hemisphere brain damage and presents with a heterogeneous range of symptoms. Classic models of the disorder that focus solely on impaired control of spatial attention have become increasingly inadequate in explaining the full range of symptoms observed in neglect. Characterising many of the deficits discussed in this chapter as an impairment in the construction, use or updating of mental models represents one potentially fruitful way of explaining a relatively broad swathe of observed deficits in neglect. This is not to suggest that deficits in model creation or updating alone would be sufficient to lead to the neglect syndrome. Instead, we would suggest that deficits in the use of mental models will represent one feature of a disorder that is best characterised by a constellation of core symptoms. When coupled with spatial biases in attention, any difficulty in generating or updating mental models will hamper the patient's ability to accurately process the constantly changing sensory data from the environment. One function of a mental model is to contrast predictions arising from the model with incoming sensory information. Neglect patients who are already biased towards exploring and processing information from a restricted range of right visual space will not have the wherewithal to sample information from the rest of the environment and will not register that lack of information as alarming in any way (i.e., the lack of information from left space will not seem 'unusual' to the patient). The severity of any deficit in utilising mental models should correlate with the severity of neglect on clinical measures of the disorder. This in turn should relate not only to the cortical and subcortical structures involved in the patient's lesion but to the white matter pathways compromised by the lesion (Table 1). Exploration of these relationships represents an important direction for future research on the neglect syndrome that has to date resisted the development of any simple theoretical account.

REFERENCES

Aboulafia-Brakha, T., Christe, B., Martory, M.D., & Annoni, J.M. (2011). Theory of mind tasks and executive function *Journal of Neuropsychology, 5,* 39–55.

Adair, J.C., & Barrett, A.M. (2008). Spatial neglect *Annals of the New York Academy of Sciences, 1142,* 21–43.

Albert, M.L. (1973). A simple test of visual neglect. *Neurology, 23,* 658–664.

Alexander, I., Cowey, A., & Walsh, V. (2005). The right parietal cortex and time perception: Back to Critchley and the Zeitraffer phenomenon. *Cognitive Neuropsychology, 22,* 306–315.

Anderson, B. (1993). Spared awareness *Neurology, 43,* 213–216.

Barrett, A.M., Buxbaum, L.J., Coslett, H.B., Edwards, E., Heilman, K.M., Hillis, A.E., Milberg, W.P., & Robertson, I.H. (2006). Cognitive rehabilitation *Journal of Cognitive Neuroscience, 18,* 1223–36.

Bartolomeo, P., Thiebaut de Schotten, M., & Doricchi, F. (2007). Left unilateral neglect as a disconnection syndrome. *Cerebral Cortex, 17,* 2479–2490.

Bartolomeo, P., & Chokron, S. (2002). Orienting of attention in left unilateral neglect. *Neuroscience and Biobehavioural Reviews, 26,* 217–234.

Basso, G., Nichelli, P., Frassinetti, F., & di Pellegrino, G. (1996). Time perception in a neglected space. *NeuroReport, 7,* 2111–2114.

Battelli, L., Pascual-Leone, A., & Cavanagh, P. (2007). The 'when' pathway of the right parietal lobe. *Trends in Cognitive Sciences, 11,* 204–210.

Battelli, L., Cavanagh, P., Martini, P., & Barton, J. J. S. (2003). Bilateral deficits of transient visual attention in right parietal patients. *Brain, 126,* 2164–2174.

Becchio, C., & Bertone, C. (2006). Time and neglect: Abnormal temporal dynamics in unilateral spatial neglect. *Neuropsychologia, 44,* 2775–2782.

Behrmann, M., Ghiselli-Crippa, T., Sweeney, J. A., Di Matteo, I., & Kass, R. (2002). Mechanisms underlying spatial representation revealed through studies of hemispatial neglect. *Journal of Cognitive Neuroscience, 14,* 272–290.

Bird, C.M., Malhotra, P., Parton, A., Coulthard, E., Rushworth, M.F., & Husain, M. (2006). Visual neglect following right posterior cerebral artery infarction. *Journal of Neurology, Neurosurgery and Psychiatry, 77,* 1008–1012.

Bisiach, E., & Luzzatti, C. (1978). Unilateral neglect *Cortex, 14,* 129–133.

Blakemore, S.J., Frith, C.D., & Wolpert, D.M. (2001). The cerebellum *Neuroreport, 12,* 1879–1884.

Blakemore, S.J., Goodbody, S.J., Wolpert, D.M. (1998). Predicting the consequences of our own actions: the role of sensorimotor context estimation. *Journal of Neuroscience, 18,* 7511–7518.

Bowen, A., McKenna, K., & Tallis, R.C. (1999). Reasons for variability in the reported rate of occurrence of unilateral spatial neglect after stroke. *Stroke, 30,* 1196–1202.

Brain, W.R. (1941). Visual dsorientation with special reference to lesions of the right cerebral hemisphere. *Brain, 64,* 224–272.

Buxbaum, L.J., Ferraro, M.K., Veramonti, T., Farne, A., Whyte, J., Ladavas, E., Frassinetti, F., & Coslett, H.B. (2004). Hemispatial neglect: Subtypes, neuroanatomy, and disability. *Neurology, 62,* 749–756.

Chechlacz, M., Rotshtein, P., Bickerton, W.-L., Hansen, P.C., Deb, S., & Humphreys, G.W. (2010). Separating neural correlates of allocentric and egocentric neglect: Distinct cortical sites and common white matter disconnections. *Cognitive Neuropsychology, 27,* 277–303.

Chun, M. M., & Potter, M. C. (1995). A two-stage model for multiple target detection in rapid serial visual presentation. *Journal of Experimental Psychology: Human Perception and Performance, 21,* 109–127.

Colby, C.L., & Goldberg, M.E. (1999). Space and attention in parietal cortex Annual Review of Neuroscience, 22, 319–349.

Colby CL, Duhamel JR, Goldberg ME. (1996). Visual, presaccadic, and cognitive activation of single neurons *Journal of Neurophysiology, 76,* 2841–2852.

Corbetta, M., Kincade, J. M., & Shulman, G. L. (2002). Neural systems for visual orienting and their relationships to spatial working memory. *Journal of Cognitive Neuroscience, 14,* 508–523.

Corbetta, M., & Shulman, G. L. (2002). Control of goal-directed and stimulus-driven attention in the brain. *Nature Reviews Neuroscience, 3,* 201–215.

Craik, K. (1943). *The Nature of Explanation.* Cambridge University Press, New York.

Danckert, J., Stottinger, E., Quehl, N., & Anderson, B. (under consideration). Right hemisphere brain damage impairs strategy updating. *PLoS ONE.*

Danckert, J., Ferber, S., Pun, C., Broderick, C., Striemer, C., Rock, S., & Stewart, D. (2007). Neglected time: Impaired temporal perception of multisecond intervals in unilateral neglect. *Journal of Cognitive Neuroscience, 19,* 1706–1720.

Danckert, J., & Ferber, S. (2006) Revisiting unilateral neglect. *Neuropsychologia, 44,* 987–1006.

Danckert, J., Ferber, S., Doherty, T., Steinmetz, H., Nicolle, D., & Goodale, M.A. (2002). Selective, non- lateralized impairment of motor imagery following right parietal damage. *Neurocase, 8,* 194–204.

Decety, J., Jeannerod, M., & Prablanc, C. (1989). The timing of mentally represented actions. *Behavioural Brain Research, 34,* 35–42.

Dehaene, S. (2003). The neural basis of the Weber–Fechner law: a logarithmic mental number line. *Trends in Cognitive Science, 7,* 145–147.

De Renzi, E., Gentilini, M., Faglioni, P., & Barbieri, C. (1989). Attentional shift towards the rightmost stimuli in patients with left visual neglect *Cortex, 25,* 231–237.

Desmurget, M., Epstein, C.M., Turner, R.S., Prablanc, C., Alexander, G.E., & Grafton, S.T. (1999). Role of the posterior parietal cortex in updating reaching movements to a visual target. *Nature Neuroscience, 2,* 563–567.

Doricchi, F., Thiebaut de Schotten, M., Tomaiuolo, F., & Bartolomeo, P. (2008). White matter (dis)connections and gray matter (dys)functions in visual neglect: Gaining insights into the brain networks of spatial awareness. *Cortex, 44,* 983–995.

Doricchi, F., & Tomaiuolo, F. (2003). The anatomy of neglect without hemianopia: a key role for parietal-frontal disconnection? *NeuroReport, 14,* 2239–2243.

Driver, J., & Mattingley, J. B. (1998). Parietal neglect and visual awareness. *Nature Neuroscience, 1,* 17–22.

Druker, M., & Anderson, B. (2010). Spatial probability *Frontiers in Human Neuroscience, 4,* pii: 63.

Duhamel, J.-R., Goldberg, M.E., Fitzgibbon, E.J., Sirigu, A., & Grafman, J. (1992b). Saccadic dysmetria in a patient with a right fronto-parietal lesion: the importance of corollary discharge for accurate   spatial behaviour. *Brain, 115,* 1387–1402.

Ferber, S., & Danckert, J. (2006). Lost in space—The fate of memory representations for non-neglected stimuli. *Neuropsychologia, 44,* 320–325.

Fitts, P.M. (1954). The informed capacity of the human motor system in controlling the amplitude of movements. *Journal of Experimental Psychology, 47,* 381– 391.

Fleming, M.K., Stinear, C.M., & Byblow, W.D. (2010) Bilateral parietal cortex function during motor imagery. *Experimental Brain Research, 201,* 499–508.

Frith, C.D., Blakemore, S.J., & Wolpert, D.M. (2000). Abnormalities in the awareness *Philosophical Transactions of the Royal Society of London, B: Biological Sciences, 355*, 1771–1788.

Gerardin, E., Sirigu, A., Lehericy, S., Poline, J.B., Gaymard, B., Marsault, C., Agid, Y., & Le Bihan, D. (2000). Partially overlapping neural networks for real and imagined hand movements. *Cerebral Cortex, 10,* 1093–1104.

Halligan, P. W., Fink, G. R., Marshall, J. C., & Vallar, G. (2003). Spatial cognition: Evidence from visual neglect. *Trends in Cognitive Science, 7,* 125–133.

Harrington, D. L., Haaland, K. Y., & Knight, R. T. (1998). Cortical networks underlying mechanisms of time perception. *Journal of Neuroscience, 18,* 1085–1095.

Heide, W., Blankenburg, M., Zimmermann, E., & K¨ompf, D. (1995). Cortical control of double-step saccades: Implications for spatial orientation. *Annals of Neurology, 38*, 739–748.

Heilman, K. M., Watson, R. T., & Valenstein, E. (1993). Neglect and related disorders. In K. M. Heilman & E. Valenstein (Eds.), *Clinical neuropsychology* (pp. 279–336). New York: Oxford University Press.

Heller, W., & Levy, J. (1981). Perception and expression of emotion in righthanders and left-handers. *Neuropsychologia, 19*, 263–272.

Husain, M., Mannan, S., Hodgson, T., Wojciulik, E., Driver, J., & Kennard, C. (2001). Impaired spatial working memory across saccades contributes to abnormal search in parietal neglect. *Brain, 124*, 941–952.

Husain, M., & Rorden, C. (2003). Non-spatially lateralised mechanisms in neglect. *Nature Neuroscience Reviews, 4*, 26–36.

Husain, M., & Nachev, P. (2007). Space and the parietal cortex *Trends in Cognitive Sciences, 11*, 30–36.

Husain, M., Shapiro, K., Martin, J., & Kennard, C. (1997). Abnormal temporal dynamics of visual attention in spatial neglect patients. *Nature, 385*, 154–156.

Jeannerod, M. (1997). *The Cognitive Neuroscience of Action.* Blackwell, Cambridge, MA.

Johnson-Laird, P.N. (2010). Mental models *Proceedings of the National Academy of Science, U S A, 107*, 18243–18250.

Karnath, H.-O., Ferber, S., & Himmelbach, M. (2001). Spatial awareness is a function of the temporal not the posterior parietal lobe. *Nature, 411*, 950–953.

Karnath, H.-O., Fruhmann-Berger, M., Küker, W., & Rorden, C. (2004). The anatomy of spatial neglect based on voxelwise statistical analysis: a study of 140 patients. *Cerebral Cortex, 14,* 1164–1172.

Karnath, H.-O., Rorden, C., & Ticini, L.F. (2009). Damaage to whiute matter fiber tracts in acute spatial neglect. *Cerebral Cortex, 19,* 2331–2337.

Karnath, H.-O., Rennig, J., Johannsen, L., & Rorden, C. (2011). The anatomy underlying acute versus chronic spatial neglect: a longitudinal study. *Brain, 134,* 903–912.

Kerkhoff, G. (2001). Spatial hemineglect in humans. *Progress in Neurobiology,63,* 1–27.

Kinsbourne, M. (1970). A model for the mechanism of unilateral neglect of space. *Transactions of the American Neurological Association, 95,* 143–146.

Kinsbourne, M. (1993). Orienting bias model of unilateral neglect: evidence from attentional gradients within hemispace. In I.H. Robertson & J.C. Marshall (Eds.), *Unilateral Neglect: Clinical and Experimental Studies* (pp.63-86). Hove, UK: Lawrence Erlbaum.

Levy, J., Heller, W., Banich, M. T., & Burton, L. A. (1983). Asymmetry of perception in free viewing of chimaeric faces. *Brain and Cognition, 2,* 404–419.

Losier, B. J., & Klein, R. M. (2001). A review of the evidence for a disengage deficit following parietal lobe damage. *Neuroscience and Biobehavioural Review, 25,* 1–13.

Malhotra, P., Mannan, S., Driver, J., & Husain, M. (2004). Impaired spatial working memory *Cortex, 40,* 667–676.

Mattingley, J. B. (1996). Paterson and Zangwill's (1944) case of unilateral neglect: Insights from 50 years of experimental inquiry. In C. Code, C-W. Wallesch, Y. Joanette, & A. R. Lecours (Eds.), *Classic cases in neuropsychology* (pp. 173–188). United Kingdom: Psychology Press.

Mattingley, J. B., Bradshaw, J. L., Nettleton, N. C., & Bradshaw, J. A. (1994). Can task specific perceptual bias be distinguished from unilateral neglect? *Neuropsychologia, 32,* 805–817.

Merrifield, C., Hurwitz, M., & Danckert, J. (2010) Multimodal Temporal Perception Deficits in a Patient with Left Spatial Neglect. *Cognitive Neuroscience, 4,* 244-253.

Mesulam, M. (1981). A cortical network for directed attention and unilateral neglect. *Annals of Neurology, 10,* 309–325.

Mort, D. J., Malhotra, P., Mannan, S. K., Rorden, C., Pambakian, A., Kennard, C., & Husain, M. (2003). The anatomy of visual neglect. *Brain, 126,* 1986–1997.

Natale, E., Marzi, C.A., Bricolo, E., Johannsen, L., & Karnath, H.-O. (2007). Abnormally speeded saccades to ipsilesional targets in patients with spatial neglect. *Neuropsychologia, 45,* 263–272

O'Connell, R.G., Bellgrove, M.A., Dockree, P.M., Lau, A., Fitzgerald, M., & Robertson, I.H. (2008). Self- Alert Training: volitional modulation of autonomic arousal *Neuropsychologia, 46,* 1379–1390.

Ogden, J.A. (1985). Antero-posterior interhemispheric differences in the loci of lesions producing visual   hemineglect. *Brain and Cognition, 4,* 59–75.

Parton, A., Malhotra, P., Nachev, P., Ames, D., Ball, J., Chataway, J., & Husain, M. (2006). Space re- exploration   in   hemispatial   neglect *Neuroreport, 17,* 833–836.

Paterson, A., & Zangwill, O.L. (1944). Disorders of visual space perception associated with lesions of the right cerebral hemisphere. *Brain, 67,* 331– 358.

Pisella, L., & Mattingley, J. B. (2004). The contribution of spatial remapping to unilateral visual neglect. *Neuroscience and Biobehavioural Reviews, 28,* 181–200.

Posner, M.I. (1980). Orienting of attention. *Quarterly Journal of Experimental Psychology, 32,* 3–25.

Posner, M.I., Walker, J. A., Friedrich, F. A., & Rafal, R. D. (1984). Effects of parietal injury on covert orienting of attention. *Journal of Neuroscience, 4,* 1863–1874.

Posner, M.I., Walker, J. A., Friedrich, F. A., & Rafal, R. D. (1987). How do the parietal lobes direct covert attention? *Neuropsychologia, 25,* 135–145.

Raymond, J.E., Shapiro, K. L., & Arnell, K. M. (1992). Temporary suppression of visual processing in an RSVP task: An attentional blink? *Journal of Experimental Psychology, 18,* 849–860.

Ringman, J.M., Saver, J.L., Woolson, R.F., Clarke, W.R., Adams, H.P. (2004). Frequency, risk factors, anatomy, and course of unilateral neglect in an acute stroke cohort. *Neurology, 63,* 468–474.

Rizzo, M., Akutsu, H., & Dawson, J. (2001). Increased attentional blink after focal cerebral lesions. *Neurology, 57,* 795–800.

Robertson, I.H., Manly, T., Beschin, N., Daini, R., Haeske-Dewick, H., Hömberg, V., Jehkonen, M., Pizzamiglio, G., Shiel, A., & Weber, E. (1997). Auditory sustained attention is a marker of unilateral spatial neglect *Neuropsychologia, 35,* 1527–1532.

Robertson, I.H., Tegnér, R., Tham, K., Lo, A., & Nimmo-Smith, I. (1995). Sustained attention training *Journal of Clinical and Experimental Neuropsychology, 17*, 416–430.

Robertson, I.H. (2001). Do we need the "lateral" in unilateral neglect *Neuroimage, 14*, S85–S90.

Schweizer, T.A., Alexander, M.P., Cusimano, M., & Stuss, D.T. (2007). Fast and efficient visuotemporal attention requires the cerebellum. *Neuropsychologia, 45*, 3068–3074.

Shapiro, K., Hillstrom, A. P., & Husain, M. (2002). Control of visuotemporal attention by inferior parietal and superior temporal cortex. *Current Biology, 12*, 1320–1325.

Sirigu, A., Duhamel, J., Cohen, L., Pillon, B., Dubios, B., & Agid, Y. (1996). The mental representation of hand movements after parietal cortex damage. *Science, 273*, 1564–1567.

Stinear CM, Fleming MK, Barber PA, & Byblow, W.D. (2007). Lateralization of motor imagery following stroke. *Clinical Neurophysiology, 118*, 1794–1801.

Striemer, C., & Danckert, J. (2010). Through a prism darkly: re-evaluating prisms and neglect. *Trends in Cognitive Sciences, 14*, 308–316.

Striemer, C. and Danckert, J. (2007) Prism adaptation reduces the disengage deficit in right brain damage patients. *Neuroreport, 18*, 99–103.

Tenenbaum, J.B., Kemp, C., Griffiths, T.L., & Goodman, N.D. (2011). How to grow a mind: statistics *Science, 331*, 1279–1285.

Thiebaut de Schotten, M., Urbanski, M., Duffau, H., Volle, E., Lévy, R., Dubois, B., & Bartolomeo, P. (2005). Direct evidence for a parietalfrontal pathway subserving spatial awareness in humans. *Science, 309*, 2226–2228.

Umiltà, C., Priftis, K., & Zorzi, M. (2009). The spatial representation of numbers: evidence from neglect and pseudoneglect. *Experimental Brain Research, 192*, 561–569.

Urbanski, M., Thiebaut de Schotten, M., Rodrigo, S., Catani, M., Oppenheim, C., Touzé, E., Méder, J.-F., Moreau, K., Loeper-Jeny, C., Dubois, B., & Bartolomeo, P. (2011). DTI-MR tractography of white matter damage in stroke patients with neglect. *Experimental Brain Research, 208*, 491–505.

Urbanski, M., Thiebaut de Schotten, M., Rodrigo, S., Catani, M., Oppenheim, C., Touzé, E., Chokron, S., Méder, J.-F., Lévy, R., Dubois, B., & Bartolomeo, P. (2008). Brain networks of spatial awareness: Evidence from diffusion tensor imaging tractography. *Journal of Neurology, Neurosurgery and Psychiatry, 79*, 598–601.

Vallar, G., & Perani, D. (1986). The anatomy of unilateral neglect after righthemisphere stroke lesions. A clinical/CT-scan correlation study in man. *Neuropsychologia, 24,* 609–622.

Verdon, V., Schwartz, S., Lovblad, K.-O., Hauert, C.-A., & Vuilleumier, P. (2010). Neuroanatomy of hemispatial neglect and its functional components: A study using voxel-based lesion-symptom mapping. *Brain, 133,* 880–894.

Wojciulik, E., Husain, M., Clarke, K., & Driver, J. (2001). Spatial working memory deficit in unilateral neglect. *Neuropsychologia, 39,* 390–396.

Wojciulik, E., Rorden, C., Clarke, K., Husain, M., & Driver, J. (2004). Group study of an "undercover" test for visuospatial neglect: Invisible cancellation can reveal more neglect than standard   cancellation. *Journal of Neurology, Neurosurgery and Psychiatry, 75,* 1356–1358.

Wolpert, D.M., Miall, R.C., & Kawato, M. (1998a). Internal models *Trends in Cognitive   Sciences, 2,* 338–347.

Wolpert, D.M., Goodbody, S.J., & Husain, M. (1998b). Maintaining internal representations: the role of   the human *Nature Neuroscience, 1,* 529–533.

Zorzi, M., Priftis, K., Meneghello, F., Marenzi, R., & Umiltà, C. (2006). The spatial representation of numerical and non-numerical sequences: evidence from neglect. *Neuropsychologia, 44,* 1061–1067.

Zorzi, M., Priftis, K., & Umiltà, C. (2002). Brain damage: neglect disrupts the mental number line. *Nature, 417,* 138–139.

In: Psychology of Neglect
Editors: Y. Spiteri, E. Galea, 29-46

ISBN 978-1-62100-180-5
© 2012 Nova Science Publishers, Inc.

Chapter 2

TRAUMA OF SEXUAL ABUSE AND THE FAMILY

Tanja Repic Slavic[1], Christian Gostecnik[2] and Robert Cvetek[3]

[1] PhD of Marriage and Family Therapy, Franciscan Family Institute, Assistant Professor, University of Ljubljana, Slovenia
[2] PhD of clinical psychology, PhD of theology and PhD of psychology; Franciscan Family Institute, Professor, University of Ljubljana, Slovenia
[3] PhD of Psychology; Franciscan Family Institute, Assistant Professor, University of Ljubljana, Slovenia

ABSTRACT

Our research investigated the difference in functioning within families of sexually abused children and families with no sexual abuse experience. We did not focus, however, on the fact whether the person was sexually abused within the family or outside of it. We used FOS (Family-of-Origin) scale by Hovestadt, Anderson, Piercy, Cochran and

[1] Mailing address: Presernov trg 4, 1000 Ljubljana, Slovenia
E-mail: tanja.repic1@guest.arnes.si
[2] Mailing address: Presernov trg 4, 1000 Ljubljana, Slovenia
E-mail: christian.gostecnik@guest.arnes.si
[3] Mailing address: Presernov trg 4, 1000 Ljubljana, Slovenia
E-mail: robert.cvetek@guest.arnes.si

Fine (1985) to measure the degree of healthy functioning in the family. 339 people completed the questionnaire (M = 22.5 years, SD = 3.5), 202 girls and 137 boys. 17 % of participants have experienced sexual abuse, which is approximately one in five girls (5.2) and one in seven boys (6.8). 78 % of all sexually abused participants in our survey were girls and 22 % were boys. The families of sexually abused participants show statistically significant differences in the way of functioning when compared to families with no experience in sexual child abuse.

Keywords: Sexual abuse, intergenerational transmission, secondary traumatization, functioning in the family

INTRODUCTION

Diverse definitions of sexual abuse cause large differences in its prevalence between studies. Some studies exclude cases where the victim was pressured to "voluntarily" agree to cooperate, most studies do not include children in different institutions (hospitals), where they are more subject to abuse, some studies do not count inappropriate touching as sexual abuse except in case of forced sexual assaults (The Invisible Boy, 1996). Williams (1994) defines sexual abuse as involuntary sexual contact including force or coercive measures on the part of other person, who is at least 5 years older than the victim. Finkelhor (1988, cited from Rojsek, 2002) defines sexual abuse as every sexual contact between an adult and sexually immature child (physical and mental or emotional and social immaturity) with the intention of satisfying sexual needs of the adult, or every sexual act using force, threats, deceit or abuse of power. Studies show that girls are most often (twice as often as boys) victims of sexual abuse (Finkelhor, 1990), whereas some say even three times as often as boys (Little and Hamby, 1999). Other data shows that almost one out of three women and one out of six men experienced some form of sexual abuse in their childhood (Finkelhor and Korbin, 1988, cited from Evans, Hawton and Rodham, 2005). It also shows that sexual abuse with boys more often occurs outside the family (79-83 %) (Finkelhor, 1984; Lisak, Hopper and Song, 1996), whereas sexual abuse with girls usually happens within the family (Finkelhor, 1990). Family is the factor for providing a child with feelings of safety, belonging, acceptance and love (Gostecnik, 1998, 2001, 2004, 2005). If the family climate instead is prevailed by abuse, trauma, violence, fear and similar frightening and violent behaviour, the child will not feel safe and loved and will continue his life looking for situations which arouse and repeat the familiar atmosphere and basic affects, which in his mental world represent the feeling of belonging and comfort (Cvetek, 2004; Gostecnik, 1997, 2004, 2005).

When one of the family members is involved in a traumatic experience of sexual abuse, its influence can spread to the whole family, not just the individual, and affect its functioning regardless of the time which has passed since the experience. This transmission to other family members is also known as secondary traumatization (Lebow and Rekart, 2005). Studies show that caring for persons who were affected by great stress and living with them presents a large risk of developing similar symptoms for the victim guardians (parents, partner, other family members). These persons can experience secondary traumatic stress (STS) or secondary traumatic stress disorder (STSD) with similar symptoms as the post-traumatic stress disorder (PTSD) (Figley, 1995). Dynamics of families (Courtois, 1988; Muller, Sicoli in Lemieux, 2000) which have experienced some kind of trauma (including sexual abuse) can differ. Abuse victims can become scape goats to blame for all the problems in the family. Some families can become more organized, supportive and protective of their members, which sometimes demands of other family members to neglect their own needs and goals. Families can form subsystems with a group of family members turning against the others, often leading to jealousy between children, especially when their need are not cared for. Steinberg (1998) claims in one of his studies that negative or inappropriate reaction from parents to different traumatic experience of their child can have a more negative impact on the child than the seriousness of the traumatic experience itself. Otherwise the connection and sympathy between members of the family helps them in dealing with traumatic experiences. Parents who are too taken over by the event of sexual abuse are at the same time disabled and not capable of reacting adequately to minimize the event and its consequences (Marans, Berkman and Cohen, 1996). Minimizing (such as "It's no big deal if he/she touched your private parts a little.") can occur when parents themselves experienced a similar traumatic event in their past or because they feel unable to help the child. Parents who are able to regulate their reactions to the child's traumatic event, are more efficient and successful in supporting and protecting the victim (Monahon, 1993).

Consequences of trauma, caused by sexual abuse, can also transmit to future generations (Barocas and Barocas, 1973; Epstein, 1979; Figley, 1995; Howell, 2002; Rosenheck and Fontana, 1998), even to their children who were not yet born at the time of the incident (Catherall, 2004). Some authors (Hanson and Slater, 1988; Kaufman and Zigler, 1987) estimate that approximately one out of three abused people will continue to abuse others and approximately two thirds of abuse victims will never be the inducer of sexual abuse, especially when provided with love and support in their family. Johnson (2002) finds that those who were victims of emotional, physical or sexual abuse in the past have a six-times greater chance of incurring the abuse they have felt. Other studies (Collin-Vezina, 2003) show that half of mothers of sexually abused children were sexually abused in the past. If the act of sexual abuse is not transmitted forward, it doesn't mean that the children of sexually abused parents will be safe from sexual abusers. Relational family theory (Gostecnik, 2004, 2005) mentions unprocessed affects, mostly disgust, shame and anger, which uses the projective identification to vertically transmit itself from an abused parent to a child. Even if this parent tries to warn the child about the dangers of abuse (Howell, 2002), he will not be in contact with his unprocessed affects and will not be able to protect himself and set limits, therefore his child will have a greater chance of becoming a victim of sexual abuse (Gostecnik, 2004, 2005). Similar to Miller (2005), who says childhood abuse is solved in one of two ways: adult who was sexually abused as a child will transfer his unresolved emotions to his child and other people around him, or the consequences can be seen on the body of the abused person in the form of psychosomatics and chronic disease. Cross (2001) finds in his study that 34 % of mothers of abused children were themselves victims of sexual abuse. McCloskey and Bailey (2000) stress out that in cases, where the mother was a victim of sexual abuse, there was a 3.4-times greater possibility that her daughter will be sexually abused, when compared to mothers who had no previous experience with sexual abuse. Authors believe the common reason for transmitting sexual abuse to future generations is also that children preserve contacts with the same family members who were also present at the time of the mother's abuse and then the daughter's. The mothers of children, who were also abused, show a greater level of experiencing stress and the symptoms of post-traumatic stress disorder (Timmons-Mitchell, Chandler-Holtz and Semple, 1996), expressing fear of being incompetent mothers and experiencing more hostility and frustrations toward the children (Cross, 2001) when compared to mothers of sexually abused children who were not abused themselves. sexually abused mothers also had more problems in creating structure, expressing feelings and love to their children, had many ambivalent feelings towards them and fear of their children also becoming victims, which often led to socialy isolating their children with the intention of protecting them (Cross, 2001). Hall, Sachs and Rayens (1998) concluded that mothers with a history of sexual abuse used physical punishments for their children 6-

times more often that those mothers who had no abuse history. Cohen (1994) summarizes that sexually abused mothers are less skilful and functional in their parental role, if they haven't processed the abuse.

Many authors study and write about other risk factors in families with one or more sexually abused members within or outside the family, beside intergenerational transmission and secondary traumatization. Trepper and Barrett (1989) describe a family with a large possibility of sexual abuse, where the characteristics include rigid sexual roles, no limitations (especially emotional), dark secrets, non-functional communication, no security and frequent conflicts between parents. They also believe an emotionally abused or neglected father and sexually abused or neglected mother to be a strong risk factor. However they stress that regardless of the number of risk factors in the family, sexual abuse will not occur, if the family used efficient strategies of dealing with stressful events. Figley (1983) and Catherall (1998) similarly agree that successful dealing with the stress is the main criteria for differentiating between functional and dysfunctional families.

Dysfunctional families use dysfunctional strategies of coping with stress which involve inefficient problem solving, indirect communication, structural deficits (lack of cohesion, rigid roles) and strategies that produce violence and drug abuse. Contrary to dysfunctional families, Olson (2000) speaks of three dimensions which are essential in functional families: connection between family members, flexibility and effective communication. Hobfoll and Spielberger (1992) also note essential dimensions in the family, which help in coping with stress and trauma: flexibility and adaptability as opposed to rigidity, closeness as opposed division, communication as opposed to secrecy, clear boundaries as opposed to incoherence, and structure and control as opposed to chaos and helplessness. Rosenbloom and Williams (1999) define typical responses in traumatized families as lack of intimacy, predominant emotional apathy or excessive outbursts of anger, substance abuse and frequent problems with the five basic psychological needs (security, trust, power/control, respect and intimacy).

Parker and Parker (1986) reveal that nurturing and presence of a person in the child's earliest years are factors which mean a lesser possibility of sexually abusing this child, as opposed to a person (parent) which was not present in this period of child's life. On the basis of this theory they deduct that mothers are more rarely the perpetrators of sexual abuse than fathers, because their nature itself means they will be more present in the child's life than fathers. Finkelhor (1980) adds that step-fathers are guilty of sexual abusing a child five-times more frequently than the child's natural fathers. Paveza (1988) adds dissatisfaction in marital relationship as a risk factor for sexual abuse since it increases the possibility of sexual abuse by 7.19-times, relationship gaps between mother and daughter increase this possibility by 11.61-times and a mother suffering partner's abuse increases this possibility by 6.51-times. Olson, Russel and Sprenkle (1983) put special focus on the functioning of incestuous families and reveal that these families show specific communication problems: secrecy, inconsistent and unclear messages between family members, little or no empathy and lack of skills for problem solving. Trepper and Barrett (1989) add that these families lack any kind of structure, include mixed roles, have no defined boundaries and operate in chaos. The other extreme are stiff and rigid patterns, where the father is very dominant and bad at controlling his impulse and the mother has passive-addictive personality. Whereas Ball, Bourdeaudhuij, Crombez and Cost (2004) do not distinguish betwen families with internal and external abuse experience, since their studies show that they show no statistically significant differences in the functioning of incestuous families and those who experienced abuse outside of the family circle.

Mollestrom, Patchner and Miller (1992) in their study point out that the level of family cohesion is most inversely proportioned to the share of child abuse. Family cohesion is described by the level of attachment, help and support between family members. Results of many other studies stress that support of the family (Burt, Cohen and Bjorck, 1988; Holohan and Moos, 1981; Kazak, 1989; Wilcox, 1986; Woodall and Mathews, 1989) is the most important factor for family members to cope with life changes. Moos and Moos (1986) define family support as low level of family conflicts, high level of attachment and moderate level of dependence. Lack of support from the family can cause an even greater terror and fear in every traumatic experience at any level of development and can turn every slightest with for independence into a need for complete union and closeness and intimacy (Gostecnik, 2001). The same happens when parents force the child into greater independence too early and do not provide him with security when he needs it. This will create a fear of being rejected and an extreme need for closeness, union and intimacy. However, if parents repress the child's need for greater independence due to their anxieties, a child will evolve deep feelings of confinement and with it a very intense need for independence and autonomy (Gostecnik, 2001). Hovestad, Anderson, Piercy, Cochran and Fine (1985) claim that the level of autonomy and intimacy is the sign of healthy functioning between family members being present in the family. In their opinion, autonomy consists of five elements: clarity of expression, responsibility, respect for others, openness to others, acceptance of separation and loss, as well as intimacy, range of feelings, mood and tone, conflict resolution, empathy and trust.

Foubert, Nixon, Sisson in Barnes (2005) in their articles believe that autonomy is tied to individual's successful development, taking responsibility for his own actions and tasks and independence of other people's opinions. On the other hand, autonomy also means intimacy, which is a process of attaching yourself to another person until you reach mutual attachment between two equals (Foubert et al., 2005). Autonomy in a child depends on the number and quality of his parent's competences, specifically communication skills, setting the structure in time and space and providing security and boundaries (Tomanovic, 2003). Autonomy and intimacy together present two components of mature interpersonal relations later on in life (Gostecnik, 2001).

As we can see, many studies have been made and many articles written on the functioning of families and sexual abuse, however we found no evidence of studies on how autonomy and intimacy as elements of healthy functioning in the family (Hovestadt et al., 1985) are connected to sexual abuse. We will not focus on the fact whether the abuse occurred within the family or outside of it. We want to study the level of autonomy and intimacy in families of the sexual abuse victims. We predict that sexually abused children more frequently originate from families with lower levels of autonomy and intimacy when compared to families of children with no experience in sexual abuse. Our conclusion is therefore that the functioning in latter is healthier than in the families of sexually abused children.

METHODS

Participants

339 participants were involved in the study, 137 boys (40 % of the sample, M = 24 years, SD = 4.4) and 202 girls (60 % of the sample, M = 22 years, SD = 2.5). They were divided into two groups (not according to gender): the group of sexually abused (SZ, N = 59, 17 % of the sample) and the group of never sexually abused (NSZ, N = 280, 83 % of the sample). Average age in the group of sexually abused persons was 22 (SD = 2.2) and the average age in the other group was 23 (SD = 3.7). The participants gave informed consent for participating in the research and everything has been done in accordance to the ethical and institutional standards.

Instruments

We used the Family-of-origin scale (FOS) to measure healthy functioning in the family (when we speak of family, we mean the original family where the child develops). This five-level scale (Hovestadt, Anderson, Piercy, Cochran and Fine, 1985) is used to measure two key factors of healthy functional families: autonomy and intimacy. It contains 40 statements and participants were able to scale every statement (agree-not agree) according to the level, to which the statement described their family. Hovestad et al. (1985) stress that elements of autonomy in healthy functional families are shown as:

1) clarity of expression (CE - thoughts and feelings are clear in the family),
2) responsibility (R - family members claim responsibility for their own actions),
3) respect for others (RO - Family members are allowed to speak for themselves),
4) openness to others (O - family members are receptive to one another) and in acceptance of separation and loss (A - separation and loss are dealt with openly in the family).

Elements of intimacy are shown as:

- range of feelings (RF - family members express a wide range of feelings),
- mood and tone (MT - warm, positive atmosphere exists in the family),
- conflict resolution (C - normal conflicts are resolved without undue stress),
- empathy (E - family members are sensitive to one another) and in
- trust (T - the family sees human nature as basically good).

Each statement provided 4 to 20 points. This means that the minimum possible number of points for autonomy and intimacy statements was 20 and the maximum was 100 points (total sum of sums for all five elements in individual risk factors). Families with a higher score show a more developed autonomy and intimacy skills, which is a sign of its healthy functioning. Finally, all points were summed up (for autonomy and intimacy) and could provide 40 to 200 points. Hovestadt et al. (1985) report a test-retest coefficient (two weeks) with 0.97 reliability. Cronbach alpha is 0.75, whereas alpha on standardized items is 0.97. Authors of the original questionnaire (Hovestadt et al., 1985) claim that it is good at distinguishing between the groups (i.e. parent relationships where men were alcoholics and those where men were not alcoholics). Our study also proved that the translated questionnaire was good at distinguishing between the group of sexually abused people and the group of people with no experience in sexual abuse (results of t-test). We established sexual abuse experience using the question: „Have you ever been sexually abused?" If the answer was YES, the person was allocated to the group of sexually abused people, otherwise they were classified as people with no sexual abuse experience. Here we must point out that prior to the question we explained to the participants that by sexual abuse we mean every sexual contact between an adult and sexually immature child with the intention of satisfying sexual needs of the adult, or every sexual contact involving the use of force, threats, deceit or power (Finkelhor, 1988, cited from Rojsek, 2002). The question was valid because the participants were explained the definition of sexual abuse and were able to place themselves in the appropriate group.

Procedures

Study participants were faculty students. After previous arrangement with professors at these faculties we showed up during class and took the last 10 minutes to explain the instructions and distributed questionnaires to those who were willing to voluntarily participate in the study. Students were informed that all answers were anonymous and will be used only for research purposes. A professor lecturer was present during the time students took the questionnaire.

For results analysis we mostly used the *t*-test statistical method for independent samples with equal or unequal variance. We formed two groups according to the question whether the person was sexually abused or not. (We did not distinguish the two groups by gender because the minority of male participants - 137 total male participants, 20 of them sexually abused - would make the results unreliable.) Using t-tests we compared all five elements of autonomy and all five elements of intimacy between the two groups.

RESULTS

Results show that 17 % of all participants (N = 339) were sexually abused (N = 59), which averaged to one out of five people experiencing sexual abuse (5.7). 83 % of participants (N = 280) have never experienced sexual abuse.

Of all the girls participating in the study (N = 202, 60 %), 19 % (N = 39) were sexually abused, which makes it approximately one out of five girls (5.2). Of all the male participants (N = 137, 40 %), 15 % (N = 20) or approximately one out of seven (6.8) were sexually abused.

Among all sexually abused participants (N = 59) 66 % were girls (N = 39) and 34 % were boys (N = 20).

The study shows that mean values for individual elements of autonomy and intimacy are lower in the group of sexually abused people, when compared to the group of people who never experienced sexual abuse (see Table 1).

Results show a statistically significant difference $(t(76) = -6,57, p = 0,000)$ in autonomy between the sexually abused and never abused people. All five elements of autonomy also strongly reflects many surprising statistically significant differences between the two groups. These differences show in the clarity of expression $(t(72) = -6,21, p = 0,000)$, responsibility $(t(73) = -6,40, p = 0,000)$, respect for others $(t(337) = -6,84, p = 0,000)$, openness to others $(t(76) = -2,53, p = 0,014)$ and in acceptance of separation and loss $(t(76) = -4,30, p = 0,000)$.

Results also point out statistically significant differences between intimacy in the families of both participant groups $(t(337) = -7,45, p = 0,000)$. Individual intimacy elements also show many statistically significant differences, mostly in: stimulation of expressing feelings $(t(337) = -5,90, p = 0,000)$, creating a comfortable family atmosphere $(t(337) = -6,41, p = 0,000)$, dealing with conflicts without stress $(t(337) = -7,63, p = 0,000)$, empathy $(t(337) = -7,09, p = 0,000)$ and in trust and developing trust $(t(337) = -5,52, p = 0,000)$.

Finally, we used t-tests to compare the mean of both sums (sum of all elements for autonomy and all elements of intimacy). We then added both sums together and compared them between the two groups. We noticed statistically significant differences between the group of sexually abused and never abused participants $(t(337) = -7,71, p=0,000)$.

**Table 1. Mean and standard deviation of elements of autonomy
and intimacy in the group of sexually abused and never sexually
abused participants**

	Sexually abused (N=59)		Never sexually abused (N=280)	
	M	SD	M	SD
Sum autonomy and intimacy	102,66	29,24	132,40	26,40
Sum autonomy	50,63	14,12	63,54	11,65
- clarity of expression	10,05	3,25	12,83	2,43
- responsibility	9,58	3,26	12,72	2,46
- respect for others	9,54	3,91	13,06	3,52
- openness to others	11,14	3,27	12,29	2,70
- acceptance of separation and loss	10,05	4,31	12,64	3,63
Sum intimacy	52,03	16,40	68,87	15,59
- range of feelings	10,61	4,06	13,70	3,57
- mood and tone	11,28	4,28	14,20	3,84
- conflict resolution	8,73	3,33	12,65	3,64
- empathy	10,46	3,43	14,13	3,66
- trust	11,13	3,12	13,49	3,16

Notes. M – mean, SD – standard deviation.

DISCUSSION

Results showed that 17 % (N = 59) of all participants in our study (N = 339) were sexually abused, which means approximately one out of six persons (5.7). As in other studies (Finkelhor and Korbin, 1988, cited from Evans et al., 2005; Little and Hamby, 1999), our study also proved that girls are more often victims of sexual abuse (approximately one out of five; 5.2) than boys (approximately one out of seven; 6.8). When compared to studies that claim girls are twice more often victims of sexual abuse (Finkelhor, 1990) than boys, our study shows a factor of 1,31, from which we could conclude that gender does not make a relevant difference.

In general, we found many statistically significant differences in a healthier functioning in the families of those individuals with no sexual abuse experience. Some authors (Catherall, 1998; Figley, 1983; Olson, 2000) attribute this difference to distinguishing between functional and dysfunctional families and emphasize that families with traumatic experience are more dysfunctional.

A comparison of autonomy and its five elements between the families of both groups also showed many statistically significant differences. When compared to the families with no experience of sexual abuse, other families show a statistically significant lower level at all five elements: clarity of expression, responsibility, respect for others, openness to others and acceptance of separation and loss. These results can be tied to the Trepper and Barrett theory, which describes a family with higher risk of sexual abuse as having no emotional boundaries, or as Hobfoll and Spielberger (1992) say, family with unclear and rigid or chaotic boundaries. From this we can assume that family members express their feelings harder, because they will not know how to link these feelings to people and who feels what. Also, many authors (Catherall, 1998; Figley, 1983; Trepper and Berrett, 1989) point out that these families suffer from inefficient communication, dark secrets and frequent conflicts between the married couple. We might be able to explain our results on the basis of these findings in areas where we got a lower level of responsibility and mutual respect, because children will not be able to learn about being responsible and respecting others if their role models for building future relationships (father and mother) show no respect for each other (Gostecnik, 1998) and experience frequent conflicts. These conflicts probably also point to dissatisfaction in their marriage, which increases the chances for sexual abuse by factor of 7.19 (Paveza, 1988). Furthermore, dark secrets and inefficient communication within the family (Olson et al. 1983; Trepper and Barrett, 1989) show that family members are not too open to other members. If there were more empathy, mutual respect and efficient communication between family members, they would be able to speak about painful things called dark secrets. Our results show a lower level of acceptance of separation and loss in the families of sexually abused participants. Similarly, other authors (Burt et al., 1988; Holohan and Moos, 1981; Kazak, 1989; Wilcox, 1986; Woodall and Mathews, 1989) find in their studies that increased family support makes it easier for family members to cope with traumatic events and changes in their lives. Of course we have to stress that previous studies show that family support, attachment and mutual help in the family are inversely proportioned to the share of child abuse (Mollestrom et al., 1992).

Our results also show that families of sexually abused participants, when compared to families of other participants, show statistically significant lower level of intimacy in all five elements. Similarly, Rosenbloom and Williams (1999) write that trauma-affected families lack intimacy and are prevailed by anger outbursts, where family members often experience problems with their five basic psychological needs (security, trust, power/control, respect and intimacy). In our case we could link this to a lower level of trust and developing trust and with creating familiar atmosphere, which is far from comfortable in families with frequent outbursts of anger and lack of security and respect.

When the families with traumatic experience lack security, trust (Rosenbloom and Williams, 1999) and empathy and sympathy (Olson et al., 1983), it is very hard to say that the family stimulates expressing feelings, but rather the opposite, especially when using rigid and stiff models with one dominant parent (Trapper and Barrett, 1989). We also established a statistically significant lower level of dealing with conflicts without stress in families of sexually abused participants in comparison to families of other participants. Other authors (Catherall, 1998; Figley, 1983; Gostecnik, 2004, 2005; Olson et al., 1983) have made similar observations and claim that families with one-time or repeated traumatic experiences (including sexual abuse) predominantly use dysfunctional strategies of coping with stress and inefficient problem solving techniques, mostly due to lack of problem solving skills.

CONCLUSION

In general, our results show that healthy functioning, represented by the level of autonomy and intimacy, is at statistically significant lower level within families of sexual abuse victims than within families which have no sexual abuse experience. In other words, families, not affected by a traumatic experience of sexual abuse, function healthier than those with trauma experience caused by sexual abuse. From this we can conclude that healthy functioning within the family is, amongst other things, a very strong factor in preventing sexual abuse of children within the family or outside of it.

The study and results analysis itself has some limitations, which need to be taken into account. It would be practical to distinguish between incestuous families and families where the perpetrator is not a family member, even though Ball et al. (2004) established that there are no statistically significant differences between the functioning of these two family groups. Due to different sexual abuse definitions (Finkelhor, 1988, cited from Rojsek, 2002; Williams, 1994) in society, we cannot tell for sure if every victim of sexual abuse sees himself or herself as one - they are likely to minimize the traumatic experience because of pain (Marans, Berkman and Cohen, 1996) and no longer see this kind of inappropriate behaviour by an adult as sexual abuse. It is also possible that they have lost memory of the traumatic event (meanings and pictures) due to shock, however they replay the trauma in their actions, sensations and affects, because the body remembers everything, even abuse (Rothschild, 2000). On the other hand we must take into consideration that some members of the family where another family member experienced sexual abuse were subject to secondary traumatization and therefore experience similar symptomatology than the sexually abused member (Catherall, 2004; Figley, 1995; Lebow and Rekart, 2005). For these reasons we believe the questionnaire should be further supplemented by additional questions to cover the whole family. This way we could see if there were sexual abuse or other traumas present in the family, which would influence the results. The study would also be further enriched and more complex if we also considered the possible influences of intergenerational transmission besides the original family, which would include another generation besides parents (grandparents), because we know this presents a great risk factor of sexual abuse (Barocas and Barocas, 1973; Epstein, 1979; Figley, 1995; Howell, 2002; Gostecnik, 2004, 2005; Rosenheck and Fontana, 1998).

REFERENCES

Ball, S., Bourdeaudhuij, J., Crombez, G., & Cost, P. (2004). Differences in trauma symptoms and family functioning in intra-and extrafamilial sexually abused adolescents. *Journal of Interpersonal Violence*, 19, 108-123.

Barocas, H., & Barocas, C. (1973). Manifestations of concentration camp effects on the second generation. *American Journal of Psychiatry*, 130, 820-821.

Burt, C. E., Cohen, L. H., & Bjorck, J. P. (1988). Perceived family environment as a moderator of young adolescents' life stress adjustment. *American Journal of Comunity Psychology*, 16, 101-122.

Catherall, D. R. (1998). Treating traumatized families. In C. R. Figley (Ed.), Burnout in families: The systemic cost of caring (pp. 187-215). New York: CRC Press.

Catherall, D. R. (2004). Handbook of stress, trauma and the family. New York: Brunner-Routledge.

Cohen, T. (1995). Motherhood among incest survivors. *Child Abuse and Neglect*, 19, 1423–1429.

Collin-Vezina, D. (2003). Current understanding about intergenerational transmission of child sexual abuse. *Child Abuse Neglect*, 27(5), 489-507.

Courtois, C. (1988). Healing the incest wound: Adult survivors in therapy. New York: Norton.

Cross, W. (2001). A personal history of childhood sexual abuse: Parenting patterns and problems. *Clinical Child Psychology and Psychiatry*, 6(4), 563-574.

Cvetek, R. (2004). Predelava disfunkcionalno shranjenih stresnih izkusenj ter metoda desenzitizacije in ponovne predelave z ocesnim gibanjem [The processing of disfunctionally stored stressful experiences and Eye Movement Desenzitization and Reprocessing method]. Neobjavljena doktorska disertacija [Unpublished doctoral dissertation], University of Ljubljana, Department of Psychology.

Epstein, H. (1979). Children of the Holocaust. New York: Putnam.

Evans, E., Hawton, K., & Rodham, K. (2005). Suicidal phenomena and abuse in adolescents: A review of epidemiological studies. *Child Abuse & Neglect*, 29(11), 45-58.

Figley, C. R. (1983). Catastrophes: An overview of family reactions. In C. R. Figley & H. I. McCubbin (Eds.), Stress and the family, Vol. II: Coping with catastrophe (pp. 3-20). New York: Brunner/Mazel.

Figley, C. R. (Ed.) (1995). Compassion fatigue: Coping with secondary traumatic stress disorder in those who treat the traumatized. New York: Brunner/Mazel.

Figley, C. R. (1995). Systematic traumatology: Family therapy with trauma survivors. Presentation at the Maryland Psychological Association, Rockville, MD.

Finkelhor, D. (1980). Risk factors in the sexual victimization of children. *Child Abuse and Neglect*, 4, 265-273.

Finkelhor, D. (1984). Child sexual abuse: New theory and research. New York: Free Press.

Finkelhor, D. (1990). Early and long term effects of child sexual abuse: An update. *Professional Psychology: Research and Practice*, 21, 325-330.

Foubert, J. D., Nixon, M. L., Sisson, V. S., & Barnes, A. C. (2005). A longitudinal study of Chickering and Reisser's vectors: Exploring gender differences and implications for refining the theory. Journal of College Student Development, 46, 461 – 471.

Gostecnik, C. (1997). Clovek v zacaranem krogu [Human in perpetual cycle]. Ljubljana: Brat Francisek and Franciscan Family Institute.

Gostecnik, C. (1998). Ne grenite svojih otrok [Don't be the Bane of your Children's Lifes]. Ljubljana: Brat Francisek and Franciscan Family Institute.

Gostecnik, C. (2001). Poskusiva znova [Let's try it again]. Ljubljana: Brat Francisek and Franciscan Family Institute.

Gostecnik, C. (2004). Relacijska druzinska terapija [Relational Family Therapy]. Ljubljana: Brat Francisek and Franciscan Family Institute.

Gostecnik, C. (2005). Preobrat v psihoanalizo in religiozno izkustvo [Radical Changes in Psychoanalysis and Religious Experience]. Ljubljana: Brat Francisek and Franciscan Family Institute.

Hall, L. A., Sachs, B., & Rayens, M.K. (1998). Mothers' potential for child abuse: The roles of childhood abuse and social resources. *Nursing Research*, 47, 87–95.

Hanson, R. K., & Slater, S. (1988). Sexual victimization in the history of sexual abusers: A review. *Annals of Sex Research*, 1, 485-499.

Hobfoll, S. E., & Spielberger, C. D. (1992). Family stress: Integrating theory and measurment. *Journal of Family Psychology*, 6 (2), 99-112.

Holohan, C. J., & Moos, R. H. (1981). Social support and psychological distress: A longitudinal analysis. *Journal of Abnormal Psychology*, 90, 365-370.

Hovestadt, A. J., Anderson, W. T., Piercy, F. A., Cochran, S. W., & Fine, M. (1985). A family-of-origin scale. *Journal of Marital and Family Therapy*, 11(3), 287-297.

Howell, E. F. (2002). »Good girls,« sexy »Bad girls,« and warriors: The role of trauma and dissociation in the creation and reproduction of gender. In Chu, J. & E. S. Bowman (Eds.), Trauma and sexuality: The effects of childhood sexual, physical, and emotional abuse on sexual identity and behavior (pp. 5-32). New York: The Haworth Medical Press.

Johnson, C. T. (2002). Some considerations about sexual abuse and children with sexual behavior problems. In Chu, J. & E. S. Bowman (Eds.), Trauma and sexuality the effects of childhood sexual, physical, and emotional abuse on sexual identity and behavior (pp. 83-106). New York: The Haworth Medical Press.

Kaufman, J., & Zigler, E. (1987). Do abused children become abusive parents? *American Journal of Orthopsychiatry*, 57, 186-191.

Kazak, A. E. (1989). Families of chronically ill children: A systems and social-ecological model of adjustment and challenge. *Journal of Consulting and Clinical Psychology*, 57, 25-30.

Lebow, J., & Rekart, K. N. (2005). Research assessing couple and family therapies for posttraumatic stress disorder. In D. R. Catherall (Ed.), Handbook of stress, trauma and the family (pp. 261-279). New York: Brunner-Routledge.

Lisak, D., Hopper, J., & Song, P. (1996). Factors in the cycle of violence: Gender rigidity and emotional construction. *Journal of Traumatic Stress*, 4, 721-743.

Little, L., & Hamby, S. L. (1999). Gender differences in sexual abuse outcomes and recovery experiences: A survey of therapist-survivors. *Professional Psychology: Research and Practice,* 30(4), 378-385.

Marans, S., Berkman, M., & Cohen, D. (1996). Child development and adoption to catastrophic circumstances. In R. J. Apfel & B. Simon (Ed.), Minefields in their hearts: The mental health of children in war and communal violence (pp.104-127). New Haven, CT: Yale University Press.

McCloskey, L. A., & Bailey, J. A. (2000). The intergenerational transmission of risk for child sexual abuse. *Journal of Interpersonal Violence*, 15, 1019-1035.

Miller, A. (2005). Upor telesa: Telo terja resnico [The body never lies]. Ljubljana: Tangram.

Mollestrom, W. W., Patchner, M. A., & Milner, J. S. (1992). Family functioning and child abuse potential. *Journal of Clinical Psychology*, 48(4), 445-454.

Monahon, C. (1993). Children and trauma: A guide for parents and professionals. San Francisco: Jossey-Bass.

Moos, R. H., & Moos, B. S. (1986). Family environment scale manual. Palo Alto, CA: Consulting Psychologists Press.

Muller, R., Sicoli, L., & Lemieux, K. (2000). Relationship between attachment style and posttraumatic stress symptomatology among adults who report the experience of childhood abuse. *Journal of Traumatic Stress*, 13, 32-332.

Olson, D. H., Russell, C. S., & Sprenkle, D. H. (1983). Circumplex model of merital and family systems. VI. Theoretical update. *Family Process*, 22, 69-83.

Olson, D. H. (2000). Circumplex model of marital and family systems. *Journal of Family Therapy*, 22(2), 144-167.

Parker, H., & Parker, S. (1986). Father-daughter sexual abuse: An emerging perspective. *American Journal of Orthopsychiatry*, 56, 531-549.

Paveza, G. (1988). Risk factors in father-daughter child sexual abuse. *Journal of Interpersonal Violence*, 3(3), 290-306.

Rojsek, J. (2002). Spolna zloraba otrok – psiholoske in psihodinamicne lastnosti ter dogajanja pri storilcu, partnerju in zrtvi [Sexual abuse of children - psychological and psychodynamic traits and functioning of the perpetrator, the partner and the victim]. Psiholoska obzorja [*Horizons of psychology*], 11(3), 39-53.

Rosenbloom, D., & Williams, M. B. (1999). Life after trauma: A workbook for healing. New York: Guilford Press.

Rosenheck, R., & Fontana, A. (1998). Transgenerational effects of abusive violence on the children of vietnam combat veterans. *Journal of Traumatic stress*, 11, 731-742.

Rothschild, B. (2000). The body remembers. The psychophysiology of trauma and trauma treatment. New York: Norton.

Steinberg, A. (1998). Understanding the secondary traumatic stress of children. In C. R. Figley (Ed.), Burnout in families: The sistemic costs of caring (pp. 29-46). Boca Raton, FL: CRC.

The Invisible Boy (1996). Health Canada. Retrieved Oktober 24, 2005 from the National Clearinghouse in Family Violence Web site: http://www.canadiancrc.com/PDFs/The_Invisible_Boy_Report.pdf.

Timmons-Mitchell, J., Chander-Holtz, D., & Semple, W. E. (1996). Post-traumatic stress symptoms in mothers following children's reports of sexual abuse: An exploratory study. *American Journal of Orthopsychiatry*, 66, 463-467.

Tomanovic, S. (2003). Negotiating children's participation and autonomy within familie. *The international Journal of Children's Rights*, 11, 51-71.

Trepper, T. S., & Barrett, J. M. (1989). Systemic treatment of incest: A therapeutic handbook. New York: Brunner-Routledge.

Wilcox, B. L. (1986). Stress, coping and the social milieu of divorced women. In S. E. Hobfoll (Ed.), Stress, social support and women (pp. 171-200). Beverly Hills, CA: Sage.

Williams, L. M. (1994). Recall of childhood trauma: A prospective study of women's memories of child sexual abuse. *Journal of Consulting and Clinical Psychology*, 62, 1167-1176.

Woodall, K. L., & Mathews, K. A. (1989). Familial environment associated with type A behavoirs and psychophysiological responses to stress in children. *Health Psychology*, 8, 403-426.

In: Psychology of Neglect
Editors: Y. Spiteri, E. Galea, 47-64

Chapter 3

WHEN HELL IS FOR CHILDREN: THE RELATIONSHIP BETWEEN NEGLECT AND OTHER CHILDHOOD ADVERSITIES IN AN ITALIAN SAMPLE

Adriano Schimmenti[*] and Ugo Pace
Kore University, Enna

ABSTRACT

Experiences of neglect typically create a threat to a child's health and well-being. On the one hand, neglectful parents show a lack of interest in relation to material care (e.g. feeding, clothing, cleanliness, hunger), friendships, school work and career prospects of their children; on the other hand, they fail to meet the emotional needs of their children, being unsuccessful in providing a secure base for the development of competent social behaviours. For these reasons, neglect can play a critical role in the origins of psychological maladjustment and in the early onset of psychiatric disorders. In the present study, the Childhood Experience of Care and Abuse interview (CECA; Bifulco, Brown, & Harris, 1994) was administered to 100 Italian non-clinical respondents, aged from 19 to 50,

[*] Correspondence:
Prof. Adriano Schimmenti, PhD
Faculty of Psychology and Educational Science, Kore University, Enna
Cittadella Universitaria, 94100 Enna (Italy)
E-mail: adriano.schimmenti@libero.it

in order to assess how neglect combines with other childhood adversities in generating a fertile ground where psychological risk grows and produces poisoned fruits. Results of the study show that severe experiences of neglect were always associated with other types of maltreatment and failures of care. Adults who were neglected during their childhood were exposed to a number of other adversities, including prolonged separation from mother, financial problems, parental discord and violence, and less involvement with peers. Neglected individuals also experienced more hostility and coldness from their parents, were more likely to be physically abused, were more often left alone without supervision, and had responsibilities of running the household and caring for the emotional and material needs of parents and siblings. A discriminant analysis showed that severe experiences of neglect (those rated at 'marked' or 'moderate' levels in the CECA) were predicted by family discord, role reversal/parentification by mother, and a prolonged separation (more than 12 months) from her, leading to 95% of cases correctly classified. The present findings are consistent with the research literature, underlining that childhood neglect merges with other parental abuses and failures of care, leading to a condition of psychological risk in the child. Results also show the possibility for early detection –and, in the most fortunate cases, even a prevention– of such a risk. This is crucial for avoiding the negative effects of neglect on the development of personality and behaviour.

INTRODUCTION

A long standing tradition of psychological theory and research has offered a consistent model for understanding the effects of parenting styles during infancy and childhood. Findings from these studies have underlined that variations in parental care have lasting effects on the offspring's behaviour through "environmental programming" (Gunnar & Quevedo, 2007; McGowan et al., 2009; Shea et al., 2005; Van Voorhees & Scarpa, 2004). This means that variations in parenting can even cause enduring alterations in child's gene expression that can be passed on to future generations. So, as in a chain reaction, individual factors interact with risks from the social environment – such as family discord, poor parenting, child abuse and neglect, family poverty and unemployment, alienated neighbourhood– in determining maladaptive patterns of development during infancy and adolescence.

These opening considerations immediately highlight that childhood adversities can play an important, perhaps critical, role in the origins of psychological maladjustment and in the onset of psychiatric disorders

(Bifulco, Brown & Harris, 1994). They also suggest that scientific research on adverse childhood experiences is necessary to identify the specific developmental pathways that lead to psychopathology. It follows that an effective evaluation of negative childhood experiences is imperative for research purposes, but this requires a great degree of accuracy in the operationalization of abuse and neglect concepts, to avoid theoretical confusion and inappropriate generalization of results. Such precision in the definition of abuse and neglect can be difficult, since these phenomena are very complex, and overlapping.

A NEED FOR CLEAR DEFINITIONS

Although the great impact of neglect experiences on child development is well established, even now there is lack of agreement about its precise definition. In fact, definitions of neglect are broad, and its boundaries are unclear. Indeed, the term "neglect" has so many variants that a one-word label is more obfuscating than clarifying. Neglect experiences have ranged from the failure to provide food, clothing, or medical care, to the failure to provide supervision or emotional support. Neglect has also been described as a persistent or severe abandonment of a child, or as the failure to protect a child from exposure to any kind of danger. At severe levels it has been described as failure to carry out important aspects of care resulting in the significant impairment of the child's health or development.

The persistent ambiguity and inconsistency of neglect definitions have lead some clinicians and researchers in this area to suggest simply a general theme or direction of study. There can be so much heterogeneity in how neglect may present itself, that even legal definitions can be inadequate. The following points can add clarity.

First, a theoretical distinction between child abuse and neglect is possible: abuse is an act or set of behaviours involving the *commission* of acts entailing violence toward a child, while neglect involves the *omission* of acts around nurturing which are critical to a child's health and well-being (Ammerman, 1990). Neglect is less what parents or caregivers do, than what they fail to do: it refers to the failure to act, and occurs when there is a deficiency in appropriate parenting behaviours, rather than the presence of inappropriate parenting behaviour.

Second, an extreme form of neglect, or "medical neglect", can be readily identified when a parent refuses or is unable, for reasons other than poverty, to provide medical care so as to seriously endanger the physical health of the child (Jenny et al., 2007). Instances of medical neglect can result from a variety of conditions considered intentional or unintentional. In cases of intentional neglect, caregivers might show features that foresee an inability to empathize with the child's need, such as through lack of empathy or clear hostility. It can also occur as a consequence of religious tradition, for which medical care is not considered essential or in some cases, where survivals down to faith regulated by a High Power (Asser & Swan, 1998).

However, the "non-medical" neglect is less clear than medical neglect. Neglect is generally branded in several different ways. For example, the second National Incidence Survey (NIS-2) has categorized children as physically or educationally neglected. Physical neglect involved delay in health care, abandonment, being thrown out of the home, other custody issues, inadequate supervision, and inattention to physical needs. Educational neglect involved parental lack of interest in the children's education, in their development of knowledge, schoolwork, career, and so on (Sedlak, 1997).

Shmitt (1981) divided neglect into five categories: medical neglect, safety neglect, educational neglect, physical neglect, and emotional neglect. Zuravin and Taylor (1987) go further and have identified eight types of neglect: physical health care, mental health care, supervision, substitute child care, housing hazards, household sanitation, personal hygiene, and nutrition. Further rating was linked both to specific parents' behaviours and to the age of the child concerned.

The lack of scientific certainties about the real meaning of the construct of neglect has lead to different means of assessment. Moreover, it is not only parents that have been labelled as neglectful for a wide variety of acts of omission, but also categories and definitions of neglect differ across jurisdictions and researchers. Thus Zuravin (1989) has affirmed that our understanding of child neglect is limited by the complexity of this construct. However, progress in this field is possible, when satisfactorily definition and operationalization of the construct are formalised, described and discussed in research. Theoretical and research advances are hindered by the lack of common definitions and the use of inappropriate, non specific, measures.

PRECONDITIONS AND DEVELOPMENTAL TRAJECTORIES ASSOCIATED WITH NEGLECT

Despite the above points illustrating the limits of research on child neglect, several psychological and environmental factors have been associated with neglect in the literature: particularly around poverty, serious caregiving deficits, parental psychopathology, substance abuse, family breakup, poor prenatal or postnatal care. These represent the most important risk factors that increase children's vulnerability to psychopathology, especially in the absence of social or psychological protective factors (McCall & Groark, 2000).

As regard sociological and sociocultural explanations, conditions such as poverty, unemployment and poor housing have been recognized as associated with child neglect. Other family risk factors such as violence and inconsistent or chaotic childrearing are closely linked to the development of parental neglect (Loeber & Farrington, 2000). Neglectful parents may also be less emotionally involved in their children's development. Thus social risk factors include those involving family violence, alcoholism, and harsh family circumstances related to frequent moves, unemployment, and poverty (Wolfe, 1999). In such circumstances the care of children can be an unrewarding experience that may lead over time to real experiences of neglect.

The developmental-ecological model, proposed by Belsky (1993), has underlined the role of the sociocultural context underlying child maltreatment. This model conceives maltreatment as the result of the interaction of different risk factors that can be grouped through four domains: the individual, family, environment, and culture. The individual ones involve personal psychological features such as a parent's low self-esteem, poor impulse control, difficult temperament, or disability. Factors concerning the family may comprise strained relationships and violent behaviours among family members. Factors involving the community include negative interactions between families' and their living environments, such as the neighbourhood or workplace. The final level involves the beliefs and traditions that characterize the culture in which families live.

This model provides a general approach for child education and growth, and involves a series of ongoing interactions; consequently the interrelation of factors may serve to increase, decrease, or maintain the likelihood of abuse or neglect within families (Ammerman, 1990).

Neglect generally represents a threat for children development. Neglectful parents refuse or delay providing for physical needs, for health care, education, or material needs as well as for psychological needs such as for kindliness and attention. Such parents fail to provide to the child a secure base (Bowlby, 1988) for the development of competent social behaviours. In particular, the interpersonal regulation of affect in a healthy family helps children to gain competence in their environment, including strategies that can be used in every day social contexts in which children are involved; thus several empirical studies have highlighted that neglected children are characterized by insecure attachment and show poorer social and emotional functioning during the different phases of growth (Azar et al., 1998). During the first two years of life, children with experiences of physical and psychological neglect show lack of motivation or enthusiasm, a high level of irritation and a low level of patience in problem-solving tasks. During the successive two years, the neglected child shows a lack of impulse control and less flexibility in problem-solving than the non-neglected child (Egeland, Sroufe, & Erickson, 1983). By kindergarten age, neglected children's performance of intellectual functioning and school achievement are the lowest even in comparison with children who experienced other failures of care or abuse (Erickson, Egeland, & Pianta, 1989). Later, during childhood and adolescence, neglected individuals suffer disruptions in interpersonal functioning that includes peer rejection and social withdrawal (Salzinger et al., 2001), bullying victimization (Shields & Cicchetti 2001), and conflict in peer and romantic relationships (Egeland et al. 2002).

In terms of parental characteristics that lead to neglectful parenting, several studies have examined parenting beliefs and attitudes and psychological variables. For example, Azar and Rohrbeck (1986) have underlined that neglectful parents have unrealistic expectations of their pupils, believing that a 2-year-old child can play quietly for hours alone, that a 3-year-old child can attend to the parent's own emotional needs, and that a 4-year-old child can get dressed and ready for school by themselves. As regards the personal characteristics that differentiate neglectful parents from non-neglecting ones, Schumacher, Slep and Heyman (2001) have stressed the importance of parenting behaviours involving attributions and expectations for child's behaviour as well as parental personality variables such as anger, confidence, self-esteem, and impulse control.

Attachment theory has provided a comprehensive framework to cover problem parenting. Attachment theory is a lifespan approach whereby the origins of insecure attachment style stem from adverse childhood experience leading to problems in parenting the next generation (Bifulco et al., 2002). Inconsistent and insensitive parenting, along with parental separation and more extreme experiences of neglect and abuse, have been identified as aetiological precursors of latter attachment difficulties. As with abused children, neglected children have been found to have significantly raised rates of insecure attachment to their caregivers compared to non-maltreated children (Crittenden & Ainsworth, 1989). Children who experience early emotional neglect seem to be particularly at risk for attachment problems. For example 57% of emotionally neglected children participating in the Minnesota Mother-Child Project whilst securely attached at 12 months of age, at 18 months of age had changed classifications to insecure attachment (Egeland & Sroufe, 1981). Compared to their non-maltreated or abused counterparts, physically and emotionally neglected preschoolers demonstrated notable problems in coping, personality development, and emotion regulation. Such neglected preschoolers have been shown to be confused by the emotional displays of others and less able to discriminate emotions than their non-maltreated counterparts (Pollack et al., 2000). When they find themselves in stressful situations, neglected preschoolers tend to be more hopeless than physically abused children, who in turn tend to be angrier (Crittenden, 1985, 1992). However, high levels of insecure attachment style have been significantly associated with a variety of childhood maltreatment, involving not only neglect but also physical or sexual abuse. In particular, fearful and angry-dismissive styles showed the highest association with such adverse childhood experience (Bifulco et al., 2002).

Children who suffer abuse or neglect may sustain a variety of devastating physical, psychological, cognitive, and behavioural problems. The effects vary with the age and personality of the victim and also with the type and duration of the abuse. Physical consequences may range from minor injuries to severe brain damage, while psychological harm ranges from lack of self-esteem, learning disorders or serious mental illness. For particular concern of neglected children, are behavioural problems that interfere with their development and education. Thus neglected children may run away from home, get involved with drugs, alcohol and delinquency, experience intimacy problems, self-harm, and they can even attempt suicide (Enns et al., 2006). Interestingly, the findings from a longitudinal study by Maxfield and Widom (1996), who followed a group of maltreated children into adulthood, show similar outcomes for both physical abuse and neglect associated with criminal behaviour, personality disorders, and substance abuse.

However, it is important to note that some factors can protect children from neglect: parental recognition of problems and their increased capacity to receive practical and emotional support may represent the first step to overcome the at-risk developmental context for the child (Dubowitz & Bennett, 2007).

In summary, understanding how neglect is associated with other childhood adversities and failures of care in childhood is necessary from both a psychosocial and clinical perspective, for preventing neglect producing its poisoned fruits later in life.

THE RESEARCH

The research presented in this chapter is aimed at investigating the association between neglect and other childhood adversities, including experiences of abuse and problems in the family, in a community sample in Italy. It is imperative to understand the environment in which neglect emerges in order to identify the best policies and practice for preventing or reducing the dreadful impact of neglect experiences in the life of an individual.

Participants

One hundred individuals, aged from 19 to 50 (M=29.3; SD=9.6), who reported no current or chronic medical or psychiatric illnesses in the past 5 years, and were not under medication (except for common minor health problems) participated in this study. Participants were recruited through a combination of convenience sampling and snowball sampling (Goodman, 1961). The group consisted of 36 men and 64 women. The socio-demographic characteristics of this group are illustrated in Table 1.

As Table 1 shows, the sample mostly entailed young adults; with almost half of participants (46) students aged less than 25 years old. Most of the individuals were single, with a medium or high degree of education, although there were some who did not go to high school or even complete post-elementary courses. Almost all subjects (99) had lived with their biological parents during their childhood, and only one of them grew up with mother alone. However, some participants experienced prolonged separation (more than a year) from father (10 participants) or mother (2) mostly due to parents working in other cities.

This group was contacted for the Italian validation (Giannone et al., 2011) of the Childhood Experience of Care and Abuse interview (CECA, Bifulco, Brown & Harris, 1994) used in this study.

Table 1. Socio-demographic characteristics of the sample (N=100)

	Frequencies
Gender	
Male	36
Female	64
Age	
19-24 years	49
25-32 years	18
33-40 years	17
41-50 years	16
Education *	
5 years or less	1
5 to 8 years	10
9 to 13 years	59
More than 13 years (degree or more)	30
Civil Status	
Single	70
Married	28
Divorced	2
Employment	
Student	50
Part-time worker	16
Full-time worker	22
Unemployed	12

* This variable is coded according to the Italian educational system.

Measure

The CECA interview was administered to the sample in order to assess neglect and other childhood adversities. The CECA is a retrospective semi-structured interview, administered to adults or late adolescents, and measures adverse experience in childhood and adolescence up to age 17. The CECA is well known in the international literature, where it is considered the 'gold standard' criterion for investigating the experiences of care and abuse in childhood and adolescence. It is also commonly used within psychological and psychiatric practice, as well as in clinical and psychosocial research. The CECA reflects objective features of early life experience with probing questions to ascertain details of context and time-sequence of experience. The interview assesses experiences of lack of care (in terms of neglect, antipathy, and role reversal) and abuse (physical abuse, sexual abuse and psychological abuse) from different parent figures during childhood and adolescence. These scales form the Core CECA. Several additional scales can be utilized to assess loss of parent, family arrangements, discord in the home, violence between parents, problem with peers, and supervision and control of children. The interview has high levels of reliability and validity (Bifulco, Brown & Harris, 1994; Bifulco et al., 1997). Since the CECA is used retrospectively, it uses procedures to enhance recall by (*i*) allowing the respondent time to talk at length by using a number of general open questions in addition to detailed probing ones for further detail, and (*ii*) dealing with childhood experience chronologically and using sequence to further trigger memory. The interview has been translated into different languages, and is used in research in United Kingdom, Portugal, Belgium and Italy as well as in Canada and USA.

All experiences reflected in the CECA are rated by the interviewer on 4-point scales of severity ('marked', 'moderate', 'mild' or 'little/none') according to predetermined criteria and manualised threshold examples. For case classification, results on the CECA scales were dichotomised between 'severe' (marked or moderate score) and 'non-severe' (mild or little-none score), since previous analyses showed that dichotomies best discriminate between binary case and non-case outcomes of disorder (Bifulco & Moran, 1998).

Full description of scales and scoring procedures are given elsewhere (Bifulco & Moran, 1998), but brief definitions of the Core CECA scales are given below.

Neglect

This involves parental lack of interest in relation to material care (e.g. feeding, clothing), friendships, schoolwork or career prospects and child's concerns. So, the parental neglect scale reflects the amount of neglect shown by parents in terms of providing for the child's material, social, educational and emotional needs. Severe neglect typically involves parental disinterest in two or more of these domains. Interview material relevant for neglect includes ascertaining whether the child could go to the parents if upset or unhappy, whether the parents made sure the child was fed and clothed adequately, whether the parents attended to the child when ill, how much interest was taken in school work, whether the parents knew who child's friend were and who s/he associated with, whether the parents remembered and celebrated the child's birthday.

Antipathy

This assesses parental hostility, coldness or rejection shown to the child, including scapegoating in relation to siblings. Severe antipathy typically involves pervasive hostility or dislike of the child.

Role Reversal/Parentification

This assesses the extent to which the child takes over practical and/or emotional responsibility of the parent. Role reversal has two distinct strands: a practical one where the child is expected to run the household and an emotional one where the child is expected to take emotional responsibility for the inadequate parents and their wellbeing. Severe role reversal typically involves complete responsibility for the household for a period, together with emotional responsibility for the parents.

Physical Abuse

This includes violence towards the child from adults in the household, usually parents but also occasionally from other adults or older siblings. Assessment is based on type of attack (e.g. with implement such as belt or stick or punching or kicking the child) and frequency (e.g. weekly or more). Severe physical abuse usually involved repeated and frequent attacks with an implement.

Sexual Abuse

This assesses sexual contact from an adult or older peer, including both household and non-household members. Scoring criteria for the sexual abuse scale include the amount of sexual contact such as touching of breasts or genitals, sexual or oral intercourse or being made to watch sexual activity. Severe experiences were those with a higher degree of sexual intrusiveness, perpetrated by close others and with higher frequency and duration.

Psychological Abuse

This includes cruelty with potential for damaging the social, cognitive and emotional development of the child. Psychological abuse is demonstrated by either verbal or non-verbal act, and can take the form of humiliation, cognitive disorientation, extreme rejection, emotional blackmail, corruption, deprivation of basic needs and valued objects, voluntarily inflicting marked distress and terrorizing the child. Severe psychological abuse typically involves more than one of these types of behaviour toward the child and the pervasiveness in the relationship with parents.

Results

In the entire sample composed of 100 participants from normal population, 8 participants (2 men, 6 women) were exposed to severe neglect during their childhood (peak scores of "marked" or "moderate" on mother's and/or father's scale of neglect on the CECA interview).

Neglect occurred in the most cases from father (7 cases), while mothers were seriously neglecting in two cases. One individual was neglected by both mother and father.

No differences were detected in relation to neglect and gender (Fisher's exact test p=NS).

Experiences of severe parental neglect were associated with a number of other childhood adversities. Results of Fisher's exact test showed that participants who were neglected during their childhood were more likely to be separated for more than a year from their mother (p=.006), they were more exposed to parental discord (p<.001), they experienced more antipathy (i.e. coldness and hostility) (p=.002), more role reversal/parentification (p<.001), more forms of inadequate supervision and discipline (p=.001), and more physical abuse (p=.03) from parents. At trend level, they were also exposed to more scenes of violence between parents (p=.07) and their parents had more financial problems (p=.07).

More specifically in relation to other maltreatment, neglect from mother was associated with experiences of antipathy (p=.02), role reversal/parentification (p=.03) and physical abuse (p=.001). Neglect from father was associated with antipathy (p=.009), role reversal/parentification (p=.003), lax supervision (p=.02) and problem discipline (i.e., non predictable, inconsistent, lax or harsh, p<0.001), financial difficulties in the family (p=.04), and the presence of discord between parents (p=.02). Interestingly, a separation of more than a year from mother was associated with both mother's and father's neglect (p=.04 and p=.004, respectively). Furthermore, it can be important to underline that in all the 8 cases where severe neglect was experienced, at least one other childhood adversity at marked or moderate level was present concurrently.

Table 2 illustrates how neglect associates with other failures of care and abuses at the scale level (four-point scores on Core CECA scales).

Table 2. Associations among neglect and other failures of care/abuses (Pearson's *r*)

	Antipathy	Role reversal	Physical abuse	Psychological abuse	Sexual abuse
Neglect by mother	.33*	.31*	.12	.17	.01
Neglect by father	.48**	.32*	.15	.18	.03
Neglect peak score (mother or father)	.54**	.40**	.10	.26*	.10

* $p<.01$; ** $p<.001$

Pearson's *r* correlations confirmed that peaks of neglect was in association with other difficulties in the participants' relationship with parents, such as antipathy, role reversal/parentification, and psychological abuse, but even with a lack of social involvement and other problems with peers ($r=.21$, $p=.03$). At the scale level, no significant association were found among neglect and physical or psychological abuse. Furthermore, it is interesting to note that neglect by mother was significantly associated with neglect by father ($r=.31$, $p=.002$).

A discriminant function analysis was performed using the exploratory stepwise method to detect which variables, among those related to childhood adversities considered in this study, would predict severe neglect. Results of this analysis showed that separation from mother, mother's role reversal/parentification and parental discord produced a canonical discriminant function accounting for 66.9% of the between group variability (Wilk's Lambda=.60, $X^2(3)=48.41$, $p<.001$), with 95% of cases correctly classified. The correlation for these scales and the canonical discriminant function was high (.68, .66, and .53 for separation from mother, mother's role reversal/parentification and parental discord, respectively), qualifying these scales as interpretable predictors of childhood experiences of neglect. This means that prolonged separations from mother, inappropriate demands for child taking care of material and emotional needs of the mother, and lasting arguments between parents dramatically increase the probability that a child would be neglected.

DISCUSSION AND CONCLUSION

The present study sought to investigate the interrelationships between neglect and other childhood adversities, including abuse, failure of care and features of social arena. Results have clearly showed that neglected individuals have experienced a plethora of childhood adversities, including hostility and coldness from parents, physical abuse, parentification, prolonged separation with their caretakers, together with financial problems, parental discord involving even violence between parents. Neglect never occurred alone: this suggests that such form of parental lack of care is one of the most notable for marking a range of family difficulties, where inappropriate parenting interacts with problem environment determining dangerous conditions for the child development.

As Rutter has affirmed in past decades (1972), some characteristics are necessary for adequate parenting, the absence of which can lead to emotional deprivation and problem development. The relationship between the children and their caregivers should be a loving relationship that leads to secure attachment, which should provide satisfactory emotional stimulation for the children and should be provided consistently and predicatably. Children need to have their needs met, such as the provision of adequate nutrition, opportunities for conversations and play, being protected from danger and having discipline based mainly on teaching and role models (Oates, 1996).

A relationship with a neglectful parent provides the opposite: in fact, "if the behaviour of neglecting parents toward their children could be summed up in one word, that would be indifference" (Young, 1964, p. 31). Such indifference can invoke feelings of inadequacy, worthlessness and mistrust in the child. It is a basic tenet of attachment theory (Bowlby, 1973), that ways of relating to others result from childhood interpersonal experiences which shape what one feels but also what one does in the social arena and what one expects from relationships and the interpersonal world. Neglected children often develop a low self-esteem and they have negative expectations toward people and relationships. Their potential to form a positive representation of themselves as good and lovable is dramatically impaired by the indifference from their parents: neglected children will expect others to be equally indifferent or damaging because they have not learned acceptance and benevolence toward themselves but instead they have seen themselves in the eyes of their parents as bad and unlovable.

On the base of these considerations, it is rather clear that childhood neglect has the potential to affect a child's ability to interact with the world across multiple domains of functioning. Although there is a group of neglected children who may be resilient to psychopathology and the other negative outcomes discussed earlier in the chapter, the clear implication of the findings of the study is that there is a need for prevention or, at the least, an early intervention in the lives of neglected children.

Findings from the study suggest that the early detection of the risk for a child being neglected is possible, even when the physical evidences of medical neglect are not present. Results from discriminant analysis showed that if there is discord and criticism between parents, if children have suffered from prolonged separation from their caregivers, and if parents made inappropriate to age requests to their children for they being emotionally and practically responsible for all the family well-being, it is very likely that neglect at moderate or even marked level might occur. This provides a family marker for neglect. Thus social services should be particularly alert about children who live in a family where is known to be discord or violence and for children who are growing up with one parent, especially when these children frequently fail to attend school and do not participate in community life, because it is possible that they are living a condition of neglect and parentification, being left alone to answer parental problems and demands, up to forget their own needs, desires, and their rights to live a normal, healthy, life. We need to ensure children are given back their childhood and rights to love and care.

REFERENCES

Ammerman, R. T. (1990). Etiological models of child maltreatment: A behavioral perspective. *Behavior Modification,*14, 230-254.

Asser, S. M., & Swan, M. (1998). Child fatalities from religion-motivated medical neglect. *Pediatrics*, 101, 625-629.

Azar, S. T., & Rohrbeck, C. A. (1986). Child abuse and unrealistic expectations: Further validation of the Parent Opinion Questionnaire. *Journal of Consulting and Clinical Psychology*, 54, 867–868

Azar, S. T., Povilaitis, T. Y., Lauretti, A. F., & Pouquette, C. L. (1998). "The current status of etiological theories in intrafamilial child maltreatment".

In J. R. Lutzker (Ed.), *Handbook of Child Abuse Research and Treatment* (pp. 3-30). New York: Plenum Press.

Belsky, J. (1993). Etiology of child maltreatment: A development-ecological analysis. *Psychological Bulletin*, 114, 413–434.

Bifulco, A., Brown, G. W., & Harris, T. (1994). Childhood experiences of care and abuse (CECA). A retrospective interview measure. *Child Psychology and Psychiatry*, 35, 1419-1435.

Bifulco, A., Brown, G. W., Lillie, A., & Jarvis, J. (1997). Memories of childhood neglect and abuse: corroboration in a series of sisters. *Journal of Child Psychology and Psychiatry*, 38, 365-374.

Bifulco, A., & Moran, P. (1998). *Wednesday's Child: Research into Women's Experience of Neglect and Abuse in Childhood, and Adult Depression.* London: Routledge.

Bifulco, A., Moran, P., Ball, C., & Lillie, A. (2002) Adult Attachment Style II. Its relationship to psychosocial depressive-vulnerability. *Social Psychiatry and Psychiatric Epidemiology*, 37, 60-67.

Bowlby, J. (1973). *Attachment and Loss,* Vol. II. *Separation: Anxiety and Anger.* London: Hogarth Press.

Bowlby, J. (1988). *A Secure Base: Parent-child Attachment and Healthy Human Development.* London: Routledge.

Crittenden, P. M. (1985). Maltreated infants: vulnerability and resilience. *Journal of Child Psychology and Psychiatry*, 26, 85–96.

Crittenden, P. M. (1992). Children's strategies for coping with adverse home environments: an interpretation using attachment theory. *Child Abuse & Neglect*, 16, 329–343.

Crittenden, P. M., & Ainsworth M. D. S. (1989). "Child maltreatment and attachment theory". In D. Cicchetti and V. Carlson (Eds.), *Child Maltreatment: Theory and Research on the Causes and Consequences of Child Abuse and Neglect* (pp. 432-463). New York: Cambridge University Press.

Dubowitz, H., & Bennett, S. (2007). Physical abuse and neglect of children: Key health issues. *Lancet*, 369 (9576),1891-1899.

Egeland, B., Sroufe, A., & Erickson, M. F. (1983). The developmental consequences of different patterns of maltreatment. *Child Abuse & Neglect*, 7, 459–469.

Egeland, B., Yates, T., Appleyard, K., & van Dulman, M. (2002). The long-term consequences of maltreatment in the early years: A developmental pathway model to antisocial behavior. *Children's Services: Social Policy, Research, and Practice*, 5, 249-260.

Egeland, E., & Sroufe, A. (1981). "Developmental sequelae of maltreatment in infancy". In R. Rizley & D. Cicchetti (Eds.), *New Directions for Child Development: Developmental Perspective on Child Maltreatment* (Vol. 11, pp. 77–92). San Francisco: Jossey-Bass.

Enns, M. W., Cox, B. J., Afifi, T.O., de Graaf, R., ten Have, M., & Sareen, J. (2006). Childhood adversities and risk for suicidal ideation and attempts: A longitudinal population-based study. *Psychological Medicine*, 32, 1769-1778.

Erickson, M. F., Egeland, B., & Pianta, R. (1989). "The effects of maltreatment on the development of young children". In D. Cicchetti & V. Carlson (Eds.), *Child Maltreatment: Theory and Research on the Causes and Consequences of Child Abuse and Neglect* (pp. 647–684). New York: Cambridge University Press.

Giannone, F., Schimmenti, A., Caretti, V., Chiarenza, A., Ferraro, A., Guarino, S., Guarnaccia, C., Lucarelli, L., Mancuso, L., Mulé, A., Petrocchi, M., Pruiti, F., Ragonese, N., & Bifulco, A. (2011). Validità, attendibilità e proprietà psicometriche della versione italiana dell'intervista CECA (Childhood Experience of Care and Abuse). *Psichiatria e Psicoterapia*, 30, 3-21.

Goodman, L. A. (1961). Snowball sampling. *Annals of Mathematical Statistics*, 32, 148–170.

Gunnar, M., & Quevedo, K. (2007). The neurobiology of stress and development. *Annual Review of Psychology*, 58, 145-173.

Jenny, C., Christian, C. Hibbard, R.A., Kellogg, N. D, Spivak, B. S., Stirling, J. Jr, Corwin, D. L., Mercy J., & Hurley, T. P. (2007). Recognizing and responding to medical neglect. Pediatrics, 120, 1385-1389.

Loeber R., Farrington D. P. (2000): Young children who commit crime: Epidemiology, developmental origins, risk factors, early interventions, and policy implications. *Development and Psychopathology*, 12, 737-762.

Maxfield, M. G., & Widom, C. S. (1996). The cycle of violence: revisited six years later. *Archives of Pediatrics and Adolescent Medicine*, 150, 390–395.

McCall, R. B., & Groark, C. J. (2000). The future of applied child development research and public policy. *Child Development*, 71, 197-204.

McGowan, P., Sasaki, A., D'Alessio, A., Dymov, S., Labonté, B., Szyf, M., Turecki, G., & Meaney, M. (2009). Epigenetic regulation of the glucocorticoid receptor in human brain associates with childhood abuse. *Nature Neuroscience*, 12, 342-348.

Oates, R. K. (1996). *The Spectrum of Child Abuse: Assessment, Treatment, and Prevention*. New York: Brunner/Mazel.

Pollak, S. D., Cicchetti, D., Hornung, K., & Reed, A. (2000). Recognizing emotion in faces: Developmental effects of child abuse and neglect. *Developmental Psychology*, 36, 679–688.

Rutter, M. (1972). *Maternal Deprivation Reassessed*. Harmondsworth: Penguin Books.

Salzinger, S., Feldman, R. S., Ng-Mak, D. S., Mojica, E., & Stockhammer, T. F. (2001). The effect of physical abuse on children's social and affective status: A model of cognitive and behavioral processes explaining the association. *Development and Psychopathology*, 13, 805–825.

Schmitt, B. D. (1981). "Child neglect". In N. S. Ellerstein (Ed.), *Child Abuse and Neglect: A Medical Reference* (pp. 297-306). New York: John Wiley & Sons.

Schumacher, J. A., Slep, A. M. S., & Heyman, R. E. (2001). Risk factors for child neglect. *Aggression and Violent Behavior*, 6, 231–254.

Sedlak, A. (1997). Risk factors for the occurrence of child abuse and neglect. *Journal of Aggression, Maltreatment & Trauma*, 1, 149-187.

Shea, A., Walsh, C., Macmillan, H., & Steiner, M. (2005) Child maltreatment and HPA axis dysregulation: relationship to major depressive disorder and post traumatic stress disorder in females. *Psychoneuroendocrinology*, 30, 162-178.

Shields, A., & Cicchetti, D. (2001). Parental maltreatment and emotion dysregulation as risk factors for bullying and victimization in middle childhood. *Journal of Clinical Child Psychology*, 30, 349-363.

Van Voorhees, E, & Scarpa, A. (2004).The effects of child maltreatment on the hypothalamic-pituitary-adrenal axis. *Trauma, Violence, & Abuse*, 5, 333-352.

Wolfe, D. (1999). *Child abuse: Implications for Child Development and Psychopathology* (2nd ed.). Thousand Oaks: Sage Publications.

Young, L. (1964). *Wednesday's children*. New York: McGraw-Hill.

Zuravin, S. J. (1989). The ecology of child abuse and neglect: Review of the literature and presentation of data. *Violence and Victims*, 4, 101–120.

Zuravin, S. J., & Taylor, R. (1987). The ecology of child maltreatment: Identifying and characterizing high-risk neighborhoods. *Child Welfare*, 66, 497–506.

Reviewed by: Prof. Antonia Bifulco, PhD, Lifespan Research Group, Centre for Abuse and Trauma Studies, Kingston University, London.

In: Psychology of Neglect
Editors: Y. Spiteri, E. Galea, 65-80

ISBN 978-1-62100-180-5
© 2012 Nova Science Publishers, Inc.

Chapter 4

DIETARY NEGLECT AND ITS INFLUENCE ON FEEDING

Robin Dando

Department of Physiology and Biophysics, University of Miami Miller
School of Medicine, Miami, USA

ABSTRACT

Both humans and other mammals possess an innate ability to detect
dietary deficiencies that operates at a subconscious level. This is
accomplished by alterations in specific sensitivities of the taste bud. Thus,
the sensitivity of the mammalian taste system displays a degree of
plasticity based on short term nutritional requirements. Deficiency in a
particular substance may lead to a perceived increase in palatability of
this substance, providing an additional drive to redress this nutritional
imbalance through modification of intake. This alteration occurs not only
in the brain, but before any higher level processing has occurred, in the
taste buds themselves. Many studies, both psychophysical and
physiological have detailed this phenomenon. This becomes particularly
relevant in cases of neglect, where systemized patterns stereotypical of
dietary deficiency are ingrained. The same phenomenon can present itself
in something as mundane as the reduced desire of diabetics to consume
salty foods, which would exacerbate problems caused by water retention
in diabetes mellitus, or as extreme as geophagy, where subjects,
particularly small children, will seek the nutrients denied them by eating
dirt or clay. Subjects suffering from eating disorders, or denied nutrients

due to neglect will experience an alteration in the hedonics of particular taste qualities, symptoms of their neglect, but often holding clues to the source of this neglect. Even a subject's mood, of course drastically altered in cases of neglect, can affect psychophysical taste sensitivity. A review of recent thinking is offered, along with some original results.

INTRODUCTION

The mammalian taste bud possesses receptors for incoming tastant molecules at the apical pore. Receptor or type II taste cells possess the receptors for bitter, sweet and umami taste stimuli. This signal is transduced through G-protein coupled receptors (GPCRs), and the PLCβ2 and IP3 intracellular signaling molecules, leading to an increase in intracellular calcium, depolarization of the cell, and opening of hemichannels to release ATP. This neurotransmitter signal then acts on afferent nerve terminals and on neighboring Presynaptic, or type III cells. This complex multi stage process involves the synchronous action of a number of ligands, receptors and signaling molecules, before the taste signal even leaves the taste bud. Needless to say, any medical condition, or pharmacological intervention which interferes with any part of this cascade will alter the process of taste transduction. In the process of dietary neglect, the body's internal source of a number of important factors can become depleted, inherently effecting how taste signals are transduced in the neglected subject. Interestingly, however, a number of recent publications have identified modulators of specific taste qualities, factors which would therefore not simply impinge on the taste transduction process as a whole, but would have a specific target within the taste bud. In addition to this, there are many receptor interactions from food, and taste related side effects from exogenous pharmaceutical drug intake. Finally, a broad spectrum of eating disorders have been recorded to produce a profound difference in how both food tastes, and in the resultant feeding behavior, be it from isolated cellular recordings, from psychophysical testing of human subjects, or from functional brain imaging. This would seem to imply that a subject's dietary neglect can have noteworthy bearing on how this subject's ensuing feeding behavior will evolve.

Taste cells possess a variety of basolateral receptors, which enable efferent neuromodulation of taste signals. This neuromodulation may arrive through neural innervation, or via paracrine, autocrine or endocrine factors. In this manner, the physiological response to a tastant can vary from situation to situation, leading to behavioral modification dependant on these endogenous factors. Thus the body may subconsciously regulate metabolic intake based on nutrient requirements. In addition to this, mood itself has been long established to effect taste preferences, perhaps influenced by an alteration in circulating factors, or neurotransmission behavior. Although both mood and appetite regulation are principally governed through the central nervous system, often an additional target for circulating factors affecting feeding lies within the taste bud itself. Thus, the same stimulus may affect both mood/appetite and the hedonics of taste itself.

This would represent a fascinating mechanism for the governance of nutrient intake into the body, whereby our specific enjoyment of a particular taste quality may be influenced by an evolutionarily derived linkage with its perceived nutritional value. Correspondingly, a previously established program of neglect or deprivation from a particular nutrient or food source may influence how this substance is perceived. A nutritional deficiency may lead to an alteration in taste perception which seeks to redress this balance through intake. A number of advances have recently been highlighted in the field of taste physiology.

DIABETES

Diabetes mellitus is a small collection of metabolic diseases characterized by an inability to control blood sugar levels. Particularly at risk are the elderly, frequent sufferers of dietary neglect. It was estimated more than ten years ago that 40% of people over 65 have impaired glucose tolerance (Harris et al., 1998). This estimate has since risen. Diabetes, in addition to its more well known influence over blood glucose levels, also manifests in alterations in salt and water balance within the body. Water retention, exacerbated by excessive salt intake, is a serious complication in diabetes. Salty taste shows a complex sensory profile in mammals, where it is first attractive, at low concentration, and therefore presumably palatable, while later becoming strongly aversive. In a recent report, Gilbertson and Baquero (2010) described a series of experiments whereby insulin treated mice showed a marked behavioral avoidance to salt solutions at lower concentrations than control animals, presumably representing an increase in salt sensitivity. Blockage of the epithelial sodium channel (ENaC), thought to be the mammalian salt receptor (Heck et al., 1984; Chandrasekar et al., 2010) with amiloride abolished this enhanced behavioral avoidance. This would imply a peripheral influence of plasma insulin levels on taste preference and hedonics. Isolated taste cells were patch clamped, with sodium influx revealing insulin dependence on the nanomolar scale. Similar results were obtained using a sodium dependant fluorescent dye. Interestingly, type I diabetes model mice showed many behavioral and electrophysiological characteristics suggesting that indeed insulin was affecting the peripheral taste system. These model animals showed a higher sodium influx into taste cells, but no insulin dependent modulation of this sodium influx through ENaC. Behaviorally, these mice avoided salt at a significantly lower concentration than wild type animals. Addition of amiloride to salt solution confirmed that this was both a peripheral effect, and one which was ENaC dependant.

Thus, animals with impaired glucose tolerance avoid excess salt intake, which would exacerbate problems through upsetting osmoregulation. We can also assume that this would act as a form of failsafe in neglected diabetes patients, whereby their own taste for salt would become aversive, and reduce their intake levels. The close interplay between sugar and plasma insulin levels might represent an interesting future direction of this work. As insulin release during the cephalic phase can initiate after only a few minutes, it would seem plausible that during the course of a sugar rich meal, a subject's taste for salt would reduce.

SEROTONIN, NEGLECT AND THE TASTE BUD

Neglect is inherently linked with underlying or ensuing depression. Sensitivity to taste quality as a whole is dependent peripherally upon the entire taste transduction process which precedes report to the primary afferent nerve. Serotonin has been postulated to play some role in taste signal transduction (Huang et al., 2005), as well as more established roles in mood and social behavior. Plasma serotonin concentration can greatly vary, based on mood, health, and in particular with pharmacological treatment. Serotonin is at present a popular target for psychological intervention, with prescription of selective serotonin reuptake inhibitors (SSRIs), tricyclic antidepressants (TCAs) and serotonin and norepinephrine reuptake inhibitors (SNRIs) widespread. Prevalent side effects of these treatments are dysgeusia and ageusia. As there are serotonin receptors expressed within the taste bud (Kaya et al., 2004), perhaps a potent target for drug interaction would not be in the CNS, but in the taste bud itself.

Recently, details on a paracrine inhibitory role for serotonin originating from type III cells, with the intended target of type II cells was laid out (Huang et al., 2009). Serotonin was observed to be released on detection of ATP, presumably arising from activation of taste receptors on type II taste cells. Whether this serotonin acts purely in a neuromodulatory role, as some form of secondary afferent taste transmitter, or merely as an intricate mechanism of inactivation of ATP release, is yet to be clarified. Intriguingly, however, alterations in plasma serotonin levels in humans results in a marked plasticity of taste thresholds (Heath et al., 2006). Application of an SSRI (paroxetine) resulting in an increase in plasma serotonin, was found to decrease the detection thresholds of both bitter and sweet compounds. Both the time scale of interaction and the fact that this effect was observed in taste qualities that share a common pathway indicate this is a peripheral effect, and not one occurring at higher levels. Taste sensitivity was selectively raised for bitter and sweet compounds, which are detected by receptors on type II taste cells. Comparatively, sour compounds, which are detected by type III cells (Richter et al., 2003), and salt taste, which is thought to be transduced primarily through type I cells (Vandenbeuch et al., 2008), were not affected by serotonin, consistent with serotonin disrupting paracrine signaling between type II and type III taste cells.

Kaya et al (2004) report that the serotonin receptors found in taste are 5-HT_{1A} receptors. Changes in the binding properties of these same 5-HT_{1A} receptors is heavily implicated in the study of depression (Drevets et al., 2000). Much remains to be discovered on the role of serotonin in the taste system, however with what is known at this point, there can be little doubt that the resultant depression brought on by neglect would affect serotonergic mechanisms of taste transduction.

EATING DISORDERS AND TASTE

Eating disorders are a broad and poorly defined group of disorders, for the most part considered to consist primarily of Anorexia Nervosa, Bulimia Nervosa and binge eating disorder, leading to excessive obesity. There are a number of epidemiologically minor eating disorder, no less important, which will not be covered in this article. Sufferers of eating disorders are neglected of a number of essential nutrients, which can lead to an aggravation of their already fragile condition. Anorexia Nervosa (AN) is a serious multi-factorial disorder with the highest mortality rate of any psychiatric disorder (Sullivan,

1995). It can be defined by restrictive type behavior where dangerously little food is consumed, or by binge/purging behavior. Interestingly, taste thresholds are altered in anorexic patients (Aschenbrenner et al., 2008) which may contribute to abnormal appetite and feeding in these individuals.

Obesity has become a leading public health concern. Over a billion adults worldwide are now classified as obese or overweight (Haslam and James, 2005). Nearly 300,000 deaths in the United States annually can be attributed to obesity (Allison et al., 1999). Obesity correlates irrefutably with cardiovascular atherosclerosis, diabetes mellitus, coronary artery disease and hypertension. Obese individuals have notably differing taste sensitivity (Pasquet et al., 2007). As the taste of food determines its palatability and level of consumption, it is logical that alterations in taste may play a role in obesity. Obesity has profound effects on taste preference. This may be due to the altered taste sensitivities noted in obese individuals (Pasquet et al., 2007; Monneuse et al., 2008). Moreover, taste is significantly altered after surgical procedures to combat obesity, such as gastric bypass (Miras and le Roux, 2010).

Orexigenic peptides are endogenously released factors in the mammalian body which promote feeding. Key orexigenic peptides include neuropeptide Y (NPY), ghrelin, and anandamide, an endocannabinoid. Orexigenic peptides represent one of the most promising new areas for pharmacological intervention in both anorexia and obesity based research. Plasma levels of NPY and ghrelin have been found by multiple groups to be significantly lowered in patients suffering from AN, presumably leading to a lowered drive to eat. A correlation of both plasma levels of anandamide and its receptor cannabinoid1 (CB1) are found with AN. Cannabinoid agonists are currently used to alleviate anorexia and nausea in patients of both cancer and AIDS, confirming them as a valid potential target for future eating disorder therapies.

In addition to their well-established role in the central control of appetite, several recent reports propose that NPY, ghrelin and anandamide also act peripherally in taste buds. Mammalian taste is complex and multifaceted. Many neurotransmitters, including serotonin, and acetylcholine, appear to play key roles in the peripheral gustatory sensory organs—taste buds, and orexigenic peptides may be influencing taste by interfering with the actions of these taste transmitters. The mechanism(s) by which orexigenic peptides alter taste is as yet unknown. It is clear, however, that alterations in taste sensitivity contribute to the observation that ingesting food is less pleasurable for an anorexic patient (Wagner et al., 2008).

Behavioral tests show that sufferers of Anorexia Nervosa respond to taste stimuli differently than normal individuals (Eiber et al., 2002). Put simply, anorectics don't enjoy food as much as controls. Many reports show that anorectics have altered taste thresholds (Aschenbrenner et al., 2008), suggesting that these patients have reduced taste. Using fMRI, Wagner et al, (2008) demonstrated taste stimulation elicits a significantly lower neural activity in anorectics. Intriguingly, their report also showed no correlation between the pleasantness of a taste stimulus and insular activity, unlike controls. They concluded that there is a change in taste processing in anorectics and that food tastes differently to an anorexic patient. Altered taste thresholds in anorectics might be related to changes in the levels of various orexigenic factors measured in these individuals. Behavioral testing also highlights differing response to taste stimuli in obese individuals. Obese patients show higher degrees of enjoyment, measured through fMRI, to pleasant tasting solutions than non-obese subjects (Stice et al., 2008). BMI in this study was in fact found to linearly correlate with consummatory food reward. Put simply, obese subjects enjoy food more than control groups. Many reports show that obese patients have altered taste thresholds (Pasquet et al., 2007; Monneuse et al., 2008) suggesting that these patients have altered taste acuity. Patients who have undergone obesity surgery find certain foods less appetizing and have altered taste detection (Miras and le Roux, 2010). Altered taste thresholds in obesity may well be related to the changes in the levels of orexigenic factors that have already been established in these individuals.

Specifically, several labs have reported an association between plasma NPY levels and anorexia nervosa (Baranowska et al., 2001; Baranowska et al., 2003). In addition to this, a wealth of research indicates a correlation between fasting plasma ghrelin levels and both anorexia nervosa and nutritional status (Tanaka et al., 2003; Tolle et al., 2003). Add to this the observation that both anandamide plasma levels (Monteleone et al., 2005), and CB1 receptor mRNA (Frieling et al., 2009) are correlated to AN, and the link between orexigenic peptides and anorexia nervosa is irrefutable. Plasma ghrelin levels are also notably lower in obese individuals (Ukkola and Poykko, 2002). Hypothalamic NPY levels and their relevant receptors are significantly higher in obese rats (Wang et al., 2007). Hippocampal anandamide levels and cannabinoid receptor expression are also notably higher in obese mice (Massa et al., 2010). The anorexigenic nature of the cannabinoid antagonist Rimonabant was first noted several years ago (Ravinet Trillou et al., 2003), and is now used to treat obesity. Cannabinoid agonists are currently used to alleviate anorexia and nausea in patients of both cancer and AIDS, confirming them as a valid potential target for future eating disorder therapy.

Importantly, these same neurochemical pathways are also implicated in peripheral taste processing. That is, alteration in circulating levels of orexigenic factors will alter taste. Because the taste of food determines its palatability and acceptance, altering taste can profoundly affect the drive to eat. Receptors for NPY have been found in mammalian taste buds through both immunohistochemistry and RT-PCR (Herness and Zhao, 2009). Also, ghrelin, its cognate receptor (GHSR), and the enzymes responsible for its synthesis and activation are present in taste cells (Shin et al., 2010). Ghrelin-null mice have reduced sensitivity to many tastants. Finally, cannabinoid receptors have been localized within the mouse taste bud (Stoving et al., 2009) with the effects of endocannabinoids on taste thresholds well documented (Dando, 2010; Jyotaki et al., 2010).

In a recent series of excellent publications, the lab of Ninomiya has detailed interactions of both Leptin (Kawai et al., 2000; Nakamura et al., 2008) and a variety of endocannabinoids (Yoshida et al., 2010) with receptors located peripherally, in the taste bud. Though both endocannabinoids and leptin are principally known as influencing appetite through central action on hypothalamic receptors, the group displayed data on the expression of receptors for these endogenous circulating factors in sweet sensitive taste cells. Behaviorally, endocannabinoids and leptin play opposing roles in the stimulation and suppression of appetite respectively. The data presented, however, suggest an additional physiological target for these factors within the taste bud itself, in addition to this appetite regulation. Both CB1 and Ob-Rb receptors, sensitive to endocannabinoids and leptin respectively, were localized specifically in sweet sensitive type II taste cells, and not cells sensitive to other taste modalities. The fact that receptors were not found in bitter sensitive cells would seem to suggest a peripheral control of caloric intake, through modulating the palatability of energy rich foods.

Plasma leptin variation is a control of appetite regulation in the CNS. In addition to its action in the brain, leptin also acts directly on receptors in the taste bud, inhibiting sweet taste, in both behavioral and electrophysiological nerve recordings. Endocannabinoids such as anandamide and 2-arachidonyl glycerol are endogenously produced in the body. Elevation in plasma leptin levels leads to a subsequent reduction in endocannabinoids, and the two display inverse variation in the body. However, an increase in sweet taste palatability has been shown to rely also on endocannabinoids themselves, rather than simply on an indirect effect of a reduction in leptin. Both nerve recording and behavioral measurements of living animals showed an enhancement in sweet sensitivity with endocannabinoid treatment, an effect which was not observed with other taste qualities. Mice undergoing genetic deletion or pharmacological inhibition of either CB1 or Ob-Rb receptors showed none of the effects seen in their wild type counterparts to sweet sensitivity when endocannabinoids or leptin respectively were applied. In fact, mice lacking a functional leptin receptor actually showed an increased response to sweet substances. These mice were of course already hyperphagic, which has previously been ascribed purely to disturbances in leptin related appetite regulation.

Humans are known to be subject to a diurnal variation in plasma leptin levels throughout the day. This would in turn suggest a variation in circulating endocannabinoids. In an intriguing set of experiments, Nakamura et al showed a variation in sweet taste sensitivity throughout the course of the day which mirrored measured circulating leptin levels. Overweight individuals did not undergo this modulation in taste sensitivity. When meal times were varied, both leptin levels and taste thresholds followed this variation. Truly then it seems, the body influences our taste for a specific food quality when it senses a homeostatic need for a particular nutrient. Neglected individuals, with inadequate dietary intake to maintain a healthy life, may find their own taste preferences altering over time in an attempt to correct this imbalance.

ALZHEIMER'S DISEASE AND TASTE, A PUTATIVE LINK

Alzheimer's disease is a progressive and debilitating disease, characterized by a gradual onset, during which patients may have difficulty in caring for themselves. This difficulty is often exemplified by loss of appetite, a progressively lowered desire to eat, and resulting emaciation. A key component to the pathophysiology of Alzheimer's disease is a decline in the synthesis of acetylcholine (ACh), a neurotransmitter key to the formation of memories.

Recently, ACh was implicated in the taste transduction process (Ogura, 2002). The application of ACh to isolated taste buds was found to mobilize calcium from internal stores, in a manner similar to the detection of a sweet, bitter or umami compound. The specific role of this neurotransmitter in taste, and from where it would originate in the taste bud is however, unknown. Even whether it is itself a tastant, or merely serves a neuromodulatory role is not known. ACh is primarily identified in the peripheral nervous system as a marker for the parasympathetic nervous system. Therefore it would seem a reasonable assumption that ACh in the taste bud could come from parasympathetic innervation.

Recently, my own work has shown that taste buds secrete acetylcholine (ACh). This occurs in native cells as part of the taste transduction process. This acetylcholine is secreted from type II taste cells, which express the enzyme Choline Acetyltransferase, which is responsible for the synthesis of ACh. This ACh then feeds back onto Muscarinic type 3 receptors on the same type II taste cells, further increasing calcium levels in these cells, thus boosting the taste signal. Targeted genetic deletion of Muscarinic receptors in mice results in a fundamentally lowered taste detection consistent with an important amplification occurring within the taste bud through Acetylcholine. These knockout animals are hypophagic, possibly due to this alteration in taste transduction. These receptors are, however, widely expressed and therefore genetic deletion would give rise to many other changes.

ACh seems to play a role related to signal amplification in the taste bud, enhancing our ability to taste sweet, umami and bitter substances. When mouse taste buds are simulated with tastants such as this in the presence of acetylcholine, at concentrations similar to those at which it is secreted from taste buds, the calcium mobilization within the taste cells is enhanced. In addition to this, the amount of ATP, the afferent neurotransmitter in taste buds, is increased significantly by the presence of ACh. Mice lacking the muscarinic receptors present in the taste bud have an inherently lowered taste responses to these substances. Thus, it would make sense that with the resultant depletion of ACh stores in Alzheimer's disease, would come an accompanying form of dysgeusia due to the lack of this cholinergic amplification. It has been noted that many Alzheimer's patients do indeed suffer from altered taste detection consistent with this lowering of taste sensitivity (Steinbach et al., 2010). This could lead in turn to the lowered drive to eat observed in many patients. A lowered desire to eat will invariably increase mortality, due to the patient not receiving the nutrients needed for survival.

Choline, the nutrient from which ACh is synthesized cannot be manufactured in the body, and hence must be taken in through diet. Sources of choline include eggs and red meat. Dietary neglect of choline regularly leads to necrosis of the kidney, and he accumulation of fat in the liver. As choline is essential to alleviate the symptoms of Alzheimer's disease, it is even essential in its treatment, failure to maintain an adequate daily intake, as found in neglected patients, would lead to deficiencies in taste. This in turn is likely to lead to a subsequent reduced impetus to eat, further exacerbating the problem.

Thus, further study leading to a characterization of this effect may help with treatment strategies for Alzheimer's patients.

This work would suggest a possible link between the reduced desire to eat in Alzheimer's disease and this missing ACh amplification pathway in the taste bud.

CONCLUSION

The taste system represents the first point of encounter between nutrients from the external environment and our body. Thus, the primary role of the taste bud is twofold. Firstly it must keep us safe from dangerous or spoiled foods and toxic agents. Concurrently, the nutritional quality and value of substances must be assessed, with selection made depending on what is necessary for maintenance of bodily wellbeing. We as higher level animals are able to make educated choices based on perceived needs and experience. In lower level animals there are many instances of seemingly astonishing perception of dietary requirement, presumably based on inherited experience. Elephants remove intestinal parasites through licking clay. Chimpanzees have been known to eat dirt, which leads to an increase in the antimalarial qualities of the foods they eat. However, for the most part this process must enter into the realms of instinct.

Herein lies the principle advantage of modulation at the peripheral level, acting directly in the taste bud. Affecting the taste hedonics of a substance leads to an animal's own wellbeing being tied to its own desires. Thus, we are driven without our knowing selectively towards the foods our body needs. A subject of dietary neglect, whether it be an elderly or infirm individual, or an infant inadequately cared for, is at an elevated risk of further deterioration due to this nutritional impairment. Their neglect implies that they do not have the capability or the knowledge to adequately regulate nutritional input to a level which would begin to alleviate any symptoms. Thus, the subject can, in the manner noted above, experience an increased desire to consume a particular substance of which they are being deprived, all the while not realizing that basic metabolic need underlies this craving. In this manner, our taste buds act as a form of failsafe to the neglected individual, guiding them away from foods which would exacerbate their condition at a subconscious level. This is by no means adequate in most regards, however will act as a form of first line defense.

The taste system is complicated and multi-faceted. Although usually taken somewhat for granted, the degree of complexity can actually provide us with clues to concepts as complex as a subject's mood, or the progression of neurological impairment, through psychophysical testing. Due to their being roles for so many neurotransmitters in the taste bud, the decline of one transmitter, or its cogent receptors, could be monitored through carefully controlled taste testing. The commercial availability of readily implemented and user friendly testing solutions such as "taste strips" make this a tractable clinical possibility, with large scale studies now readily establishing clinical standards (Landis et al., 2009). Taste disturbances have long been viewed as an unfortunate but neglected symptom of depression. It now seems possible that the two could be inexorably linked, to the degree that researchers now highlight the possibility of taste testing as a measure of mood and anxiety (Heath et al., 2006). Due to serotonergic medications being so widely prescribed currently, it would stand to reason that taste thresholds could be used to accurately define dosages of these medications. Steinback et al (2010) suggest that taste testing could be used to distinguish healthy patients with those suffering from either Alzheimer's disease of mild cognitive impairment. It is clear that this relatively new field of taste psychophysics in clinical testing, while in its infancy, could have a bright future in diagnostic medicine.

REFERENCES

Chandrashekar J, Kuhn C, Oka Y, Yarmolinsky DA, Hummler E, Ryba NJ, Zuker CS (2010) The cells and peripheral representation of sodium taste in mice. *Nature*, 464:297-301.

Gilbertson TA, Baquero AF (2010) Insulin regulates the function of epithelial sodium channels and salt taste preference. Association for chemoreception sciences 37th annual meeting, St Petersburg, FL, USA

Heck GL, Mierson S, DeSimone JA (1984) Salt taste transduction occurs through an amiloride-sensitive sodium transport pathway. *Science*, 223:403-405.

Allison DB, Fontaine KR, Manson JE, Stevens J, VanItallie TB (1999) Annual deaths attributable to obesity in the United States. *JAMA*, 282:1530-1538.

Aschenbrenner K, Scholze N, Joraschky P, Hummel T (2008) Gustatory and olfactory sensitivity in patients with anorexia and bulimia in the course of treatment. *J Psychiatr Res*. 43:129-137.

Baranowska B, Wolinska-Witort E, Wasilewska-Dziubinska E, Roguski K, Chmielowska M (2001) Plasma leptin, neuropeptide Y (NPY) and galanin concentrations in bulimia nervosa and in anorexia nervosa. *Neuro Endocrinol Lett.* 22:356-358.

Baranowska B, Wolinska-Witort E, Wasilewska-Dziubinska E, Roguski K, Martynska L, Chmielowska M (2003) The role of neuropeptides in the disturbed control of appetite and hormone secretion in eating disorders. *Neuro Endocrinol Lett.* 24:431-434.

Dando R (2010) Endogenous peripheral neuromodulators of the mammalian taste bud. *J Neurophysiol.* 104:1835-1837.

Eiber R, Berlin I, de Brettes B, Foulon C, Guelfi JD (2002) Hedonic response to sucrose solutions and the fear of weight gain in patients with eating disorders. *Psychiatry Res.* 113:173-180.

Frieling H, Albrecht H, Jedtberg S, Gozner A, Lenz B, Wilhelm J, Hillemacher T, de Zwaan M, Kornhuber J, Bleich S (2009) Elevated cannabinoid 1 receptor mRNA is linked to eating disorder related behavior and attitudes in females with eating disorders. *Psychoneuroendocrinology,* 34:620-624.

Harris MI, Flegal KM, Cowie CC, Eberhardt MS, Goldstein DE, Little RR, Wiedmeyer HM, Byrd-Holt DD (1998) Prevalence of diabetes, impaired fasting glucose, and impaired glucose tolerance in U.S. adults. The Third National Health and Nutrition Examination Survey, 1988-1994. *Diabetes Care,* 21:518-524.

Haslam DW, James WP (2005) Obesity. *Lancet,* 366:1197-1209.

Heath TP, Melichar JK, Nutt DJ, Donaldson LF (2006) Human taste thresholds are modulated by serotonin and noradrenaline. *J Neurosci.* 26:12664-12671.

Herness S, Zhao FL (2009). The neuropeptides CCK and NPY and the changing view of cell-to-cell communication in the taste bud. *Physiol Behav.* 97:581-591.

Huang YA, Dando R, Roper SD (2009) Autocrine and paracrine roles for ATP and serotonin in mouse taste buds. *J Neurosci.* 29:13909-13918.

Huang YJ, Maruyama Y, Lu KS, Pereira E, Plonsky I, Baur JE, Wu D, Roper SD (2005) Mouse taste buds use serotonin as a neurotransmitter. *J Neurosci.* 25:843-847.

Jyotaki M, Shigemura N, Ninomiya Y (2010) Modulation of sweet taste sensitivity by orexigenic and anorexigenic factors. *Endocr J.*

Kawai K, Sugimoto K, Nakashima K, Miura H, Ninomiya Y (2000) Leptin as a modulator of sweet taste sensitivities in mice. *Proceedings of the*

National Academy of Sciences of the United States of America, 97:11044-11049.

Kaya N, Shen T, Lu SG, Zhao FL, Herness S (2004) A paracrine signaling role for serotonin in rat taste buds: expression and localization of serotonin receptor subtypes. *Am J Physiol Regul Integr Comp Physiol.* 286:R649-658.

Massa F, Mancini G, Schmidt H, Steindel F, Mackie K, Angioni C, Oliet SH, Geisslinger G, Lutz B (2010) Alterations in the hippocampal endocannabinoid system in diet-induced obese mice. *J Neurosci.* 30:6273-6281.

Miras AD, le Roux CW (2010) Bariatric surgery and taste: novel mechanisms of weight loss. *Curr Opin Gastroenterol.* 26:140-145.

Monneuse MO, Rigal N, Frelut ML, Hladik CM, Simmen B, Pasquet P (2008) Taste acuity of obese adolescents and changes in food neophobia and food preferences during a weight reduction session. *Appetite*, 50:302-307.

Monteleone P, Matias I, Martiadis V, De Petrocellis L, Maj M, Di Marzo V (2005) Blood levels of the endocannabinoid anandamide are increased in anorexia nervosa and in binge-eating disorder, but not in bulimia nervosa. *Neuropsychopharmacology*, 30:1216-1221.

Nakamura Y, Sanematsu K, Ohta R, Shirosaki S, Koyano K, Nonaka K, Shigemura N, Ninomiya Y (2008) Diurnal variation of human sweet taste recognition thresholds is correlated with plasma leptin levels. *Diabetes*, 57:2661-2665.

Pasquet P, Frelut ML, Simmen B, Hladik CM, Monneuse MO (2007) Taste perception in massively obese and in non-obese adolescents. *Int J Pediatr Obes.* 2:242-248.

Ravinet Trillou C, Arnone M, Delgorge C, Gonalons N, Keane P, Maffrand JP, Soubrie P (2003) Anti-obesity effect of SR141716, a CB1 receptor antagonist, in diet-induced obese mice. *Am J Physiol Regul Integr Comp Physiol.* 284:R345-353.

Richter TA, Caicedo A, Roper SD (2003) Sour taste stimuli evoke Ca2+ and pH responses in mouse taste cells. *J Physiol.* 547:475-483.

Shin YK, Martin B, Kim W, White CM, Ji S, Sun Y, Smith RG, Sevigny J, Tschop MH, Maudsley S, Egan JM (2010) Ghrelin is produced in taste cells and ghrelin receptor null mice show reduced taste responsivity to salty (NaCl) and sour (citric acid) tastants. *PLoS One*, 5:e12729.

Stice E, Spoor S, Bohon C, Veldhuizen MG, Small DM (2008) Relation of reward from food intake and anticipated food intake to obesity: a functional magnetic resonance imaging study. *J Abnorm Psychol.* 117:924-935.

Stoving RK, Andries A, Brixen K, Flyvbjerg A, Horder K, Frystyk J (2009) Leptin, ghrelin, and endocannabinoids: potential therapeutic targets in anorexia nervosa. *J Psychiatr Res.* 43:671-679.

Sullivan PF (1995) Mortality in anorexia nervosa. *Am J Psychiatry*, 152:1073-1074.

Tanaka M, Naruo T, Yasuhara D, Tatebe Y, Nagai N, Shiiya T, Nakazato M, Matsukura S, Nozoe S (2003) Fasting plasma ghrelin levels in subtypes of anorexia nervosa. *Psychoneuroendocrinology*, 28:829-835.

Tolle V, Kadem M, Bluet-Pajot MT, Frere D, Foulon C, Bossu C, Dardennes R, Mounier C, Zizzari P, Lang F, Epelbaum J, Estour B (2003) Balance in ghrelin and leptin plasma levels in anorexia nervosa patients and constitutionally thin women. *J Clin Endocrinol Metab.* 88:109-116.

Ukkola O, Poykko S (2002) Ghrelin, growth and obesity. *Ann Med.* 34:102-108.

Vandenbeuch A, Clapp TR, Kinnamon SC (2008) Amiloride-sensitive channels in type I fungiform taste cells in mouse. *BMC Neurosci.* 9:1.

Wagner A, Aizenstein H, Mazurkewicz L, Fudge J, Frank GK, Putnam K, Bailer UF, Fischer L, Kaye WH (2008) Altered insula response to taste stimuli in individuals recovered from restricting-type anorexia nervosa. *Neuropsychopharmacology*, 33:513-523.

Wang C, Yang N, Wu S, Liu L, Sun X, Nie S (2007) Difference of NPY and its receptor gene expressions between obesity and obesity-resistant rats in response to high-fat diet. *Horm Metab Res.* 39:262-267.

Drevets WC, Frank E, Price JC, Kupfer DJ, Greer PJ, Mathis C (2000) Serotonin type-1A receptor imaging in depression. Nucl Med Biol 27:499-507.

Heath TP, Melichar JK, Nutt DJ, Donaldson LF (2006) Human taste thresholds are modulated by serotonin and noradrenaline. *J Neurosci.* 26:12664-12671.

Landis BN, Welge-Luessen A, Bramerson A, Bende M, Mueller CA, Nordin S, Hummel T (2009) "Taste Strips" - a rapid, lateralized, gustatory bedside identification test based on impregnated filter papers. *J Neurol.* 256:242-248.

Ogura T (2002) Acetylcholine increases intracellular Ca2+ in taste cells via activation of muscarinic receptors. *J Neurophysiol.* 87:2643-2649.

Steinbach S, Hundt W, Vaitl A, Heinrich P, Forster S, Burger K, Zahnert T (2010) Taste in mild cognitive impairment and Alzheimer's disease. *J Neurol*. 257:238-246.

In: Psychology of Neglect
Editors: Y. Spiteri, E. Galea, 81-103

ISBN 978-1-62100-180-5
© 2012 Nova Science Publishers, Inc.

Chapter 5

LANDMARK RECOGNITION AND MENTAL ROUTE NAVIGATION DISORDERS IN PATIENTS WITH IMAGERY NEGLECT AND PERCEPTUAL NEGLECT

Laura Piccardi[1,2], Liana Palermo[3,2], Raffaella Nori[4], Fiorella Giusberti[4] and Cecilia Guariglia[3,2]

[1]Dipartimento di Scienze della Salute, Università degli Studi de L'Aquila
[2]I.R.C.C.S., Fondazione Santa Lucia, Roma
[3]Dipartimento di Psicologia, Università Sapienza degli Studi di Roma
[4] Dipartimento di Psicologia, Università degli Studi di Bologna

ABSTRACT

The complex relationship between perceptual neglect and imagery neglect is still not completely understand because, at least in part, these disorders depend on are associated with, different neural systems and can be dissociated even in the same patient (Beschin, Basso, & Della Sala, 2000).

Recent studies show that imagery neglect affects specific mechanisms underlying human orientation. In particular, it impairs the ability to manipulate mental representations of the environment and thus prevents the use of previous navigational experience (see for instance Guariglia et al., 2005; Piccardi, 2009; Guariglia & Piccardi, 2010).

In this study, we compared the route learning and delayed recall task performance of imagery neglect patients with pure perceptual neglect patients, patients with no neglect and healthy participants.

They had to learn a circular pathway in an unexplored area of the hospital; it included 13 landmarks and five turning points (three on the right and two on the left). During the learning phase, the participants explored the pathway three times with the examiner, who pointed out the landmarks. At the end of this phase, the participants performed two different tasks: a) Landmark Recognition Task and b) Navigational Questions. The first task included 26 pictures of landmarks (13 target pictures and 13 fillers) located along the pathway that the participants had to recognize. Fillers were the same type of stimuli as the target, but with different characteristics (e.g., two different doors). The second, delayed recall task consisted of 30 questions investigating the participants' ability to recall a learned pathway and the landmarks encountered along the way.

We assessed 23 right brain-damaged patients (4 patients with pure perceptual neglect, 8 patients with imagery neglect and 11 patients without neglect) and 17 healthy participants matched for age and education.

Our results showed that only patients with imagery neglect had a pervasive disorder in recognizing landmarks met along the route and in mentally navigating the previously learned pathway. Specifically, they were unable to answer navigational questions investigating their mental representation of the pathway. Differently, perceptual neglect patients were able to recognize landmarks as well as answer navigational questions in spite of their exploration disorder. Right brain-damaged patients without neglect showed no deficit on the tasks.

In summary, only the imagery neglect patients were unable to build or retrieve a mental representation of the new environment and, thus, failed in performing these tasks. In fact, results showed they were deficient in using a cognitive map of the environment. It is still unknown whether the deficit observed in imagery neglect patients is due to difficulty in building a mental map, recalling it from memory or using it during navigation, leaving unknown the exact point in which the navigational process is compromised.

INTRODUCTION

Hemineglect is a pervasive disorder of space representation that occurs following lesions of posterior areas of the right hemisphere (Bisiach & Vallar, 2000). It is characterised by the inability to orient attention or consider events in the contralesional side of extrapersonal or personal-body space. Difficulty in conjuring up the left side of mental images, which was described separately from other neglect symptoms (Guariglia et al., 1993), may also be present (Bisiach and Luzzatti, 1978). When hemineglect selectively affects the mental image of an inner representation (Guariglia et al. 1993; Beschin et al. 1997; Ortigue et al. 2001, 2003), patients do not report the left-side details of familiar places from memory or omit the left side of drawings from memory (Bisiach and Luzzatti, 1978; Chokron et al., 2004).

In a seminal paper, Bisiach and Luzzatti (1978) described two patients who were unable to imagine Piazza del Duomo in Milan, Italy, from two different perspectives. When they were asked to describe the landmarks in the city square, they only reported those to the right of their imagined position. This difficulty was present even when they had to form new contralateral representations (Bisiach, Luzzatti, & Perani, 1979).

Several hypotheses have been proposed to explain the nature of imagery neglect. First, imagery neglect has been considered analogous to perceptual neglect, that is, the same exploration bias that affects visual perception in neglect impedes the exploration of the contralesional side of visual mental images (Bisiach, 1993). In fact, imagery neglect has usually been described in patients also affected by perceptual neglect. Nevertheless, the existence of dissociated cases of representational neglect in the absence of perceptual neglect undermines this interpretation (Guariglia et al., 1993; Beschin et al., 1997; Coslett, 1997).

A deficit in directing attention toward the left side of mental images or damage to the mental representation system, which consists of "tearing" the left side of the mental screen, has also been hypothesized (Bisiach, 1993). Logie et al. (2005) investigated these two hypotheses in a study in which a set of ten arrays, each composed of four objects, was shown to two patients affected by imagery neglect. The patients had to describe each array from memory. They could start from the same perspective they had seen it or from the opposite (180° rotation) perspective. Both patients consistently failed to report the left-sided objects from both perspectives, but showed no deficit in reporting objects on the right side, even after mental rotation of the visual arrays. According to the authors, these results strongly support the hypothesis of a deficit in generating the left side of mental images, because a deficit in directing attention toward the left side of mental images would negatively affect mental rotations. Other authors have suggested that representational neglect results from a) damage to a system involved in the generation of mental images that is independent from systems involved in exploring and representing visuo-spatial percepts (Guariglia et al., 1993); b) damage to an egocentric spatial representation involved in the maintenance of visual information across saccades and time (Coslett, 1997); and c) unilateral damage to visuo-spatial working memory (Beschin et al., 1997).

Alternative explanations interpret imagery neglect by considering its effect on navigation (Guariglia et al., 2005; Nico et al., 2008; Byrne et al., 2007). In the BBB model (Byrne et al., 2007), which describes interactions between brain regions involved in spatial memory and mental imagery, the spatial orientation difficulties of patients with imagery neglect are considered to arise from a specific deficit in a mechanism that transforms allocentric representations into egocentric ones and vice-versa. An alternative interpretation of navigational deficits in imagery neglect patients (Guariglia et al., 2005) is that these individuals have a specific deficit in building up cognitive maps (Tolman, 1948), that is, mental representations of the environment. Indeed, the former authors reported that only patients with perceptual neglect build a stable spatial representation of the environment and use a navigational strategy based on the geometric characteristics of the environment. By contrast, they found that patients with imagery neglect were unable to build or use a mental map or implement a navigational strategy based on the geometric shape of the experimental setting. This was also supported by the findings of Nico et al. (2008) in a landmark re-orientation study in which the patients' task was to find a target location using landmarks after they had been disoriented. The authors found that the patients with imagery neglect failed to store the target location in long-term memory, whereas the patients with perceptual neglect were able to find the target location in a long-term recall condition in spite of their poor learning performance. Also in this study, the imagery neglect patients' failure seemed due to an impairment in building cognitive maps and retrieving information from them. Piccardi (2009) reported similar results in a task involving a virtual maze with and without landmarks in which patients with imagery neglect were unable to build a mental representation of the virtual space. Navigational deficits seem to co-occur in patients with imagery neglect but not in patients with perceptual neglect. Indeed, there are reports that patients with perceptual neglect successfully replicated distances when proprioceptive and vestibular information was available and were particularly efficient in navigation in a blindfolded condition and in using Euclidean information (Philbeck, Behrmann, Black, & Ebert, 2000; Pizzamiglio, Iaria, Berthoz, Galati, & Guariglia, 2003; Guariglia et al., 2005).

Until now, the ability of imagery neglect patients to build a cognitive map has been assessed in simple experimental settings, that is, in a human model of the Morris Water Maze with and without landmarks (Guariglia et al., 2005; Nico et al., 2008) and in virtual mazes with and without landmarks (Piccardi, 2009). Therefore we do not know whether patients with perceptual neglect would also show deficits linked to the presence of several left turnings and left points of repere in a real ecological and generally more complex environment full of stimuli.

In the present study, we aimed to use an ecological task to assess the ability of imagery neglect patients to recognize landmarks without considering their spatial position and to mentally navigate a previously learned pathway (i.e., in a previously unexplored area of the hospital). In particular, we were interested in studying their use of egocentric coordinates, which are based on the individual position in respect of environmental landmarks for maintaining the perspective in which spatial information has been experienced (e.g., Iachini, Ruggiero, Conson, & Trojano, 2009; Kosslyn, 1994) both in acquiring and retrieval spatial information in ecological settings. We compared the performance of imagery neglect patients with that of pure perceptual neglect patients, patients without neglect and healthy participants. We expected that imagery neglect patients would evidence a specific deficit in building egocentric cognitive maps also in ecological environments.

METHOD

Participants

Four groups of participants took part in the study:

1) 17 healthy participants with no signs of neurological or psychiatric impairment (HP);
2) 4 right brain-damaged patients affected by visuo-spatial neglect (RN+);
3) 8 right brain-damaged patients affected by pure imagery neglect or both visuo-spatial neglect and imagery neglect (RI+);
4) 11 right brain-damaged patients with no signs of visuo-spatial and/or imagery neglect (RN-).

All participants gave their informed consent to take part in the study, which was approved by the local ethics committee.

Table 1. Participants' demographic and clinical data

Participants	Group	Sex	Age (years)	Education (years)	Stroke onset (days)	Lesion site
Patients						
Case 1	RN+	F	51	13	259	F + T + P
Case 2	RN+	M	53	18	62	F + P
Case 3	RN+	M	70	8	77	ln + cn
Case 4	RN+	M	35	17	55	F + T + P
mean (s.d.)			52.25 (14.31)	14 (4.55)	113.25 (97.6)	
Case 5	RI+	M	79	17	41	cr
Case 6	RI+	F	76	5	387	T + P
Case 7	RI+	F	46	13	52	F + P + i
Case 8	RI+	M	76	4	190	F + T
Case 9	RI+	F	75	5	39	F + T + P
Case 10	RI+	M	52	13	45	F + T + P
Case 11	RI+	M	49	13	66	F + T + P
Case 12	RI+	M	40	13	4010	F + P
mean (s.d.)	RI+		61.63 (16.29)	10.38 (4.93)	603.75 (1381.62)	
Case 13	RN-	M	65	5	423	i + cr
Case 14	RN-	M	80	5	28	P
Case 15	RN-	F	74	3	44	i + th
Case 16	RN-	F	48	17	72	ic+ u
mean (s.d.)	RN-		64 (10.77)	11.2 (5.55)	82 (120.5)	

Case 18	RN-	M	56	13	49	F + T
Case 19	RN-	M	63	13	38	F + T
Case 20	RN-	M	62	18	55	F + T+ P
Case 21	RN-	M	49	17	36	ic
Case 22	RN-	M	75	13	45	cs + pons
Case 23	RN-	F	56	8	180	P+O
mean (s.d.)	RN-		64 (10.77)	11.2 (5.55)	82 (120.5)	

Healthy Participants (n 17)

mean (s.d.)	HP	61.47 (14.07)	12.35 (4.85)	

cn= caudate nucleus; cp= cerebral peduncle, cr= corona radiata, cs= centrum semiovale; F= frontal lobe; i=insula; ic= internal capsule; ln= lenticular nucleus; O=occipital lobe; P= parietal lobe; T= temporal lobe; th= thalamus; u=uncus.

Table 2. Patients' results on the visuo-spatial neglect and imagery neglect tests

Subject	Group	Letter cancellation (hits)		Line cancellation (hits)		Wundt-Jastrow illusion test (unexpected responses)^		Sentence reading (hits)	LQ Familiar Squares Description	LQ O' Clock Test
		Left (53)	Right (51)	Left (11)	Right (10)	Left	Right			
Case 1	RN+	0	13	0	9	12	1	0	-16.66	-11.11
Case 2	RN+	5	50	11	10	10	1	6	-12	-6.66

Table 2. Continued

Case				2	10	10	1	6		
Case 3	RN+	0	19	9	10	10	1	6	5.88	0
Case 4	RN+	5	34	11	10	4	0	5	-9.09	6.66
Case 5	RI+	53	51	11	10	0	0	6	-27.27*	4.76
Case 6	RI+	47	53	11	10	0	0	6	-21.21*	-41.18*
Case 7	RI+	1	16	10	10	12	0	3	-41.93*	25
Case 8	RI+	5	47	11	10	0	0	4	-60*	-10
Case 9	RI+	0	8	10	11	14	0	0	-27.27*	14.28
Case 10	RI+	0	10	1	9	17	5	0	-25*	-18.18*
Case 11	RI+	0	16	0	7	19	0	0	3	-18.51*
Case 12	RI+	53	51	11	10	0	0	6	-69.23*	0
Case 13	RN-	53	51	11	10	0	0	6	-7.14	-3.23
Case 14	RN-	52	49	11	10	0	0	6	0	-15.79
Case 15	RN-	53	51	11	10	0	0	6	-4.6	-6.67
Case 16	RN-	53	51	11	10	0	0	6	-6.25	0
Case 17	RN-	50	47	11	10	0	0	6	-5.6	0
Case 18	RN-	53	49	11	10	0	0	6	4.76	-12
Case 19	RN-	53	51	11	10	0	0	6	15.79	-11.11
Case 20	RN-	53	45	11	10	0	0	6	-6.66	-3.03
Case 21	RN-	53	51	11	10	0	0	6	0	-3.22
Case 22	RN-	53	51	11	10	0	0	6	-4.54	-3.22
Case 23	RN-	53	51	11	10	0	0	6	-8.33	-11.11

* Asymmetric performance.

Patients were recruited from a population of in-patients at the I.R.C.C.S. Fondazione Santa Lucia (Rome) hospital who were being treated for hemiparesis or hemiplegia following a cerebrovascular accident (CVA). Exclusion criteria were the following: two or more CVA, neoplastic or traumatic aetiology, cognitive deterioration or the presence of global amnesia.

Personal data and lesion site are reported in Table 1.

NEUROPSYCHOLOGICAL ASSESSMENT

The right brain-damaged patients were subdivided into three groups (RN–, RI+ and RN+) according to their performance on the Standard Battery for the Evaluation of Hemineglect (Pizzamiglio et al., 1989) and two tests of representational neglect (Bisiach and Luzzatti, 1978; Grossi et al., 1989).

The Standardized Battery for the Evaluation of Hemineglect (Pizzamiglio et al., 1989) includes the following tests:

Line Cancellation Test

The patient has to cross out 21 slanted lines (2.5 cm) distributed randomly on A3 sheet, 11 on the left half and 10 on the right half. The score is the number of lines crossed out on each half of the stimulus array. The cut-off is >2 omissions on the left side;

Letter Cancellation Test

The patient has to cross out 104 upper-case letter H's interspersed with 208 fillers; 53 targets are distributed over the left and 51 over the right half of A3 sheet. The score is the number of letters crossed out on each half. The cut-off is a difference >4 between omissions on the left and the right side;

Wundt–Jastrow Area Illusion Test

The patient is presented with a picture of two identical black fans placed one above the other, so that one of them appears to be horizontal, and has to point to the stimulus that seems longest (illusionary effect). In neglect patients, the illusory effect is reduced on the contralesional side (see Massironi et al., 1988). The score is the number of trials in which the normal illusory effect is present on each side. The cut-off is the difference >2 between unexpected responses (i.e., responses in the direction opposite the illusory effect in controls) for left oriented minus right oriented stimuli.

Sentence Reading Test

The patient has to read aloud six sentences ranging from five to 11 words (21-42 letters). The score is the number of correctly read sentences. The cut-off is one or more sentences incompletely read on the left side.

Patients who scored below the cut-off on at least two of these tests were considered to have an extrapersonal deficit.

The presence of representational neglect was evaluated using specific tests:

O'Clock Test (Grossi et al., 1989)

The patient has to image two different times on two analogical clocks and judge on which clock the hands form the widest angle. Sixteen pairs of times on the left hemiface (i.e., 7:30 and 8:00) and 16 pairs of times on the right hemiface (i.e., 3:30 and 2:00) were used. Scores were the number of correct responses. A laterality quotient was calculated as follows: LQ= (correct responses on the left − correct responses on the right/ correct responses on the left + correct responses on the right)*100;

Familiar Squares Description Test (Bisiach & Luzzatti, 1978)

The patient is asked to describe two familiar public squares from memory as they would appear from opposite vantage points. The elements described on each side of the square are recorded. When a patient was familiar with a square unknown to the examiners, a relative was asked to describe the square in detail before the patient was submitted to the test. The relative's description was used to decide the vantage points in the two descriptions and to score the patient's performance. The number of elements reported on the left and the right side of the imagined squares was transformed into a laterality quotient as follows: LQs: [(left answers – right answers)/(left answers + right answers)] x 100 (see also Bartolomeo et al., 1994).

An LQ below –18 (i.e., 2 standard deviations below the controls' means) on one of these tests was considered an index of representational neglect.

Patients whose performance was below the cut-off on at least one of the two tests were included in the group of right brain-damaged patients with imagery neglect (RI+). Three patients showed pure imagery neglect. All brain-damaged patients also underwent an extensive neuropsychological evaluation to assess their verbal and visuo-spatial short- and long-term memory (Carlesimo et al., 2002; Carlesimo, Caltagirone, & Gainotti, 1996; Novelli et al., 1986; Rey, 1958; Spinnler & Tognoni, 1987; Corsi, 1972), abstract reasoning (Basso, Capitani, & Laiacona, 1987; Raven, 1938), constructional apraxia (Spinnler & Tognoni, 1987) and visual integration ability (Spinnler & Tognoni, 1987) and visuospatial neglect (Pizzamiglio, Judica, Razzano, & Zoccolotti, 1989). All healthy participants were submitted to the Mini-Mental State Examination (MMSE; Folstein, Folstein, & McHugh, 1975; Magni, Binetti, Bianchetti, Rozzini, & Trabucchi, 1996) to verify they had no mental decay.

No participant was amnesic or had mental deterioration.

EXPERIMENTAL TASK

Once the participants had undergone the neuropsychological assessment and had been separated into the experimental groups, they were asked to learn a circular pathway in an area of the hospital they had never explored. Along this pathway, they encountered 13 landmarks and five turning points (three on the right and two on the left) (see Figure 1). During the learning phase, self-guided exploration of the pathway was performed three times. The participants had to pay attention to the landmarks along the way; the examiner pointed them out, indicating that afterwards they would have to answer questions about the pathway and the landmarks. At the end of the learning phase, the participants had to carry out two different tasks.

Table 3. Neuropsychological assessment

Subject	Group	Digit Span (max 9)	Corsi Span (max 9)	Short story (Novelli et al, 1986)	Short story: Immediate recall (Carlesimo et al, 2000)	Short story: Delayed recall (Carlesimo et al, 2000)	Rey's word: Immediate recall (Rey, 1958; Carlesimo et al, 1996)	Rey's word: Delayed recall (Rey, 1958; Carlesimo et al, 1996)	Street completion test (Spinnler & Tognoni, 1987) max 14	Constructional apraxia (Spinnler & Tognoni, 1987) max 14
Case 1	RN+	5 (n)	4 (n)	15 (n)	--	--	53 (n)	15 (n)	5 (n)	9 (d)
Case 2	RN+	5 (n)	3 (d)	17 (n)	--	--	45 (n)	12 (n)	7 (n)	11 (n)
Case 3	RN+	5 (n)	0 (d)	--	6.3 (n)	6.3 (n)	34 (n)	5 (n)	0 (d)	4 (d)
Case 4	RN+	6 (n)	3 (d)	--	6.8 (n)	6.5 (n)	48 (n)	7 (d)	2 (d)	7 (d)
Case 5	RI+	6 (n)	5 (n)	9.5 (n)	--	--	31 (n)	5 (n)	12 (n)	12 (n)
Case 6	RI+	5 (n)	4 (n)	8.5 (n)	--	--	--	--	10 (n)	10 (n)
Case 7	RI+	6 (n)	3 (d)	12.5 (n)	--	--	41 (n)	8 (n)	7 (n)	9 (d)
Case 8	RI+	4 (n)	4 (n)	11.5 (n)	--	--	17 (d)	2 (n)	2 (n)	7 (n)
Case 9	RI+	4 (n)	--	6 (n)	--	--	24 (n)	3 (n)	--	1 (d)
Case 10	RI+	4 (n)	2 (d)	14 (n)	--	--	54 (n)	11 (n)	3 (d)	9 (d)
Case 11	RI+	6 (n)	3 (d)	--	5.5 (n)	4.4 (n)	49 (n)	12 (n)	7 (n)	10 (n)
Case 12	RI+	7 (n)	4 (n)	--	--	--	Rey's figure: Immediate recall 16 (n)	Rey's figure: Delayed recall 13.5 (n)	8 (n)	14 (n)
Case 13	RN-	5 (n)	4 (n)	9 (n)	--	--	25 (n)	5 (n)	9 (n)	12 (n)
Case 14	RN-	4 (n)	4 (n)	11.5 (n)	--	--	38 (n)	8 (n)	7 (n)	8 (n)
Case 15	RN-	4 (n)	4 (n)	5.5 (n)	--	--	33 (n)	7 (n)	5 (n)	11 (n)

Case 16	RN-	5 (n)	5 (n)	12.5 (n)	--	--	42 (n)	8 (n)	13 (n)	13 (n)
Case 17	RN-	4 (n)	4 (n)	12.5 (n)	--	--	32 (n)	10 (n)	10 (n)	14 (n)
Case 18	RN-	5 (n)	5 (n)	18 (n)	--	--	40 (n)	7 (n)	9 (n)	12 (n)
Case 19	RN-	5 (n)	5 (n)	11 (n)	--	--	54 (n)	11 (n)	10 (n)	13 (n)
Case 20	RN-	--	--	10 (n)	--	--	53 (n)	14 (n)	8 (n)	13 (n)
Case 21	RN-	6 (n)	6 (n)	14 (n)	--	--	60 (n)	12 (n)	12 (n)	14 (n)
Case 22	RN-	6 (n)	4 (n)	10 (n)	--	--	35 (n)	4 (n)	11 (n)	14 (n)
Case 23	RN-	5 (n)	4 (n)	14.5 (n)	--	--	46 (n)	10 (n)	10 (n)	14 (n)

n= normal performance; d=deficit performance.

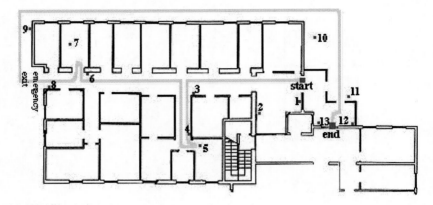

1 umbrella stand
2 sofa
3 picture depicting the map of Rome
4 hat stand
5 room 18 (Interns)
6 poster
7 room 8 (Dr. Bureca)
8 potted plant
9 electrical box
10 lamppost
11 litter basket
12 snack dispenser
13 drinks dispenser

Figure 1. Pathway, showed by the line, in the hospital with landmarks and turning points.

Landmarks Recognition Task

The participants were separately shown 26 pictures of landmarks (13 targets) met along the pathway and fillers (see Figure 2). The fillers were similar to the targets (the same object) but had different characteristics (e.g., two different chairs). The participants were asked to recognize the landmarks they had seen before (maximum score: 26).

Figure 2. Example of Landmarks Recognition Task item. Target (up) seen on the pathway and its filler (down).

Navigational Questions

The participants were asked to answer 30 questions aimed at investigating their mental representation of the learned environment (i.e., "Imagine being at the poster and looking at the emergency exit: Do you turn right or left to reach room 18?" See Appendix for a list of the questions). The maximum score was 30.

RESULTS

To assess group differences in ability to recognize previously seen landmarks and mentally navigate through the environment, we performed single analyses of variance (ANOVAs) with group (HP, RN-, RN+, RI+) as independent variable and number of correct responses on the Landmark Recognition Task and the Navigational Questions as dependent variables.

The single ANOVAs showed significant differences among groups on both of the experimental tasks (Landmark Recognition Task: $F_{3,36}=7.51$, $p<0.0005$; Navigational Questions: $F_{3,36}=12.78$, $p<0.0001$).

Post hoc comparisons were performed by means of Tukey's honestly significant difference (HSD) test for unequal N (Spjotvoll/Stoline test). In the Landmark Recognition Task, the RI+ group performed significantly worse that the HP group in determining whether a picture depicted a previously seen landmark along the pathway ($p<0.01$). No differences were observed between RI+ and RN-, RI+ and RN+, RN+ and HP, RN+ and RN-, and between RN– and HP.

Similarly, in the Navigational Questions Task the RI+ group had greater difficulty in answering questions that required mentally navigating a learned path with respect to the HP group ($p<0.0005$) and the RN- group ($p<0.001$). No differences were observed between RI+ and RN+, RN+ and HP; RN+ and RN-, or between RN– and HP.

DISCUSSION

In the present study, we investigated the ability of patients with imagery neglect and perceptual neglect to mentally navigate in a learned area of the hospital. Specifically, they had to recognize landmarks met along the pathway, and we assessed their knowledge of the egocentric spatial coordinates. The aim of the study was to assess the patients' performance in an ecological setting. We observed the performance of patients with different types of neglect in an urban environment navigation in which landmarks were plentiful and the space was generally too large to be perceived in its entirety from any one vantage point. Indeed, although a previous study (Guariglia et al., 2005) reported the co-occurrence of deficient navigation and imagery neglect, the patients had been tested in simplified experimental settings. By contrast, the present experiment allowed us to assess the strict and selective association between topographical orientation and imagery neglect in an ecological setting.

We found a pervasive disorder in landmark recognition and mental navigation only in patients with imagery neglect. In fact, patients with perceptual neglect were able to recognize landmarks and answer navigational questions in spite of their exploration disorder; and right brain-damaged patients without neglect showed no deficit in performing the tasks. One interpretation of perceptual neglect patients' performance in route learning under natural conditions, where real-world routes are full of ecological landmarks and too complex to be learned through stimulus-response contingencies, could have to do with the examiner's instructions, which forced the patients to explore the left side of the environment. In pure perceptual neglect, there is no deficit in mentally representing space, only in exploring it. Therefore, if patients are forced to pay attention on the contralesional side they can generate a mental map of the environment. Specifically, with regard to the ability to correctly solve landmark recognition tasks, according to the definition of the term, a landmark should be considered an environmental pattern that is perceptually salient or important for people, such as their home, without spatial characteristics (Siegel & White, 1975). Therefore, it is not necessary to remember exactly where the landmark is in relation to one's position in the environment, but it is necessary to remember its form, colour and so on (i.e., its structural characteristics). It can be hypothesised that during the experimental phase (and thanks to the experimental instructions) pure perceptual neglect patients acquire and represent landmarks by considering both structural and spatial information in a way that enables them to transform a landmark into a "navigational landmark" with structural and egocentric spatial information. When forced to pay attention to the environment, these patients are able to acquire and represent both structural characteristics and spatial coordinates. Furthermore, it appears that they use these two factors in recognizing landmarks and responding to egocentric spatial questions. Thus, landmarks become "navigational landmarks" with spatial information associated with them, so they are not just a visual pattern. The ability to acquire and represent egocentric information is also essential to perceptually control movement in near space, such as avoiding obstacles. Indeed, these patients may also be able to process fine-grained metric information. These results are in line with previous works by Janzen and co-workers (2004; 2007) who pointed out that people are able to recognize objects when they have specific navigational relevance even if they are not buildings. This result was also confirmed by the findings of Schinazi and Epstein (2010) who reported that buildings were more easily recognized at navigational decision (not non-decision) points, supporting the idea that landmarks and route learning may occur simultaneously when they are useful for solving navigational tasks.

By contrast, patients with imagery neglect showed a more pervasive deficit and were unable to take advantage of the examiner's instructions. Indeed, they were unable to mentally imagine themselves on the learned pathway and to recognize landmarks previously met along the pathway. Therefore, we can hypothesise that these patients are unable to build a useful cognitive map for moving successfully through the environment.

It is still unclear whether the deficit observed in patients with imagery neglect is due to difficulty in building a mental map, recalling it from memory or using it during navigation. Therefore, we do not know the exact point in which the navigational process is compromised.

A recent review by Kravitz and co-workers (2011) suggests a new neural framework for visuospatial processing that sheds some light on our results. These authors identified three pathways emerging from the dorsal stream: a parieto-prefrontal pathway, a parieto-premotor pathway and a parieto-medial temporal pathway, which mainly support spatial working memory, visually guided action and spatial navigation, respectively. As many of our patients with neglect have lesions involving the parietal cortex, their different performance on the landmark recognition task and the navigational questions might be due to the different involvement of pathways coming from the dorsal stream. Indeed, the participants with imagery neglect, who performed deficiently on the navigational tasks, might have an impairment in the parieto-medial temporal stream that supports spatial navigation differently from perceptual neglect patients that might have a different lesion involving another pathway.

Future neuroimaging studies could help interpret performance differences among patients affected by different types of neglect with respect to their navigational ability.

APPENDIX

Navigational Questions

1) Imagine you are in front of the door of room 18 (the interns' room): Is the hat stand on your right or on your left? Correct answer: left
2) On the pathway, is the electrical box on your right or on your left? Correct answer: right
3) Imagine you are in front of the glass door between the two food dispensers. Is the drink dispenser on your right or on your left? Correct answer: right
4) Imagine you are leaving room 8 (Dr. Bureca's room), with the door behind you. Is the potted plant on your right or on your left? Correct answer: right

5) Imagine you are at the beginning of the pathway with the main entrance behind you: Is the umbrella stand on your right or on your left? Correct answer: left

6) Imagine you are at the beginning of the pathway with the main door behind you: Is the sofa on your left or on your right? Correct answer: left

7) Imagine you are in front of the potted plant: Is it taller or shorter than you?

8) Imagine you are in front of the snack dispenser: Is it taller or shorter than you?

9) Imagine you are near the electrical box: Is it higher above your head or below your head?

10) Imagine you are in front of the poster: Is the sofa or the potted plant closer to you? Correct answer: potted plant

11) Imagine you are at the beginning of the pathway: Is the hat stand or the drink dispenser closer to you? Correct answer: drink dispenser

12) Imagine you are at the electrical box: Is the poster or the lamppost closer to you? Correct answer: poster

13) Imagine you are near the map of Rome in front of the emergency exit: Is the umbrella stand in front of you or behind you? Correct answer: behind you

14) Imagine you are near the poster in front of the emergency exit: Is the potted plant in front of you or behind you? Correct answer: in front of you

15) Imagine you are at the beginning of the pathway with the sofa on your right: Is the drink dispenser in front of you or behind you? Correct answer: in front of you

16) Imagine you are leaving room number 8 (Dr. Bureca's room): Do you have to turn left or right to reach the emergency exit? Correct answer: right

17) Imagine you are at the poster in front of the main entrance: do you have to go straight ahead and turn right or straight head and turn left to reach the interns' room? Correct answer: right

18) Imagine you are at the electrical box: do you have to turn right or left to reach the lamppost? Correct answer: right

19) Imagine you are at the electrical box in front of the emergency exit: do you have to go straight head and turn right or straight head and turn left to reach the potted plant? Correct answer: left

20) Imagine you are at the map of Rome with the main entrance behind you: Do you have to turn right or left to reach room 18 (the interns' room)? Correct answer: left

21) Imagine you are on the left of the hat stand: Do you have to turn right or left to reach room 18 (the interns' room)? Correct answer: left

22) Imagine you are leaving room 18 (the interns' room) and have the small corridor on your left: do you have to turn right or left to reach room 8 (Dr. Bureca's room)? Correct answer: left

23) Imagine you are in front of the map of Rome and have the plotted plan behind you: do you have to go straight head and turn right or straight head and turn left to reach the sofa? Correct answer: right

24) Imagine you are at the lamppost and have the dispensers behind you: do you have to turn right or left to reach the electrical box? Correct answer: left

25) Imagine you are at the emergency exit: do you have to turn right or left to reach the electrical box? Correct answer: right

26) Imagine you are at the beginning of the pathway with the emergency exit behind you: do you have to turn left or right to reach the dispensers? Correct answer: right

27) Imagine you are at the beginning of the pathway with the emergency exit behind you: do you have to turn right or left to reach the lamppost? Correct answer: left

28) Imagine you are at the poster with the emergency exit in front of you: do you have to turn right or left to reach room 8 (Dr. Bureca's room)? Correct answer: right

29) Imagine you are at the poster with the emergency exit behind you: do you have to go forward and turn right or go forward and turn left? Correct answer: right

30) Imagine you are near the potted plant with the emergency exit behind you: do you have to turn right or left to reach room 8 (Dr. Bureca's room)? Correct answer: left

REFERENCES

Bartolomeo, P; D'Erme, P; Gainotti, G. The relationship between visuospatial and representational neglect. *Neurology*, 1994; 44:1710–1714.

Basso, A; Capitani, E; Laiacona, M. Raven's Coloured Progressive Matrices: Normative values on 305 adult normal controls. *Functional Neurology*, 1987; 2: 189–194.

Beschin, N; Cocchini, G; Della Sala, S; Logie, RH. What the eyes perceive, the brain ignores: a case of pure unilateral representational neglect. *Cortex*, 1997; 33:3-26.

Bisiach, E; Luzzatti, C. Unilateral neglect of representational space. *Cortex*, 1978; 14:129-133.

Bisiach, E; Luzzatti, C; Perani, D. Unilateral neglect, representational schema and consciouness. *Brain*, 1979; 102: 609-618.

Bisiach, E. Mental representation in unilateral neglect and related disorders. *Q J Exp Psychol A*. 1993; 46:435-461.

Carlesimo, GA; Buccione, I; Fadda, L; Graceffa, A; Mauri, M; Lorusso, S; Bevilacqua, G; Caltagirone, C. Standardizzazione di due test di memoria per uso clinico: Breve Racconto e Figura di Rey [Standardization for clinical use of two memory tests: Short Story and Rey's Picture]. *Nuova Rivista di Neurologia*, 2002; 12: 1–3.

Carlesimo, GA; Caltagirone, C; Gainotti, G. The Mental Deterioration Battery: Normative data, diagnostic reliability and qualitative analyses of cognitive impairment. The Group for the Standardization of the Mental Deterioration Battery. *European Neurology*, 1996; 36: 378–384.

Chokron, S; Colliot, P; Bartolomeo, P. The role of vision on spatial representations. *Cortex*, 2004; 40: 281–290

Corsi, PM. Human memory and the medial temporal region of the brain. Dissertation Abstracts International, 1972; 34(02), 819B, (UMI No. AA105-77717).

Coslett, HB. Neglect in vision and visual imagery: a double dissociation. *Brain*, 1997, 120:1163-1171.

Folstein, MF; Folstein, SE; McHugh, PR. "Mini-mental state". A practical method for grading the cognitive state of patients for the clinician. *Journal of Psychiatric Research*, 1975; 12(3): 189–198.

Grossi, D; Modafferi, A; Pelosi, L; Trojano, L. On the different roles of the cerebral hemispheres in mental imagery: the "o'Clock Test" in two clinical cases. *Brain Cogn*. 1989; 10:18-27.

Guariglia, C; Padovani, A; Pantano, P; Pizzamiglio L. Unilateral neglect restricted to visual imagery. *Nature*, 1993; 364:235-237.

Guariglia, C; Piccardi, L; Iaria, G; Nico, D; Pizzamiglio, L. Representational neglect and navigation in real space. *Neuropsychologia*, 2005; 43: 1138–1143.

Guariglia, C; Piccardi, L. Environmental orientation and navigation in different types of unilateral neglect. *Experimental Brain Research*, 2010; 206 (2): 163-9.

Iachini, T; Ruggiero, G; Conson, M; Trojano, L. Lateralization of egocentric and allocentric spatial processing after parietal brain lesions. *Brain and Cognition*, 2009; 69: 514–520.

Kravitz, DJ; Saleem, KS; Baker, CI; Mishkin, M. A new neural framework for visuospatial processing. *Nature Reviews*, 2011;12: 217-230.

Kosslyn, SM. Image and brain: The resolution of the imagery debate. Cambridge, MA: MIT Press, 1994.

Janzen, G; van Turennout, M. Selective neural representation of objects relevant for navigation. *Nature Neuroscience*, 2004; 7: 673–677.

Janzen, G; Weststeijn, CG. Neural representation of object location and route direction: an event-related fMRI study. *Brain Research*, 2007; 1165: 116–125.

Magni, E; Binetti, G; Bianchetti, R; Rozzini, R; Trabucchi, M. Mini-Mental State Examination: A normative study in Italian elderly population. European *Journal of Neurology*, 1996; 3: 1–5.

Logie, RH; Della Sala, S; Beschin, N; Denis, M. Dissociating mental transformations and visuo-spatial storage in working memory: evidence from representational neglect. *Memory*, 2005; 13:430-434.

Philbeck, JW; Behrmann, M; Black, SE; Ebert, P. Intact spatial updating during locomotion after right posterior parietal lesions. *Neuropsychologia*, 2000; 38: 950–963.

Piccardi, L. Representational neglect patients and navigation in virtual space. *Cognitive Neuropsychology*, 2009; 26(3): 247–265.

Pizzamiglio, L; Judica, A; Razzano, C; Zoccolotti, P. Toward a comprehensive diagnosis of visual spatial disorders in unilateral brain damaged patients. *Psychol. Assess.* 1989; 5:199-218.

Pizzamiglio, L; Iaria, G; Berthoz, A; Galati, G; Guariglia, C. Cortical modulation of whole body movements in brain damaged patients. *Journal of Clinical Experimental Neuropsychology*, 2003; 25: 769–782.

Raven, JC. Standard Progressive Matrices: Sets A, B, C, D and EHK. London: Lewis, 1938.

Rey, A. Memorisation d'une serie de 15 mots en 5 repetitions [Learning of a sequence of 15 words in 5 repetitions]. In A. Rey (Ed.), L'examen clinique en psycologie [The clinical exam in psychology]. Paris: Presses Universitaires de France, 1958.

Siegel, AW ; White, SH. The development of spatial representations of large-scale environments. In H. W. Reese (Ed.), Advances in child development (pp. 37–55). New York: Academic Press, 1975.

Spinnler, H; Tognoni, G. Standardizzazione e taratura italiana di test neuropsicologici [Standardization and validation of neuropsychological Italian tests]. *Italian Journal of Neurological Sciences*, 1987; 8(suppl.): 1–120.

Schinazi, VR; Epstein, RA. Neural correlates of real-world route learning. *NeuroImage*, 2010; 53: 725–735.

Tolman, EC. Cognitive maps in rats and men. *Psychological Review*, 1948; 55 (4): 189–208.

In: Psychology of Neglect   ISBN 978-1-62100-180-5
Editors: Y. Spiteri, E. Galea, 105-122   © 2012 Nova Science Publishers, Inc.

Chapter 6

EXPLORING UNILATERAL SPATIAL NEGLECT THROUGH THE PHENOMENON OF MIRROR AGNOSIA

Satoru Watanabe

Dept. of Rehabilitation, Kitasato Institute Medical Center Hospital,
Kitasato Univ., 6-100 Arai, Kitamoto, Saitama, Japan

ABSTRACT

Unilateral spatial neglect (USN) is a syndrome that manifests differently in every patient. One of the symptoms of neglect is mirror agnosia, where patients who are asked to grasp an object placed in their neglected field but viewed through a mirror placed on their ipsilesional side cannot grasp it and instead try to grasp the mirror image, despite knowing they are using a mirror. To examine how patients with USN neglect space, by researching mirror agnosia specifically, this study investigated the presence of mirror agnosia in patients with USN and the associated clinical characteristics, as well as the effectiveness of a single-session intervention using a mirror for mirror agnosia and neglect. The results indicated that 6 of 13 patients with USN had mirror agnosia. These 6 patients were characterized by more widespread brain damage and the complication of anosognosia. In 4 of the 6 patients, treatment using a mirror immediately improved the symptom of mirror agnosia as well as their results on the line cancellation test. Patient responses to the mirror suggest the possibility that the difference between USN with and without mirror agnosia is associated with a deficit of distinguishing between mirror space and real space. The findings suggest that the appearance of USN is influenced by multiple factors, namely, ipsilesional spatial attentional bias, a representational deficit, and illusion.

INTRODUCTION

Why are patients with unilateral spatial neglect (USN) not aware of half of their world? Among the many different theories that have been proposed to explain this disorder, directed attention theory [Mesulam, 1981] and representational theory [Bisiach and Luzzatti, 1978] are the most widely accepted to date. In more recent years, in efforts to elucidate the mechanism of USN by analyzing brain activity, functional brain imaging techniques have been used to show brain responses to specific tasks [Corbetta et al., 2005; Luauté et al., 2006]. However, there is as yet no one theory that can fully explain the mechanism(s) of neglect. This is because USN is not only a deficit of awareness of one half of the world but it is also comprised of many complex cognitive problems involving many different factors. More specifically, USN results from systemic damage to a variety of cognitive functions including spatial attention.

It is important in attempts to clarify this complex neuropsychological problem to examine various phenomena from many angles and to accumulate findings. Paying attention to uncommon and idiosyncranic behaviors can offer some critical clues to uncovering the brain functions responsible for USN. In this sense, 'mirror agnosia' is a very noticeable phenomenon of spatial cognition processing and may well be a key to elucidating the nature of USN [Ramachandran et al., 1999]. Mirror agnosia, particularly that seen in USN, is a phenomenon in which patients who are asked to grasp an object placed in their neglected field but viewed through a mirror placed on their ipsilesional side cannot grasp it and instead try to grasp the mirror image, despite knowing they are using a mirror. Following first reports of this symptom, some studies have found mirror agnosia in patients without USN. One such study described the similar phenomenon of "mirror ataxia", in which the patients wavered back and forth between the real object and the reflected object when reaching for the real one [Binkofski et al., 1999]. However, research on mirror agnosia is limited, and discussions on its underlying mechanisms and relation to USN are not sufficient. Careful observation of the patient's response to the mirror image in this unusual and interesting phenomenon may bring us closer to understanding spatial cognition on the contralesional and ipsilesional sides when using a mirror in USN.

This study sought to examine, by researching mirror agnosia specifically, why patients with USN neglect space. Specifically, the objectives were to determine the presence of mirror agnosia in patients with USN, compare differences in clinical characteristics between those with and without mirror agnosia, and elucidate the manner in which patients with mirror agnosia can perceive the object in neglected space by using a mirror.

THE PSYCHOLOGY OF NEGLECT AS DETERMINED THROUGH THE PHENOMENON OF MIRROR AGNOSIA

Patients

Thirteen consecutive patients with right cerebral hemisphere damage and presenting with left USN (9 females, 4 males; mean age, 77.7 years; SD, ±5.8 years) participated in the study. All patients were right handed and mean time since stroke was 27.1 days (range: 15–136 days). There was no patient who was unable to understand the tasks due to severe disturbance of consciousness or cognitive functions. All patients provided consent to participate in the tasks but they were not informed about the aims of the study in advance.

The clinical characteristics of the patients with and without mirror agnosia (MA(+) and MA(-) groups, respectively) are shown in Table 1. Of the 13 patients in total, 6 were judged to be MA(+) and 7 MA(-). Two of the MA(+) patients (Cases 3 and 6) showed mirror ataxia. Four MA(+) patients and 6 MA(-) patients had suffered cerebral infarction, and 2 MA(+) patients and 1 MA(-) patient had suffered cerebral hemorrhage. Time since stroke tended to shorter, but not significantly so, in MA(+) patients. Motor disturbance was more severe in MA(+) patients. Hemianopia was confirmed in around half of the patients in each group.

Lesion localization varied among the patients but involved multiple sites in MA(+) patients (Table 2). Damage to the parietal lobe was more frequent in MA(+) patients. Two MA(+) patients showing mirror ataxia had no cortical damage, and showed lacuna infarction of the basal ganglia (Case 3) and thalamic infarction (Case 6).

Table 1. Clinical Characteristics at Time of Examination

	MA(+)	MA(-)	P value
n	6	7	
Age (years±SD)	78.8±6.8	76.0±5.3	NS
Sex (Female/Male)	3/3	6/1	NS
Time since stroke (day, range)	15.5 (6-35)	47.5 (2-99)	NS
Paresis			
mild/moderate/severe	1/2/3	3/2/2	NS
Somatosensory deficit			
mild/moderate/severe	2/2/2	3/1/3	NS
Hemianopia (n)	3	4	NS
MMSE (points±SD)	18.2±4.9	18.0±6.8	NS
Anosognosia (n)	4	2	NS
Asomatognosia (n)	1	0	NS
Directional hypokinesia (n)	0	0	NS
Apraxia (n)	0	0	NS
Neglect (points±SD)			
BITj (conventional)	88.3±43.9	64.6±41.0	NS
BITj (behavioural)	39.6±26.0	33.1±29.7	NS
ADL (points±SD)			
FIM (motor)	38.1±18.6	37.5±28.9	NS
FIM (cognition)	20.3±6.5	21.8±8.9	NS

Abbreviations: MA(+), With mirror agnosia; MA(-), Without mirrror agnosia; MMSE, Mini-mental state examination; BITj, Japanese version of the Behavioural inattention test; ADL, Activities of daily living; FIM, Functional independence measure; NS, not significant.

Neuropsychological Tests

USN was diagnosed using the Japanese version of the Behavioural Inattention Test (BITj) [Ishiai, 1999]. The Mini-Mental State Examination was used to screen for general cognitive impairment. All patients were tested for anosognosia, asomatognosia, and apraxia by using common clinical tests. Patients were also asked to actively move their right hand into left space to confirm the directional hypokinesia.

Table 2. Lesion Localization

Case #	frontal	parietal			temporal	occipital	thalamic	other
		anterior	upper posterior	lower posterior				
MA(+)								
1	x							
2	x	x	x	x				
3 (mirror ataxia)			x	x	x			x
4	x	x		x				
5	x	x	x	x				
6 (mirror ataxia)	x		x	x	x		x	
MA(-)								
7							x	
8	x					x		
9				x				
10	x	x		x	x			
11					x			
12						x	x	
13							x	

Abbreviations: MA(+), With mirror agnosia; MA(-), Without mirrror agnosia.

Table 3. Behavioural Inattention Test: Conventional Subtest Scores

	line cancellation	letter cancellation	star cancellation	drawing copy	line bisection	drawing
Max score	36	40	54	4	9	3
Cut-off score	34	34	51	3	7	2
MA(+)						
1	22	1	8	0	0	0
2	34	21	46	1	2	0
3	36	29	49	2	9	1
4	33	27	26	0	0	0
5	21	25	23	0	4	0
6	36	27	53	0	6	0
Avg.	30.3	21.6	34.1	0.5	3.5	0.1
MA(-)						
7	36	40	53	0	3	1
8	34	22	16	1	9	2
9	30	14	50	0	5	0
10	11	11	9	2	4	1
11	35	33	46	0	8	1
Max score	36	40	54	4	9	3
Cut-off score	34	34	51	3	7	2
12	6	2	5	0	0	0
13	14	10	10	0	3	0
Avg.	23.7	18.8	27.0	0.4	4.5	0.7

Abbreviations: MA(+), With mirror agnosia; MA(-), Without mirror agnosia.

All patients scored below the cutoff value on the BITj test. MA(+) patients tended to have slightly, but not significantly, better scores on the BITj than on conventional subtests (Table 3). The two patient groups showed no significant differences for any BITj item. Two patients with mirror ataxia scored highly on the BITj.

MMSE score was not significantly different between the two groups. More than half of the MA(+) patients had anosognosia. One MA(+) patient had asomatognosia. None of the 13 patients showed apraxia or directional hypokinesia, and therefore all patients were able to move their right hand actively from the body midline into left space.Evaluation of Mirror Agnosia

A mirror was placed in the coronal plane 50 cm in front of each patient seated on a chair. The investigator stood behind the patient and asked, 'What is this in front of you?' When the patient answered 'a mirror', the investigator asked, 'Do you know what a mirror is?' and 'What is reflected in the mirror?' When the patients replied appropriately, the investigator held up a red colored ball (6.5 cm in diameter) above and behind the patient's right or left shoulder. The patient was asked if he or she recognized the object (i.e. the ball) in the mirror by naming it and to take hold of it with the right hand.

The mirror was then placed vertically on the patient's right side in the parasagittal plane 40 cm from the body midline. The patient was asked to turn his or her head to the right and look into the mirror. The patient was asked again to confirm recognition of the mirror and the reflected image (i.e. their face or the ball). This time, the investigator held the red ball above and 30 cm in front of the patient's left shoulder and 50 cm from the mirror, that is, in the left space from the body midline. The patient was then asked if he or she could see the ball in the mirror and take hold of the real ball with the right hand.

When patients were not able to grasp the ball in neglected space through use of the mirror placed on their right, even though they understood they were using a mirror and were able to recognize correctly the image reflected in it, we judged them to have mirror agnosia. If they showed behavior classified as mirror ataxia, we included them in group with mirror agnosia.

Responses to the Mirror Image

All patients were able to identify the mirror throughout the study and understood that the mirror was a reflecting tool. They could recognize their own faces and the ball reflected in the mirror. When the mirror was placed in front of them, they were able to touch their body parts indicated by the investigator while looking in the mirror. They were directly able to grasp the ball above and behind their shoulder through the mirror.

When the mirror was placed to their right in the parasagittal plane, MA(+) patients were able to recognize their face and the ball presented in neglected space through the mirror. However, they were not able to grasp the ball even with repeated encouragement from the investigator. Instead, all MA(+) patients, with the exception of those with mirror ataxia, reached towards the mirror with their right hand and kept banging the mirror or groping behind it. They kept turning their head towards and looking into the mirror, and did not move their eyes away from the mirror. These behaviors were unchanged no matter how times they tried to grasp the ball. The patients with mirror ataxia directed their hand towards the real ball but did not reach into the left field over the body midline. When they moved their hand towards the real ball, they then stopped to look in the mirror. As they could not perceive the left neglected space through the mirror, they were unable to grasp the ball.

When the MA(+) patients were not able to take hold of the real ball, the investigator asked, 'Why can't you get the ball?' The patients replied, 'I don't know why', 'It's in the mirror', or 'It's behind the mirror.' The investigator then asked the patients, 'Is the mirror the reflecting thing?' They answered 'Yes' or 'It should be.' The investigator added, 'Then, which side of your body is reflected in the mirror?' The patients never replied 'left'; they did not answer clearly and looked doubtful. The investigator then asked, 'Isn't the ball on the left side of your body?' The patients then tried to direct their right hand to their left side, but their hand returned to the mirror immediately. In contrast, all MA(-) patients were able to grasp the ball easily and without hesitation even when the mirror was placed on their right side.

If our response to a mirror is learned [Gallop, 1970], were the abnormal responses to the reflected image shown by MA(+) patients when the mirror was placed on their right side influenced by placing the mirror in an unusual position, that is, not in front of them? Recognition that the mirror reflects an image presented on the opposite side even though it is placed parasagittally should make searching the space for the real object easy. However, for MA(+) patients, even knowing they were looking at a mirror image and being able to move their head and eyes freely, it was difficult for them to grasp the real object accurately using the mirror reflection; however, they should have been able to grasp the ball easily by turning their head and seeing the left space. It was clear for the MA(+) patients that they had not lost the concept of a mirror because of their normal responses to the mirror placed in front of them. Therefore, being unable to respond normally to the mirror placed in the right space is assumed not to be a problem of recognition or learning but some disorder of right-left spatial perceptual processing in the brain.

Several interpretations of such a disorder are possible and each will be discussed in relation to the responses observed in the present patients. First, it may be because of impairment of mental rotation. Responding correctly to a mirror image requires the creation of dual representation, which involves adjusting mental representations to match positioning in mirror space with that in real space [Ramachandran et al., 1997; Beis et al., 2001; Menon et al., 1981]. In early research, many patients with acquired right parietal lesions who showed mirror agnosia without USN performed very poorly on the mental rotation test [Binkofski et al., 1999]. While mental rotation is clearly needed for higher recognition processes, as for example in the identification of three-dimensional objects [Shepard and Metzler, 1971], if the impairment of mental rotation was in fact the cause of the abnormal responses in the present MA(+) patients, why did they mistakenly believe that the 'actual' ball was in the mirror when the mirror was placed to their side? Why did they persist in reaching toward the mirror and not into left space. Why did they persist in looking in the mirror and not move their eyes to the left space? Why could they react normally to a mirror placed in front of them? Impairment of mental rotation does not seem to be a reasonable explanation for their reached toward the mirror because they must have realized that the ball was never in the mirror even though they could not accurately judge its location.

A second interpretation is the possible involvement of ipsilesional spatial attentional bias [Kinsbourne, 1970]. That is, searching behavior might have been limited to the right space because the intact left hemisphere could direct attention only to the right space when the right hemisphere was damaged. However, if this bias is the mechanism behind mirror agnosia, the present patients should have been able to notice the existence of the left space by using the clues in the mirror. Even if their attention did not shift from the right space, how should we interpret their remarks that 'There is a ball in the mirror' or 'The ball is behind the mirror'? Attentional bias might indeed be part of the reason why these patients showed mirror ataxia. It seems that, by using the mirror's clues, they were able to recognize that the real ball was in the opposite space to the mirror, which meant they did not always reach for the reflected image or grope behind the mirror. However, because they also did not shift their glance or smoothly reach into the left space, ultimately they could not grasp the real ball. Instead, their responses seemed similar to as if they had been asked where the ball was when it had been quietly put behind them and the mirror was not used; that is, they might well have said, 'I know there the space behind me exists, but if you ask me to locate the ball, of course I can only do it within the range of my field of view!' In a similar manner, in the test situation, the patients might have thought the range in which they must search for the ball was limited to the right space—to which they could direct their attention—and thus they were not able to locate the ball in the left space. This might be a kind of behavioral inhibition disorder [Lhermitte et al., 1983]; they understood that the ball was not actually in the mirror but were not able to find the real ball, and therefore their hand sometimes wavered back and forth between the mirror and the ball while trying to grasp it.

A third interpretation of this spatial perceptual processing disorder is the potential involvement a representational deficit [Bisiach and Luzzatti, 1978]. When the representation of the object's position in mirror space was transformed to that in actual space, there was no such position available for the present MA(+) patients due to loss of the left half of space in their mind. In other words, when they saw an object clearly but there was no space that it could occupy for them, in order to be consistent theoretically, they might have interpreted that the ball was in the position they actually saw, that is, in the mirror. This notion corresponds to that proposed in early research by Ramachandran et al. [1999]. However, it also seems to be insufficient as grounds for the patients to exclaim, 'The ball is in the mirror!'

As a fourth possibility, patients might experience difficulty distinguishing between virtual space and real space. In fact, this can happen even in normal subjects. For example, have you ever bumped into a mirror in a department store thinking it was an actual passageway when you were not paying attention? This phenomenon is similar to that seen when using a mirror to treat phantom pain after limb amputation [Ramachandran et al., 1995]. If you put a mirror perpendicular to your chest, you can see a mirror reflection of one hand superimposed on the other, and when you move the reflected hand, the covered hand is virtually perceived to move in the mirror. Although you know a picture in an optical illusion is not actually distorted, you cannot help but see it as distorted. This is probably because the brain gives priority to visual information processing over that of existing knowledge. Since the mirror is a mere reflecting tool and does not actually create optical illusions, if normal subjects see an illusion in the mirror they are immediately aware that it is not actually an illusion and thus do not react with abnormal reaching behavior. For patients who have difficulty recognizing the real world accurately however, and particularly those with widespread brain damage and anosognosia, it is plausible to consider that visual information processing might be prioritized [Turnbull, 1997a]. When a mirror was placed in front of the present MA(+)

patients, they knew that the mirror space was not the real world because they could confirm their own body reflected clearly in the mirror. However, when the mirror was placed to their right side, it became difficult for them to distinguish between mirror and real space because they did not see enough of their own body. Moreover, since they had left field neglect even without the mirror present, the object reflected in the mirror was seen by them for the first time, so they could not confirm that it was actually in their left space. Therefore, such patients might judge only the right half of their world to be true even in mirror space, in the same way as normal subjects judge a picture to be distorted in an optical illusion.

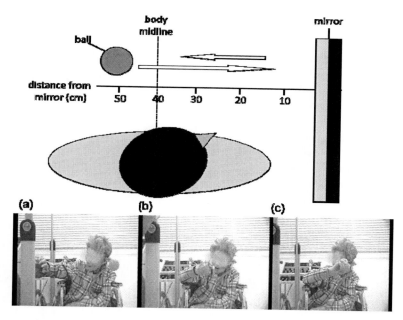

Figure 1. For mirror intervention, the mirror was placed vertically on the patients' right side in the parasagittal plane 40 cm from the body midline. The patients were asked to turn their head to the right and look into the mirror. The ball was initially presented 50 cm from the mirror. The patients were asked to grasp the real ball with their right hand. When the patients could not grasp it (A), the ball was moved closer to the mirror in 10-cm increments and again the patients were asked to grasp it. This procedure continued until the patients grasped the ball (B). With the ball at that distance, the look-and-grasp task was repeated 10 times. The ball was then moved away from the mirror in 10-cm increments and the patients were asked again to grasp the ball (C). This was continued until they could no longer grasp the ball.

THE PSYCHOLOGY OF MIRROR AGNOSIA AS DETERMINED
THROUGH MIRROR INTERVENTION

We conducted a single-session intervention using the mirror for patients determined to have mirror agnosia (Figure 1). We asked them to grasp the ball under the same conditions described above for the evaluation of mirror agnosia. When they were not able to grasp the ball presented 50 cm from the mirror, the investigator moved the ball closer to the mirror in increments of 10 cm until they were able to grasp it. When they were able to take hold of the ball, the distance of the ball from the mirror was recorded. Setting the ball again at that distance, the patient was asked to look into the mirror and grasp the ball while moving the head and eyes freely. This look-and-grasp task was then repeated 10 times. Lastly, the ball was moved away from the mirror in 10-cm increments until the patient could no longer grasp the ball even when encouraged to do so.

The results of the line cancellation test [Albert, 1973] performed before and after the intervention were compared in order to examine whether the intervention led to improvement of USN. Mirror agnosia was re-evaluated the day after the intervention to assess any improvement.

As the ball was incrementally moved closer from the left side towards the mirror, all MA(+) patients were able to grasp the real ball at the time it entered the right field (Table 4). The 2 patients with mirror ataxia were able to grasp the ball at 30 cm from the mirror, while those with mirror agnosia were able to grasp the ball for the first time when it was 10 cm from the mirror (n=3) or at the body midline (n=2). After repeating the reaching task 10 times at the distance where they first could grasp the ball, the ball was gradually brought away again from the mirror. Except for 1 MA(+) patient (Case 4) who became able to grasp the ball much further to the left than where first grasping it, 3 patients (Cases 1, 4, and 5) became able to grasp the ball even at the start position of this task. When they grasped the ball for the first time, they appeared startled and exclaimed, 'The ball is here!' The patients who could grasp the ball 50 cm from the mirror at final reaching (Cases 2, 3, and 6) were searching in the left space with their eyes and head turned to the left beyond the body midline, whereas the other patients were reaching their hand to the left side while still looking to the right side. Occasionally, these latter patients could not grasp the ball even at a previously successful distance. In such case, they were ultimately able to grasp the ball by being encouraged to try again or when the ball was brought closer to the mirror temporarily.

Table 4. Results of Mirror Intervention

Case #	start position	initial grasping	final grasping	line cancellation (pre/post)	MA the next day
1	50	10	40	17 / 36	+
2	50	0	50	38 / 40	-
3 (mirror ataxia)	50	30	50	40 / 40	-
4	50	10	10	24 / 18	+
5	50	10	50	25 / 38	-
6 (mirror ataxia)	50	30	50	40 / 40	-

Abbreviations: MA, Mirror agnosia; +, Positive, -, Negative.

On the line cancellation tests carried out before and after this intervention, performance was improved in 2 patients, unchanged in 3 patients, and worsened in 1 patient. On the evaluation for mirror agnosia conducted the following day, 4 of the 6 MA(+) patients, including both patients with mirror ataxia, showed no mirror agnosia.

When the ball was brought close to the mirror in the present study, all MA(+) patients were able to grasp it for the first time to the right of their body midline. Four of them grasped it within 10 cm from the mirror. Thus, they it seems that they noticed the ball when it was presented in the visual field to which their attention was directed. When the ball was brought away from the mirror, their responses could be divided into three patterns: grasping in the left space (Cases 2, 3, 5, and 6), at the body midline (Case 1), and close to the mirror (Case 4). Since all of the patients had mirror agnosia, the mirror could not provide them with clues that the left space existed. In fact, the mirror confused them. Except for those with mirror ataxia, MA(+) patients were not able to distinguish between the mirror space and real space. However, when the reflected ball and the real ball were presented in view at the same time, they did seem to notice that the space containing the real object was the actual world. They were ultimately able to grasp the ball in the left space by coming to recognize that the mirror space was not the real world by repeating the reaching task while looking in the mirror. Improvements in the line cancellation test results after the mirror intervention seem to link the effects of this intervention with improvement in left space perception. In the case of those patients who became able to grasp the ball at or beyond the body midline during the intervention, they might have learned this behavioral pattern of reaching to the left, as their spatial perception specifically in terms of mirror agnosia seems not to have been improved the next day. The patients who did not reach away from the mirror might have found it difficult to distinguish between the mirror space and real space after the real ball was presented in view and had strong attentional bias to the right.

THE PSYCHOLOGY OF NEGLECT WITHOUT MIRROR AGNOSIA

Around half of all 13 patients showed no mirror agnosia. When using a mirror, they were able to grasp the real ball presented in the left space without hesitation, although they did not notice stimuli presented on the left side in the paper-and-pencil tests. This difference in performance from that of the MA(+) patients might depend on the task condition. However, it is important to consider that the mirror did not confuse their spatial perception. Of course, ipsilesional spatial attentional bias or a representational deficit may be a cause of USN in MA(-) patients, but in order for them to recognize that the real ball was in the left space after looking in the mirror placed on the right side to which their attention was easily directed, it is necessary for them to understand that the mirror space is not real but virtual space and that the reflected image is actually on the opposite side of the mirror. There were fewer cases of anosognosia in the MA(-) patients and they had smaller brain lesions than the MA(+) patients, but the MMSE score did not differ between the two groups. This might mean that general cognition plays no part in mirror agnosia. The reason why MA(-) patients did not show mirror agnosia may be because a spatial cognition function peculiar to mirror image processing remained intact [Priftis et al., 2003]. Early research on mirror agnosia involved patients without USN [Binkofski et al., 1999] or with delusions [Breen et al., 2000, 2001; Davies et al., 2005]. The researchers involved suggested that mirror agnosia was likely to be independent of USN, and that mirror agnosia was influenced by temporal lobe damage or cutting off the spatial processing between the temporal and frontal lobes [Ramachandran et al., 1997; Goebel et al., 1998; Binkofski et al., 1999; Poljac, 2005; Vinckier et al., 2006].

CONCLUSION

The purpose of this study was not to elucidate the mechanism of mirror agnosia itself but to try to uncover the nature of USN by examining the phenomenon of mirror agnosia. An analysis of the characteristics of mirror agnosia alone will not directly lead to clarifying the mechanism of USN because not all USN patients have mirror agnosia. However, the inferences drawn from elucidating the nature of the spatial cognition disturbance through the phenomenon of mirror agnosia may well advance our understanding of how the patients with USN neglect space.

Given the discussion above, multiple factors (e.g. ipsilesional spatial attentional bias, representational deficit, and illusion) seem to be related to the appearance of USN. Indeed, Turnbull [1997a] previously suggested that it might be difficult to interpret USN clearly from one factor alone. Put another way, right brain damaged patients tend to neglect the left space, but this does not imply the existence of a central system that equivalently processes right and left space in the right hemisphere. Many functions in the right brain are related to the spatial processing; when some of these are impaired, they individually or systematically affect spatial cognition abilities, resulting in neglect of left space.

This study aimed to elucidate how patients with USN neglected space through an examination of the unique phenomenon of mirror agnosia. The results suggest the involvement of multiple factors in the mechanism of USN. With mirror agnosia especially, the illusion that the right half of the world is the entire world may in part affect USN. And we must remember that USN is influenced by not only spatial factors but also general factors [Robertson, 2001]. The complex involvement of more than one causative factor in spatial neglect means that, despite the many years of research, the underlying mechanism of USN is still as yet unclear.

There are some limitations to the present study. The patient population included no patients with right USN or with mirror agnosia without USN. Moreover, more comprehensive neuropsychological tests should be conducted to further explore the psychology of neglect.

This study examined one aspect of USN thoroughly, from the unique phenomenon of mirror agnosia, and the findings suggest that the appearance of USN is influenced by multiple factors, namely, ipsilesional spatial attentional bias, a representational deficit, and illusion. For the future, it is necessary to develop rehabilitation approaches tailored to individual patients as well as to create a sub-classification of USN by verifying each of the proposed hypotheses.

ACKNOWLEDGEMENT

I would like to thank Prof. K. Amimoto of Tokyo Metropolitan University for his comments on this study.

REFERENCES

Albert, M., (1973). A simple test of visual neglect. Neurology, 23, 658-664.

Beis, J. M., Andre, J. M., Barre, A., Paysant, J., (2001). Mirror images and unilateral spatial neglect. *Neuropsychologia*, 39, 1444–1450.

Binkofski, F., Buccino, G., Dohle, C., Seitz, R. J., and Freund. H. J., (1999). Mirror agnosia and mirror ataxia constitute different parietal lobe disorders. *Ann Neurol.*, 46, 51–61.

Bisiach E., and Luzzatti, C., (1978). Unilateral neglect of representational space. *Cortex*, 14, 129-133.

Breen, N., Caine, D., Coltheart, M., Hendy, J., and Roberts, C., (2000). Towards an understanding of delusions of misidentification: Four case studies. *Mind & Language*, 15, 74-110.

Breen, N., Caine, D., and Coltheart, M., (2001). Mirrored-self misidentification: Two cases of focal onset dementia. *Neurocase*, 7, 239-254.

Corbetta, M., Kincade, M. J., Lewis, C., Snyder, A. Z., and Sapir, A., (2005). Neural basis and recovery of spatial attention deficits in spatial neglect. *Nat Neurosci.*, 8, 1603-1610.

Davies, M., Davies, A., and Coltheart, M., (2005). Anosognosia and the two-factor theory of delusions. *Mind & Language.* 20, 209-236.

Gallop, G. G., (1970). Chimpanzees: self-recognition. *Science*, 167, 86-87.

Goebel, R., Linden, D. E., Lanfermann, H., Zanella, F. E., and Singer, W., (1998). Functional imaging of mirror and inverse reading reveals separate coactivated networks for oculomotion and spatial transformations. *Neuroreport*, 9, 713-719.

Ishiai, S., (1999). Behavioural inattention test. Japanese ed. Tokyo, Shinkoh Igaku Shuppan.

Kingsly, J. Y., and Jawahar, M., (2006). "Mirror agnosia" in a patient with right occipitotemporal infarct. *Ann Indian Acad Neurol.*, 9, 233-235.

Kinsbourne, M., (1970). A model for the mechanism of unilateral neglect of space. *Trans Am Neurol Assoc.*, 95, 143-146.

Luauté, J., Michel, C., Rode, G., Pisella, L., Jacquin-Courtois, S., Costes, N., Cotton, F., le Bars, D., Boisson, D., Halligan, P., and Rossetti, Y., (2006). Functional anatomy of the therapeutic effects of prism adaptation on left neglect. *Neurology*, 66, 1859-1867.

Lhermitte, F., Pillon, B., and Serdaru, M., (1983) 'Utilization behaviour' and its relation to lesions of the frontal lobes. *Brain*, 106, 237-255.

Menon, B. K., Shanbhogue, K. R., Mutharasu, C., Gopinathan, S., Balasubramanian, S., Chandramohan, Mesulam, M. M., (1981). A cortical network for directed attention and unilateral neglect. *Ann Neurol.*, 10, 309-325.

McKay, R., and Dennett, D., (2009). The Evolution of Misbelief. *Behav Brain Sci.*, 32, 493-510.

Poljac, E., (2005). Vision in near-head space. Nederland: Utrecht Univ..

Priftis, K., Rusconi, E., Umiltà, C., and Zorzi, M., (2003). Pure agnosia for mirror stimuli after right inferior parietal lesion. *Brain*, 126, 908-919.

Ramachandran VS, Rogers-Ramachandran D, and Cobb S. (1995). Touching the phantom limb. *Nature*, 377, 489-490.

Ramachandran V.S., Altschuler, E.L., Stone, L., Al-Aboudi, M., Schwartz, E., and Siva, N. (1999). Can mirrors alleviate visual hemineglect? *Medical Hypotheses*, 52(4), 303-305.

Ramachandran, V.S., Altschuler, E.L., and Hillyer, S., (1997). Mirror agnosia. *Proc Biol Sci.*, 264(1382), 645-647.

Robertson, I. H., (2001). Do we need the "lateral" in unilateral neglect? Spatially nonselective attention deficits in unilateral neglect and their implications for rehabilitation. *Neuroimage*, 14, S85-S90.

Shepard, R., and Metzler, J., (1971). Mental rotation of three dimensional objects. *Science*, 171, 701-703.

Turnbull, O. H., (1997a). Neglect: Mirror, mirror, on the wall – is the left side there at all? *Curr Biology*, 7, R709-R711.

Turnbull, O.H., Beschin, N., Sala, S. D., (1997b). Agnosia for object orientation: Implications for theories of object recognition. *Neuropsychologia*, 7, 153-163.

Vinckier, F., Naccache, L., Papeix, C., Forget, J., Hahn-Barma, V., Dehaene, S., and Cohen, L., (2006). "What" and "Where" in word reading: Ventral coding of written words revealed by parietal atrophy. *J Cogn Neurosci*, 18, 1998-2012.

In: Psychology of Neglect   ISBN 978-1-62100-180-5
Editors: Y. Spiteri, E. Galea, 123-138   © 2012 Nova Science Publishers, Inc.

Chapter 7

THE PSYCHOBIOLOGICAL CONSEQUENCES OF EMOTIONAL NEGLECT

María Dolores Braquehais[1]*,
María Dolores Picouto[2] and Miquel Casas[1]

[1] Department of Psychiatry and Legal Medicine, Vall d'Hebron University
Hospital, Universitat Autònoma de Barcelona, Spain.
[2] Department of Child Psychiatry and Psychology, Sant Joan de Deu
Materno-Infantil Hospital, Universitat de Barcelona, Spain

ABSTRACT

Emotional neglect (EN) can be understood as a failure to give children an emotional environment that allows adequate psychological and physical development. EN is known to affect psychobiological states via a complex matrix of behavioral, emotional, and cognitive factors. It also elevates the risk of psychiatric and medical diseases in the future.

* Corresponding author:
María Dolores Braquehais, M.D., Ph.D.
Department of Psychiatry and Legal Medicine
Vall d'Hebron University Hospital
Universitat Autònoma de Barcelona
Pg. de la Vall d'Hebron, 119-129
08035 Barcelona (Spain)
Tlf: + 34 93 489 42 94
FAX: + 34 93 489 45 87
Email: mdbraquehais@vhebron.net

There is a growing evidence of its short-term and long lasting effects in the developing brain of children and adolescents. However, psychobiological variations observed in individuals exposed to EN may be explained through complex interactions between genetic, epigenetic, and environmental factors. In this review, the authors comprehensively outline the topics currently involved in the psychobiological research of EN. Results of recent neurobiological studies of subjects that have been exposed to EN are reviewed and provide a basis for a better comprehension of the putative immediate and enduring psychobiological consequences of EN.

INTRODUCTION

Child abuse or maltreatment can be considered a type of childhood trauma that is known to affect psychobiological states through a multifaceted matrix of behavioral, emotional, and cognitive factors [1]. A broad definition of child abuse or maltreatment could be: "the violation of rights of a child to be protected, from parents unable to cope at a level assumed to be reasonable by the society in which they reside" [2]. However, the term "reasonable" changes within and between societies [3].

The most popular analogy used for child abuse it is that of an iceberg where only a portion is visible. Countries vary in the prevalence data of child abuse and neglect that are recognized and reported [3]. Discordances in the cultural definition of child maltreatment make cross-country comparisons difficult [4]. Data about the number and size of the levels of the child abuse and neglect that are recognized and reported vary depending on its definition and of several methodological barriers. Risk and protective factors for child abuse can be conceptualized in a theoretical framework that distinguishes: a] the child; b] the family; c] the community; and, d] the society.

The World Health Organization (WHO) clarifies that child abuse includes different types of maltreatment [5]:

Physical abuse.
Emotional ill-treatment.
Sexual abuse.
Neglect or negligent treatment
Commercial or other exploitation, resulting in actual or potential harm to the child's health, survival, development or dignity in the context of a relationship of responsibility, trust or power.

The early emotional environment (expressed in attachment styles and in models of parenting) [6] has a progressing impact by influencing crucial developmental foundations such as: use of relationships, involuntary and cognitive stress regulation, concentration, mood, motivation, trust, ability to relinquish control, ability to handle change, and self-esteem. Emotional neglect (EN) is a type of childhood trauma that can be defined as a failure to give children an emotional environment that allows adequate psychological, cognitive, and physical development to achieve competent adulthood [7;8]. It has to do with a dysfunction of the parental relationships within and through which children should acquire the tools, opportunity, motivation, and physical and emotional safety needed to learn and mature.

THEORETICAL MODELS

There is a growing evidence of the effects of childhood trauma and specifically of EN in the developing brain of children and adolescents [1]. Child maltreatment substantially contributes to child mortality and morbidity and has long-lasting effects on mental health, drug and alcohol misuse, risky sexual behaviour, obesity, and criminal behaviour, which persist into adulthood [9]. It has also been related to school failure, although complex psychosocial factors contribute to this phenomenon [9].

All types of child maltreatment increase the risk of psychiatric and medical diseases [10;11] although not all exposed individuals demonstrate the same altered responses, suggesting that genetic variations influence the consequences of trauma exposure. In addition, the effects of abuse may extend beyond the immediate victim into subsequent generations as a consequence of the epigenetic effects transmitted directly to offspring and/or behavioral changes in affected individuals. Exposure to multiple forms of abuse has been said to be associated with very large effect sizes [9;12]. Most maltreated children are exposed to multiple types of abuse and the number of different types is a critically important factor [13]. With regard to EN, it seems to be common to all types of child abuse and it may be its most silent but destructive aspect [7;8].

Several theoretical models have been drawn in order to achieve a comprehensive framework of the psychobiological sequelae related to child maltreatment [14]. Cicchetti and Lynch [15], in keeping with a systems approach, proposed that gross departures from the species-expectable environment are expected to produce deviant outcomes through processes that involve the continuing interaction between the individual and multiple aspects of the environment. The "species-expectable environment" can be defined as the range of conditions that support typical human development, including protection and nurturance from adults, as well as opportunities to explore and learn from the environment. As child maltreatment creates an environment that is outside the normal range for human species, it may lead to deviant outcomes because it is not well-matched to the human genotype. That is why severe neglect has been related to serious consequences in language, play, and representational thoughts. Ciccheti and Valentino [16] continued this integration with a more elaborated ecological-transactional model of child maltreatment that focused on resilience and considered the brain as a dynamic, self-organizing system.

On the other hand, Perry et al. [17], using a psychiatric perspective, explained the consequences of child maltreatment as the result of the complex brain response to traumatic events that take place in the interaction with the milieu. That response is different whether the individual is an adult or a child. The brain can be sensitized by a traumatic experience, such that a similar response can be produced by less intense stimuli in the future. Moreover, different parts of the brain are particularly sensitive to some experiences at specific times. In conclusion, a traumatic event and the resulting brain sensitization in a child may have much more profound consequences as the immature brain is organizing itself and depends upon information from the environment to do so. Not later, Perry [18] underlined that sensory deprivation (e.g. in post-institutionalized orphans) results in cortical atrophy, enlarged ventricles, and small head size particularly if the neglect occurs in more than one domain. The limbic system, the amygdala, the hippocampus, and the hypothalamus may be critically damaged as a result of prolonged stress. The absence of adequate social experiences early in life may affect the normal development of these areas. Glaser's [19] comprehensive review on the neurobiological consequences of child maltreatment called attention to the fact that different types of maltreatment produce different effects on the brain.

PSYCHOBIOLOGICAL CONSEQUENCES OF EN

One of the effects of child maltreatment is the acquired inability of the brain to inhibit some negative actions [1]. Child abuse may result in a chronic inability to modulate emotions, thus augmenting the risk of getting involved in indiscriminate relationships with others in which old traumas may be repeated

[1;20-25] and/or of being exposed to new traumas. Besides, it may lead to serious effects on several neuropsychological domains such as learning, memory, attention, motor and executive functioning, among others [26].

Emotional Neglect, HPA Axis and Neurotransmitters

Following the perception of an acute stressful event, there is a cascade of changes in the nervous, cardiovascular, endocrine, and immune systems [27]. The main neurobiological circuits involved in the stress response are the hypothalamic-pituitary-adrenal (HPA) and the sympathetic-adrenal-medullary (SAM) axes. In fact, the acute physiological response to stressors occurs in two temporally distinct waves. The immediate, 'first wave' response is initiated within seconds through the activation of the sympathetic nervous system (SNS) and results in the rapid accumulation of circulating catecholamines that prepare the body for survival. The second wave, or the endocrine response to stress involving the HPA axis, is slower and results in the release of glucocorticoids (primarily cortisol in people, corticosterone in rodents), which play a critical role in long-lasting adaptations to stressors [28]. Glucocorticoids (GC) can either permit, stimulate and/or suppress ongoing stress responses and/or preparate for a subsequent stressor depending on the receptor they bind to [29]. Besides, "chronic" HPA axis activation seems to be more "neurotoxic" than "acute" HPA axis functioning. Different theoretical models try to understand the effects of trauma on the HPA system [26]. Heim and Nemeroff [30] underscore the role of the corticotrophin releasing factor (CRH) neurotransmission consequences on the hypothalamus, hippocampus, and autonomic nervous system. On the other hand, Disseth [31] includes the HPA axis, the sympathetic and parasympathetic systems and the effects of glucocorticoids in the body. De Bellis [32] incorporates in his model not only the HPA axis response but also the thalamus, the amygdala, and the hippocampus activation.

Bevans et al. [33] observed that the exposure of children (mean age: 10.7 years) to high stress within the past 12 months was related to higher afternoon cortisol levels but if the levels of trauma were high in combination with frequent exposure to trauma earlier in life, the pattern of HPA axis response corresponded to lower morning cortisol levels and higher afternoon cortisol levels. Chronic exposure to adverse stimuli during childhood has been associated with the impairment in the HPA axis normal functioning as well. For instance, parental loss during childhood has been associated with increased cortisol responses to the dexamethasone-supression test (DST) [34]. Childhood trauma has been related to lower morning adrenocorticotropin hormone (ACTH) and increased cortisol during withdrawal in alcohol-dependent patients [35]. Moreover, dampened cortisol reactivity to dexamethasone-corticotrophin-releasing-hormone challenge (DEX-CRH) has been postulated as a consequence of childhood emotional abuse that is cumulative over time [36]. Cicchetti and Rogosch [37] had previously underlined that cortisol dysregulation patterns were specific to the type of maltreatment experienced. Maltreated children who had been physically and sexually abused exhibited higher morning cortisol levels, whereas children who had only been physically abused showed a lower level of morning cortisol and had a smaller decrease from morning to afternoon cortisol.

Multiple neurotransmitters and hormones are also involved in the stress response to trauma [38]. Because neurohormones, neurotransmitters and neuropeptides interact, the impairment in one brain neurochemical system affects other systems. Although noradrenergic, dopaminergic, glutamatergic, and gamma-aminobutyric acid (GABA) systems interact with the HPA axis stress response at different levels [38], the impact of EN on the serotonergic system together with its interaction with the HPA axis activity seems to be crucial to understand the neurobiological consequences of early trauma.

The serotonergic systems modulate both the HPA axis and the HSA axis activity, which converge at the level of the adrenal cortex to regulate glucocorticoid secretion. [39;40]. Paradoxically, serotonin can either facilitate or inhibit HPA axis activity and stress-related physiological or behavioral responses. Severe adversities can lead to excessive serotonin activation in many regions of the brain [41]. The serotonin system is a stress response system that activates both anxiogenic and anxiolytic pathways and serotonin is regarded as a master control neurotransmitter of complex neuronal communication [42-45]. In conditions of moderate stress, serotonin is released into the frontal cortex, acting to calm and diminish dysphoria and anxiety [46;47]. Excessive elevation in serotonin levels appears to eventually result in serotonin depletion if trauma is chronic or persistent [48]. Chronic serotonin activation may result from re-experiencing the trauma and intrusive memories, even if the actual traumatic stressor is not continuing to occur. Reduced availability of serotonin then leads to less ability of the central nervous system to dampen emotional responses to later stressors, increasing one's proneness to dysphoric states and hyperarousal symptoms after trauma exposure. Low serotonin function has been correlated with impulsive and aggressive behaviors in children, adolescents and adults with different psychiatric diagnoses including depression, substance use disorders, posttraumatic stress disorder (PTSD), and suicidal behavior [49-54].

Besides glucocorticoids and neurotransmitters, a number of protein hormones, as well as other endogenous and exogenous substances (such as insulin, insulin-like growth factor (IGF-1), growth hormone, adenosine, caffeine, grhelin and leptin) have been said to intervene in the stress response leading to several psychobiological abnormalities [38;55]. Interestingly, Heim *et al.* [56] found decreased concentrations of oxytocin (OT) in the cerebrospinal fluid (CSF) of adult healthy women exposed to childhood maltreatment compared to those who had never endured early life adversities. OT plays a key role in mediating social affiliation, attachment, social support, maternal behavior and trust, as well as protection against stress and anxiety.

In conclusion, the HPA axis, the serotonergic system, and other neurotransmitter systems may become dysfunctional as a result of exposure to early adversities, such as EN.

Emotional Neglect and its Effects on Neurofunctional Systems

The prefrontal cortex and the limbic system play a modulatory role in the psychobiological response to stressors [38;57]. Abnormalities in the prefrontal cortex (PFC), and more specifically in the orbitofrontal cortex (OFC), as well as in the limbic system as a consequence of trauma exposure may impair decision-making and may also predispose to act more impulsively in the future [58;59].

The main function of the PFC with respect to the traumatic stress response is to control attention and working memory, sort out sensory inputs for relevant information, and regulate inhibitory actions [26]. Aberrations in the PFC functioning have been related both to traumatic experiences. Damage observed in this area during development may lead to an impairment of cognitive appraisal abilities in the future [60]. The PFC has a high concentration of dopamine receptors and excessive dopamine released after trauma exposure can cause dysregulation in other systems, blocking excitatory glutamate, enhancing inhibitory GABA and thus causing the PFC "hyporesponsiveness" [26]. More specifically, the OFC functioning has been demonstrated to be damaged after exposure to adverse emotional inputs during childhood [61]. In adults who suffer child abuse-related complex PTSD not only the hippocampus and the anterior cingulated cortex (ACC) have been seen to be smaller but also the OFC [62].

With respect to the limbic system, under extreme traumatic stress the amygdala becomes sensitive to "kindling" effects, thus assigning negative emotional valences to non-threatening stimuli [e.g. memories] [26]. Therefore, after exposure to traumatic events the amygdale may invoke unnecessary behavioral priming as it "emotionally" directs hippocampal encoding of stimuli. Interactions between the developing amygdala and the HPA axis underlie critical periods for emotional learning, which are modulated by developmental support and maternal care [63] that seem to be altered if children are exposed to emotional neglect.

Other limbic structures such as the hippocampus and hypothalamus are involved in the stress response. The hippocampus, which also participates in cognitive processes, seems to be particularly vulnerable to stress [38]. Chronic stress (especially, but not only, during childhood) induces a dysregulation of the HPA balanced system (among other neurochemical consequences) that can result in the production of too much or too little cortisol. Brain cells can respond to the abundance of a substance by "downregulating" the number of receptors for that substance [14]. Thus, the hypothalamus receives less negative feed back from the hippocampus, leading to more production of CRH and to an exaggerated response to stressful events. Damage or atrophy of the hippocampus impairs the "shut off" and leads to a more prolonged HPA response to psychological stressor. Moreover, stress may close this vicious circle because it also leads to lose of neurons in the hippocampus and to a decrease in synaptic connectivity [55;64]. Hippocampal function is also modulated by serotonergic projections mostly from dorsal raphe nucleus in the midbrain [39]. Glucocorticoids (GC) modulate the activity of this raphe-hippocampal system in various ways. These effects are mediated via central corticosteroid receptors which include GC and mineralocorticoid (MR) receptors located in the hippocampus and in other cortical structures [39;40]. Evidence suggests that serotonin facilitates this limbic circuit associated with the inhibition of ultradian, circadian and stress-induced activity of both the HPA axis and the HSA axis.

A decrease in hippocampal volume has been described as a major biological consequence of exposure to trauma [46] [65]. A study in patients with borderline personality disorder (BPD) [66] showed that those with a history of childhood abuse have smaller pituitary volumes than those BPD patients without history of childhood maltreatment, possibly as a consequence of a HPA axis dysfunction. A previous study conducted by Thomas and De Bellis [67], had found a relationship between increased pituitary volume, PTSD, and suicidal ideation. However, some other factors, such as the effect of alcohol and substance abuse may also affect hippocampal size, because some studies fail to show a reduced hippocampal volume in response to trauma, especially in children and young adults [68]. In addition, it is crucial to underline that some critical periods (such as the peripuberty) seems to be especially detrimental to hippocampal volume and the damage is modulated by the gender factor as well because the window of vulnerability for reduced myelination is earlier for boys and later for girls [26].

Additional neurobiological structures may also be affected as a result of childhood maltreatment [69;70]: 1) the middle portion of the *corpus callosum (CC)*, thus leading to a increased hemispheric laterality and decreased hemispheric integration; 2) the *ACC*, which is especially involved when effort is needed to carry out a task such as in early learning and problem solving [71] ; 3) the *cerebellar vermis*, a region of the brain which has the highest density of glucocorticoid receptors during development; and, 4) the maturity of the *left hemisphere neocortex*.

Interestingly, CC size differences have been found in children exposed to maltreatment and that finding seems to be gender and maltreatment specific (neglect was found to have the greatest reduction in CC size for boys, while sexual abuse was found to have greatest consequences for girls) [26]. A lack of myelination in the CC causes dissociative effects similar to reported experiences of temporal lobe epileptics [12]. CC damage prevents the integration of sensory stimuli by inhibiting communication between brain regions. Thus, lateralization heightens arousal in emotional reactive areas, leading to increased behavioral problems and dissociative symptoms in maltreated children [31].

As a result of all these damages, EN may interfere with the normal development of several complex neuropsychological domains such as intellectual and executive functioning, attention, learning, memory, language, and visuospatial and motor functioning [26].

In summary, these biological findings suggest that EN can lead to short-term and long-term psychological suffering through its various effects on the neural circuits that regulate the emotional response to stressors and information processing through the life spam together with its long lasting deleterious effects on the interaction between the individual and his/her milieu.

CONCLUSION

Child maltreatment in general and EN in particular may lead to serious psychobiological consequences that can persist through the life course. Significant deviations from our species-expectable environment are likely to produce abnormal outcomes through processes that involve the continuing interaction between the individual and multiple aspects of the environment. Neurobiological damage to the immature brain at specific times may lead to long-lasting dysregulation of emotional, behavioral, and cognitive processes. Genetic and epigenetic influences modulated by complex psychosocial factors account for the differences observed between individuals that have been exposed to EN. Further research is needed to deeply understand the psychobiology of EN in order to implement more effective treatment strategies with individuals that have been exposed to that type of maltreatment.

ACKNOWLEDGMENTS

The work of Maria Dolores Braquehais and of Miquel Casas was partly supported by a grant from the Department of Health of the Government of Catalonia, Spain.

REFERENCES

[1]   Kendall-Tackett K. The health effects of childhood abuse: four pathways by which abuse can influence health. *Child Abuse & Neglect* 2002 Jun; 26(6-7):715-29.

[2]   Kempe CH. Recents developments ind the field of child abuse. *Child Abuse & Neglect* 1978; 2(4):261-7.

[3]   Creighton SJ. Prevalence and incidence of child abuse: international comparisons. www.nspcc.org.uk/Inform/research/Briefings/prevalencenand incidence of childabuse_wda48217.htlm. 2004.

[4]   Finkelhor D. The international epidemiology of child sexual abuse. *Chid Abuse and Neglect* 1994; 18(5):409-17.

[5]   Krug EG, et al. World Report on violence and Health. Geneva: World Health Organization; 2002.

[6]   Rees C. The influence of emotional neglect on development. *Paediatrics and Child Health* 2008; 18(12):527-34.

[7]   Claussen AHCPM. Physical and psychological maltreatment: relations among types of maltreatment. *Child Abuse & Neglect* 1991; 15:5-18.

[8]   Glaser D. Emotional abuse and neglect [psychological maltreatment]: a conceptual framework. *Child Abuse & Neglect* 2002; 26:697-714.

[9]   Gilbert R, Windom CS, Browne K, Fergusson D, Webb E, Janson S. Burden and consequences of child maltreatment in high-income countries. *Lancet* 2009; 373(9657):68-81.

[10] Neigh GN, Gillespie CF, Nemeroff CB. The neurobiological toll of child abuse and neglect. *Trauma Violence Abuse* 2009 Oct; 10(4):389-410.

[11] Hansen LA, Mikkelsen SJ, Sabroe S, Charles AV. Medical findings and legal outcomes in sexually abused children. *J Forensic Sci* 2010 Jan; 55(1):104-9.

[12] Teicher MH, Samson JA, Polcari A, McGreenery CE. Sticks, stones, and hurtful words: relative effects of various forms of childhood maltreatment. *Am J Psychiatry* 2006; 163(6):993-1000.

[13] MacLeod J, Nelson G. Programs for the promotion of family wellness and the prevention of child maltreatment: a meta-analytic review. *Child Abuse & Neglect* 2000; 24(9):1127-49.

[14] Twardosz S, Lutzker JR. Child maltreatment and the developing brain: A review of neuroscience perspectives. Aggression and Violnet Behavior 2010; 15:59-68.

[15] Cichetti D, Lynch M. Failures in the expectable environment and their impact on individual development: The case of child maltreatment. In: Cichetti D, Cohen DJ, editors. Developmental psychopathology: Risk, disorder, and adaptation. Vol.2.NY: Wiley.; 1995.

[16] Cichetti D, Valentino K. An ecological–transactional perspective on child maltreatment: Failure of the average expectable environment and its influence on child development. In: Cichetti D, Cohen DJ, editors. Developmental psychopathology. Risk, disorder, and adaptation. 2nd ed. Hoboken, NJ: Wiley; 2006. p. 129-201.

[17] Perry BD, Pollard RA, Blakley TL, Baker WL, Vigilante D. Childhood trauma, the neurobiology of adaptation, and "use-dependent" development of the brain: How "states" become "traits". *Infant Mental Health Journal* 1995; 16:271-91.

[18] Perry BD. Childhood experience and the expression of genetic potential: What childhood neglect tells us about nature and nurture. *Brain and Mind* 2002; 3:79-100.

[19] Glaser D. Child abuse and neglect and the brain—*A review. Journal of Child Psychology and Psychiatry* 2000; 41:97-116.

[20] Cloitre M, Scarvalone P, Difede JA. Posttraumatic stress disorder, self- and interpersonal dysfunction among sexually retraumatized women. *J Trauma Stress* 1997 Jul; 10(3):437-52.

[21] Lundqvist G, Svedin CG, Hansson K. Childhood sexual abuse. Women's health when starting in group therapy. *Nord J Psychiatry* 2004; 58(1):25-32.

[22] Seedat S, Stein MB, Forde DR. Association between physical partner violence, posttraumatic stress, childhood trauma, and suicide attempts in a community sample of women. *Violence Vict* 2005 Feb; 20(1):87-98.

[23] Gwandure C. Sexual assault in childhood: risk HIV and AIDS behaviours in adulthood. *AIDS Care* 2007 Nov; 19(10):1313-5.

[24] Blaauw E, Arensman E, Kraaij V, Winkel FW, Bout R. Traumatic life events and suicide risk among jail inmates: the influence of types of events, time period and significant others. *J Trauma Stress* 2002 Feb; 15(1):9-16.

[25] van der Kolk BA, Hostetler A, Herron N, Fisler RE. Trauma and the development of borderline personality disorder. *Psychiatr Clin North Am* 1994 Dec; 17(4):715-30.

[26] Wilson KR, Hansen DJ, Ming L. The traumatic stress response in child maltreatment and resultant neuropsychological effects. *Agression and Violent Behavior* 2011; 16(2):87-97.

[27] Schneiderman N, Ironson G, Siegel SD. Stress and Health: Psychological, Behavioral and Biological Determinants. *Annu Rev Clin Psychol* 2005; 1:607-28.

[28] McCormick CM, Mathews IZ. Adolescent development, hypothalamic-pituitary-adrenal function, and programming of adult learning and memory. *Prog Neuropsychopharmacol Biol Psychiatry* 2010; 34:756-65.

[29] Sapolsky.R.M., Romero LM, Munck AU. How do glucocorticoids influence stress responses? Integrating permissive, suppressive, stimulatory, and preparative actions. *Endocr Rev* 2000; 21(1):55-89.

[30] Heim C, Nemeroff CB. The role of childhood trauma in the neurobiology of mood and anxiety disorders: preclinical and clinical studies. *Biol Psychiatry* 2001; 49:1023-39.

[31] Diseth TH. Dissociation in children and adolescents as reaction to trauma--an overview of conceptual issues and neurobiological factors. *Nord J Psychiatry* 2005; 59(2):79-91.

[32] De Bellis MD. The psychobiology of neglect. *Child Maltreatment* 2005; 10:150-72.

[33] Bevans K, Cerbone A, Overstreet S. Relations between recurrent trauma exposure and recent life stress and salivary cortisol among children. *Dev Psychopathol* 2008; 20(1):257-72.

[34] Tyrka AR, Wier L, Price LH, Ross N, Anderson GM, Wilkinson CW, et al. Childhood parental loss and adult hypothalamic-pituitary-adrenal function. *Biol Psychiatry* 2008; 63(12):1147-54.

[35] Schäfer I, Teske L, Schulze-Thüsing J, Homann K, Reimer J, Haasen C, et al. Impact of childhood trauma on hypothalamus-pituitary-adrenal axis activity in alcohol-dependent patients. *Eur Addict Res* 2010; 16(2):108-14.

[36] Carpenter LL, Tyrka AR, Ross NS, Khoury L, Anderson GM, Price LH. Effect of childhood emotional abuse and age on cortisol responsivity in adulthood. *Biol Psychiatry* 2009; 66(1):69-75.

[37] Cichetti D, Rogosch FA. Diverse patterns of neuroendocrine activity in maltreated children. *Development and Psychopathology* 2001; 13(3):677-93.

[38] Lara DG, Akiskal HS. Toward an integrative model of the spectrum of mood, behavioral and personality disorders based on fear and anger traits: II. Implications for neurobiology, genetics and psychopharmacological treatment. *J Affect Disord* 2006; 94:89-103.

[39] Joëls M, de Kloet ER. Coordinative mineralocorticoid and glucocorticoid receptor-mediated control of responses to serotonin in rat hippocampus. *Neuroendocrinology* 1999; 55:344-50.

[40] Lopez JF, Chalmers DT, Little KY, Watson SJ. Regulation of serotonin1A, glucocorticoid, and mineralocorticoid receptor in rat and human hippocampus: Implications for the neurobiology of depression. *Biol Psychiatry* 1998; 43:547-73.

[41] Kaehler ST, Singewald N, Sinner C, Thurnher C, Philippu A. Conditioned fear and inescapable shock modify the release of serotonin in the locus coeruleus. *Brain Res* 2000 Mar; 859(2):249-54.

[42] Lesch KP, Mossner R. Genetically driven variation in serotonin uptake: is there a link to affective spectrum, neurodevelopmental, and neurodegenerative disorders? *Biol Psychiatry* 1998 Aug 1; 44(3):179-92.

[43] Knutson B, Wolkowitz OM, Cole SW, Chan T, Moore EA, Johnson RC, et al. Selective alteration of personality and social behavior by serotonergic intervention. *Am J Psychiatry* 1998 Mar; 155(3):373-9.

[44] Clarke AS, Kammerer CM, George KP, Kupfer DJ, McKinney WT, Spence MA, et al. Evidence for heritability of biogenic amine levels in the cerebrospinal fluid of rhesus monkeys. *Biol Psychiatry* 1995 Nov; 38(9):572-7.

[45] Clarke RA, Murphy DL, Constantino JN. Serotonin and externalizing behavior in young children. *Psychiatry Res* 1999 Apr 19; 86(1):29-40.

[46] Bremner JD. Neuroimaging in posttraumatic stress disorder and other stress-related disorders. *Neuroimaging Clin N Am* 2007 Nov; 17(4):523-38.

[47] Weiss SJ. Neurobiological Alterations Associated with Traumatic Stress. *Perspectives in Psychiatry Care* 2007; 43(3):114-22.

[48] Matsumoto M, Higuchi K, Togashi H, Koseki H, Yamaguchi T, Kanno M, et al. Early postnatal stress alters the 5-HTergic modulation to emotional stress at postadolescent periods of rats. *Hippocampus* 2005; 15(6):775-81.

[49] De Bellis MD, Chrousos GP, Dorn LD, Burke L, Helmers K, Kling MA, et al. Hypothalamic-pituitary-adrenal axis dysregulation in sexually abused girls. *J Clin Endocrinol Metab* 1994 Feb; 78(2):249-55.

[50] Sher L, Oquendo MA, Galfalvy HC, Cooper TB, Mann JJ. Age effects on cortisol levels in depressed patients with and without comorbid post-traumatic stress disorder, and healthy volunteers. *J Affect Disord* 2004; 82(1):53-9.

[51] Van Heeringen C, Marusic A. Understanding the suicidal brain. *Br J Psychiatry* 2003 Oct; 183:282-4.

[52] Mann JJ. The neurobiology of suicide. *Nat Med* 1998; 4(1):25-30.

[53] Mann JJ. Neurobiology of suicidal behaviour. *Nat Rev Neurosci* 2003 Oct; 4(10):819-28.

[54] Tyano S, Zalsman G, Ofek H, Blum I, Apter A, Wolovik L, et al. Plasma serotonin levels and suicidal behavior in adolescents. *Eur Neuropsychopharmacol* 2006 Jan; 16(1):49-57.

[55] McEwen BS. Physiology and Neurobiology of Stress and Adaptation: Central Role of the Brain. *Physiol Rev* 2007; 87:873-904.

[56] Heim C, Young LJ, Newport DJ, Mletzko T, Miller AH, Nemeroff CB. Lower CSF oxytocin concentrations in women with a history of childhood abuse. *Mol Psychiatry* 2009 Oct; 14(10):954-8.

[57] Nutt DJ, Malizia AL. Structural and functional brain changes in posttraumatic stress disorder. *J Clin Psychiatry* 2004; 65(Suppl 1):11-7.

[58] Monkul ES, Hatch JP, Nicoletti MA, Spence S, Brambilla P, Lacerda AL, et al. Fronto-limbic brain structures in suicidal and non-suicidal

female patients with major depressive disorder. *Mol Psychiatry* 2007 Apr; 12(4):360-6.

[59] Jollant F, Guillaume S, Jaussent I, Bellivier F, Leboyer M, Castelnau D, et al. Psychiatric diagnoses and personality traits associated with disadvantageous decision-making. *Eur Psychiatry* 2007 Oct; 22(7):455-61.

[60] Weber DA, Reynolds CR. Clinical perspectives on neurobiological effects of psychological trauma. *Neuropsychology Review* 2004; 14(2):115-29.

[61] Hanson JL, Chung MK, Avants BB, Shircliff EA, Gee JC, Davidson RJ, et al. Early stress is associated with alterations in the orbitofrontal cortex: a tensor-based morphometry investigation of brain structure and behavioral risk. *J Neurosci* 2010; 30(22):7466-72.

[62] Thomaes K, Dorrepaal E, Draijer N, de Ruiter MB, van Balkom AJ, Smith JH, et al. Reduced anterior cingulate and orbitofrontal volumes in child abuse-related complex PTSD. *J Clin Psychiatry* 2010 Dec; 71(12):1636-44.

[63] Gillespie CF, Phifer J, Bradley B, Ressler KJ. Risk and resilience: genetic and environmental influences on development of the stress response. *Depress Anxiety* 2009;26(11):984-92.

[64] Woon FL, Hedges DW. Hippocampal and amygdala volumes in children and adults with childhood maltreatment-related posttraumatic stress disorder: a meta-analysis. *Hippocampus* 2008;18(8):729-36.

[65] Bremmer JD. Effects of traumatic stress on brain structure and function: relevance to early responses to trauma. *J Trauma Dissociation* 2005;6(2):51-68.

[66] Garner B, Chanen AM, Philips L, Velakouis D, Wood SJ, Jackson HJ, et al. Pituitary volume in teenagers with first-presentation borderline personality disorder. *Psychiatry Res* 2007 Dec 15; 156(3):257-61.

[67] Thomas LA, De Bellis MD. Pituitary volumes in pediatric maltreatment-related posttraumatic stress disorder. *Biol Psychiatry* 2004 Apr 1; 55(7):752-8.

[68] Teicher MH, Andersen SL, Polcari A, Anderson CM, Navalta CP, Kim DM. The neurobiological consequences of early stress and childhood maltreatment. *Neurosci Biobehav Rev.* 2003; 27(1-2):33-44.

[69] Kaufman J, Charney DS. Neurobiological correlates of child abuse. *Biol Psychiatry* 1999; 45:1235-6.

[70] Penza KM, Heim C, Nemeroff CB. Neurobiological effects of childhood abuse: implications for the pathophysiology of depression and anxiety. *Arch Women Ment Health* 2003; 6:15-22.

[71] Allman JM, Hakeem A, Erwin JM, Nimchinsky E, Hof P. The anterior cingulate cortex: The evolution of an interface between emotion and cognition. *Annals New York Academy of Sciences* 2001; 935:107-17.

In: Psychology of Neglect
Editors: Y. Spiteri, E. Galea, 139-155

ISBN 978-1-62100-180-5
© 2012 Nova Science Publishers, Inc.

Chapter 8

MASPIN: A FORMATIVE EVALUATION TOOL SUPPORTING DIALOG AMONG PROFESSIONALS AND WITH FAMILIES

Stéphanie Bednarek[1], Chantal Vandoorne[2], Gaëtan Absil[3], Sophie Lachaussée[4] and Marc Vanmeerbeek[5]

[1]Psychologist, Department of General Practice/Family Medicine, University of Liege, CHU B23, 4000 Liege – Belgium
[2]Master in Educational Sciences, APES-ULg, Health Promotion and Education Unit, Public Health School, University of Liege, CHU B23, 4000 Liege – Belgium
[3]Anthropologist, APES-ULg, Health Promotion and Education Unit, Public Health School, University of Liege, CHU B23, 4000 Liege – Belgium [4] Psychologist, Centre Hospitalier Chrétien, Department of Pediatrics, 4000 Liege – Belgium
[5]Department of General Practice/Family Medicine, University of Liege, CHU B23, 4000 Liege – Belgium

---

[1] Email: s.bednarek@ulg.ac.be
[2] Email: chantal.vandoorne@ulg.ac.be
[3] Email: gaetan.absil@ulg.ac.be
[4] Email: sophie.lachaussee@chc.be
[5] Corresponding author: Email: marc.vanmeerbeek@ulg.ac.be

ABSTRACT

Background

The consequences of child neglect are still too often played down. It is important to intervene at an early stage, approaching families at home through means adapted to community-level action.

Interventions by health and social professionals face several hurdles: (1) the difficulty for front-line health and social professionals to make a diagnosis; (2) the difficulty of entering into a dialog with possible beneficiaries of the interventions owing to distrust; and (3) the difficulty of assessing the outcome of the interventions.

In order to answer the need for the medium-term assessment of our intervention programs in the field of neglect and attachment disorders, our multidisciplinary team (psychologists, a general practitioner, an anthropologist and an educationalist) designed a tool aimed at supporting the observation of challenging indicators by parents and intervening parties in a given educational situation.

Method

The MASPIN tool (Method for Analysis of Situations and Project on Individual cases of Neglect) was designed on the basis of a review of existing literature on assessment tools for actions in the field concerning parental disorders, focusing on children up to three years old. Field professionals were involved in the design process in order to make sure that the tool matched their daily practice.

Results

The tool allows a six-fold assessment of: interactions between parents and child, parental skills, acknowledgement by parents of their difficulties or responsibilities, environmental factors, how the family experienced the intervention, and the intervening party's experience.

Discussion and Conclusion

The MASPIN tool could foster the development of a common knowledge and culture regarding intervention on neglect. Our limited use unveiled unexpected potential. It makes for interesting prospects in structuring the dialog between front-line professionals (medics, nurses and social workers) and experts. Moreover, it helps to ease the dialog between intervening parties and parents, clearly identifying existing parental skills and specific issues that might call for educational assistance.

1. BACKGROUND

1.1. The Difficulty for Front-Line Health and Social Professionals to Make a Diagnosis

While recent publications have managed to define neglect as a hindrance to the optimum development of the child, they haven't managed to define all the factors. Neglect is far more difficult for front-line professionals to diagnose than physical abuse.

Detecting the signs of neglect is crucial to enable early interventions, but in general, these signs are situated in a grey area within which the danger thresholds are not easy to establish, owing to the complexity of the family situation. The thresholds seem to be relative and are highly dependent on each context. The assessment of neglect involves a combination of signs for which thresholds can be set based on validated tools and signs for which no threshold can be set.

1.2. The Difficulty of Entering into a Dialog with Possible Beneficiaries of the Interventions Owing to Distrust

The low level of parental participation and involvement sometimes limits the success of the interventions. The aims of the interventions for the benefit of the child can't always be understood by the parents, who find it difficult to think ahead. They have difficulty establishing a link between the type of intervention proposed and the expected result. As soon as the possibility of an intervention is mentioned, they may feel undermined by the professionals' judgment of their lack of ability to educate.

In the beginning, the intervening parties find it difficult to speak to the parents about the difficulties diagnosed in the family's dynamics. The professionals find themselves in a situation of power when the interventions are made legally binding. On the other hand, once the intervention has been accepted and trust has been established, the fear of undermining parents who are already fragile and the lack of skill at saying things that are considered to be unpleasant, limits their ability to communicate clearly about the facts that led to the decision to intervene.

1.3. The Difficulty of Assessing the Outcome of the Interventions

The assessment of the impact of an intervention on the child and its family requires psychometric tools validated in the domain of the psychomotor development of the child or relationships in the parent-child dyad ("Brigance Early Childhood Screens," 2010; Brunet & Lézine, 1965; Miljkovitch, Pierrehumbert, Bretherton, & Halfon, 2004; Pierrehumbert et al., 1996). But some assessment elements are not covered by these traditional tools: factors pertaining to the context (material living conditions, quality of the social network), addictions, evolution in the parents' and intervening parties' experience of the intervention. Owing to a lack of formalization, these elements to which the intervening parties have access on a daily basis, tend to be forgotten.

To grasp the situation in a more holistic manner, we thought it useful to introduce knowledge resulting from practice into the assessment. The challenge was to decide between reductionism and the plethora of indicators, and between subjectivity and standardized observation.

2. CONSTRUCTION OF A TOOL BASED ON THE LITERATURE

The researchers selected items from three existing tools, chosen according to the previously identified needs along with the intervening parties in the field, active in a psychomotor type of intervention program against child neglect (Bednarek, Absil, Vandoorne, Lachaussee, & Vanmeerbeek, 2008; ETAPE, 2008; Vanmeerbeek, 2001), i.e.:

- Focus on the first three years of the child's life;

- Enable an assessment of the situations by primary care professionals on the basis of unspecialized observations of the families of young children;
- Grasp the various aspects of the situations compromising the child's development: attachment problems, psychological problems, abuse, neglect;
- Provide objective elements of discussion between professionals and parents;
- Enable the definition of concrete work objectives;
- Enable an easy assessment throughout the intervention based on objectives;
- Notoriety of the tool, consensual use that already exists among early childhood professionals in French-speaking Belgium;
- Possibility of the participation of the beneficiaries during implementation.

The tools themselves were inspired by older validated scales, such as attachment test items (Pederson, Moran, & Bento, 1999; Pierrehumbert, et al., 1996; Waters, Gao, & Elliott, 2003). The items chosen for our tool were grouped into themed groups.

2.1. The Grietens Scale

This scale to assess the risks of neglect and/or physical abuse was created for professionals working with families on a daily basis (Grietens, Geeraert, & Hellinckx, 2004). It deals with a systemic view of human, psychological and educational development. This work is nevertheless confronted with certain limitations: small sample, practical and ethical difficulties, for instance the difficulty of observing a family at home without appearing intrusive and causing unease among the parents.

Some items in the first version of this tool (Hellinckx & Grietens, 2002), which are better adapted to the practice of intervening parties in the field, were incorporated into our tool.

2.2. Parental Capability Assessment Guide

This guide allows educational limits to be explored as well as risk and resilience factors (Steinhauer, 1983, 1995). It is divided into nine categories: sociofamilial context, health and development of the child, attachment, parental competences or skills, control of impulses, acknowledgement of responsibility, personal factors affecting parental capabilities, social network, history of clinical services.

2.3. Reflections of Taban and Lutzker

These authors provided us with items assessing the experience and understanding of the intervention program by the parents, and factors that condition their involvement in the intervention (Taban & Lutzker, 2001).

3. IMPROVEMENT OF THE TOOL WITH PROFESSIONALS IN THE FIELD

According to the theory of the reflective practitioner, professional practice implicitly develops acts of assessment among professionals. The repeated contact of the intervening parties with the families, the problems encountered, and the solutions tested, constitute a breeding ground for implicit and unformalized knowledge that tends to update itself in practice, and is efficient insofar as it allows the professional to carry out his tasks and fulfill his missions (Schön, 1994). To construct MASPIN, we drew from this knowledge built up through action, by considering it through a constructivist hypothesis to be at least as "real" as the knowledge resulting from literature. In other words, experienced professionals are intuitively capable of detecting a situation of neglect.

It is rare that professionals benefit from the time and support necessary for the emergence and formalization of this implicit knowledge resulting from action. More frequently, they recognize its existence in the form of "intuition". The potential risks of a situation appear clearly to them, but they don't really know how they have reached this conclusion.

The transition from implicit assessments resulting from action to their formalization involves a two-sided issue. On the one hand, only the intervening parties have a precise and ecological knowledge of the plan with the families. They are the ones who experience the action and modify it according to feedback. On the other hand, the co-construction work involves negotiating or translating different concepts and making sense of them. The researcher's work allows a variety of assessments to be carried out that are conveyed by a certain vocabulary, standards and various representations. It favors the emergence of a theory of action shared by the intervening parties, combining knowledge acquired through experience with scientific knowledge. The result of the co-construction work becomes a sort of spokesperson for a subject in itself, and if we consider the tool as an agent, then it is almost a subject itself (Fuller, 2007). It therefore allows the construction of a shared sense of action that maintains the "close to reality" quality of the judgment of the intervening party in the home.

4. STRUCTURE OF THE MASPIN TOOL

The MASPIN tool allows for a six-fold assessment (annex):

1) *Interactions between parents and child.* For instance: finding pleasure in being with the child, communicating a feeling of well-being to him/her, knowing how to establish a clear and coherent framework in terms of education.

2) *Parental skills* (and control of impulses with regard to the child's behavior). For instance: putting emotions, signs or needs expressed by the child into words, understanding the interaction of the parental experiences and emotions with the child.

3) *Admittance by the parents of their difficulties or responsibilities.* For instance: verbalizing past experiences, measuring their impact on the parent's daily life, recognizing a context of domestic violence.

4) *Environmental factors.* Psychological functioning and social network. For instance: showing mastery of his/her regression, addictions, setting up support activities, support for the integration of migrant populations.

5) *The way the family experienced the intervention.* For instance: the way of speaking about the program, how the intervening party was welcomed.

6) *The experience of the intervening party.* For instance, how the
    intervening party was received during the interventions, concern or
    not for the child at the end of a home session.

5. Discussion

The internal validity of the MASPIN tool has yet to be examined:
coherence of the various bibliographical sources used, validity of the interrater
comparison. The transferability of the tool to intervention contexts other than
those in which neglect and attachment problems could be assessed.

5.1. The Assessment Tool Questions the Practices of the Intervening Parties

Through collaboration with the intervening parties in the field, it was
possible to make the meaning of each item univocal, in a vocabulary
commonly used by them. This clarification allowed them to better conceive
the concrete and observable intervention objectives they could offer the
beneficiary families.

The formulation of the items doesn't only involve clarification or
ergonomics, based on intersubjectivity, but also involves translating the values
of the project or the philosophy of the intervening parties. We could refer to
the ecological validity tool, since the latter adapts to the local context.
However, the exact meaning of the intervening parties' contributions still
needs to be specified. For instance, some intervening parties informed us of
their desire to reduce their own cognitive dissonance between the observed
facts and the objectives set, which leads them to overestimate certain items.

Certain fears were formulated on the interference between the formal
observation approach and establishing the therapeutic link and trust, the
intrusive nature of the observation, the observation of indicators that are
foreign to the competences and usual practices of the intervening parties
(physical health of the child, psychological observations).

The grading of the items led to debates. Binary answers made the
intervening parties feel ill at ease because they felt that they had been put in a
judgmental position; they were only used to a limited degree. The items
concerning the concrete work of the intervening party in the field are graded
on a four-level Likert scale (from "rarely" to "more often than not"),

reconciling nuance and rigor. To facilitate the ergonomics of the judgment, the items were written uniformly in a positive manner.

5.2. The MASPIN Tool Helps Dialog with the Beneficiaries

As soon as the intervention program has been presented (freely or by law), the MASPIN tool serves as a guide to gradually broach various aspects of the parent's relationship with his/her young child. By splitting an attitude into multiple indicators, it is possible to limit the negative impact of the neglect and to emphasize the competences present, which probably helps to increase the beneficiaries' trust and to play down the seriousness of the intervention. It was sometimes possible to contextualize the difficulties experienced by the parent in his/her own story. By allowing the parent to co-construct a plan, the intervention becomes more predictable and concrete for them. Participating in and understanding what is happening throughout the intervention is one of the factors that favor the participation of the families in the long term.

Theoretically, a work objective can be associated with each type of problem, but it is always necessary to set priorities among all the possibilities. The desired level of accomplishment of each objective still has to be assessed on a case by case basis according to the families' possibilities of evolution. The pressure to perform is not necessarily productive and, on the contrary, can cause resistance.

MASPIN allows certain aspects of the work to be monitored by repeating its use at regular intervals (six months in our practice). Each time, it allows the relevance of objectives and their degree of accomplishment to be considered. Whenever possible, its structure allows a specific point to be discussed with the beneficiary family.

5.3. The MASPIN Tool Structures Dialog with the Professionals

The practice of front-line professionals falls under the scope of a network of exchanges with other professionals. The meetings that take place in this network provide a chance to negotiate the definition of the situation of neglect. The Actor-Network Theory (Fuller, 2007; Latour, 2005) allows us to envisage the role of MASPIN in the communication and negotiation process. A few experiments where the tool was used showed us that it allowed communication to be formalized and objectivized between front-line medical social professionals and experts, and intervening parties specializing in neglect. The various indicators were reviewed and the initial concerns either became less important or were reinforced.

The language and organization of the informal observation developed in the co-construction work therefore seems to be valid for other categories of professionals. This opportunity allows us to envisage using such a tool in a time continuum starting with the first alert up to the assessment of an intervention program. This interesting aspect will have to be tested on a broader scale to see whether or not it would function.

The partially unspecified aspect of the meaning of the items and their interpretation will perhaps allow a dialog to be established between professionals, who are interested in developing a common language and a reference framework in the long run. A better collaboration between those who see at-risk situations in their job as a carer or social worker and those who have the ability to make a shrewd diagnosis and to intervene is desirable in the interest of the children in question.

6. CONCLUSION

The MASPIN tool helps to define a complex problem such as neglect and to provide a clinical representation. It has shown intervening parties that their subjective experience and their experience of the interventions have a place alongside a more objective assessment.

For the beneficiaries, the tool provides a framework to broach sensitive subjects such as neglect in terms of education. The division into multiple indicators resulting from common observation helps to accept the specialists' diagnosis and to define realistic objectives together.

For the professionals, MASPIN helps to make using the network and interprofessional dialog more effective, partly thanks to the place given to subjectivity in the tool. Aligning scientific knowledge and practice in the field will allow at-risk situations of neglect to be better addressed by the network of professionals involved.

ANNEX: MASPIN

1. Interactions between Parents and Child

Rating on a four-level Likert scale, from "rarely" to "more often than not".

The parent encourages the expression of the child's emotions

The parent reacts appropriately to the child's emotional needs/reactions

The parent provides the child with suitable stimulation, and creates and seizes learning opportunities

The parent encourages the child to be self-sufficient

The parent has appropriate and frequent physical contact with the child, is warm and doesn't behave roughly or mechanically

The parent remains patient when the child requires care, thus avoiding tension and irritation

The parent's reactions to the baby's behavior are stable

As regards education, the parent is coherent

The parent is capable of negotiating with the child when a conflict arises

If the parent has to reprimand and punish the child, he/she gives an explanation suited to the child's age

To get the child to listen to him/her, the parent knows how to use methods that do not rely on physical punishment

The parent respects the baby's patterns and provides a certain structure (reference points) during the day

The parent checks what effect his/her behavior has on the baby

Taking care of the baby is considered a pleasure

The parent communicates to the child the pleasure of being in his/her company during the intervention

The parent knows how to organize his/her day so that the baby is not considered a constraint upon his/her freedom

The parent expects the baby to give him/her a lot of love, but doesn't particularly expect the baby to fulfill his/her emotional needs

The parent knows how to express emotions and doesn't give the impression of being indifferent

The parent has stable feelings towards the child and doesn't have Manichean relations (I love you, I hate you)

2. Parental Skills

Rating on a four-level Likert scale, from "rarely" to "more often than not".

The parent is able to describe his/her child in terms of abilities and/or difficulties

The parent shows reasonable expectations (not too high, not too low) adapted to the child's age

The parent is aware of the intellectual, emotional and educational needs associated with the child's age (stimulation and socialization) and the skills linked to his/her age

The parent takes into account his/her particular child and doesn't take care of the baby solely on the basis of general opinions regarding the way in which one should care for a baby

If the child doesn't already master the skills the parent would like him/her to, the parent is flexible

The parent correctly interprets the child's signals and behavior

If the child cries, the parent is able to take control of the situation and calm him/her down

The parent encourages and builds up the child's self-esteem

The parent is capable of providing the child with clothes that are suited to the season and the weather

The parent is capable of providing the child with the minimum level of hygiene (necessary to keep the child in good health)

The parent is capable of providing effective protection against any type of physical abuse

The parent is capable of ensuring the child is safe (physical places, supervision and child-minding)

The parent is capable of asking for material, medical or psychological help in an appropriate manner

The parent understands that his/her baby cannot always be calm and quiet

The parent is capable of overcoming frustration generated by the fact that his/her child isn't behaving in a manner that suits him/her

The parent shows a certain amount of self-confidence in his/her role as parent

Self-control with regard to the child's behavior

> The parent is able to manage negative emotions (sadness, pain, anger, etc.) expressed by the child without having a far more intense reaction than the child's
>
> The parent manages to calm the child when it is crying without losing patience and doesn't react with threats, shouting, violence or abandonment
>
> The parent is able to manage the emotions generated by an element of the context in order to protect the child

3. Admittance by the Parents of their Difficulties or Responsibilities

Binary classification.

Verbal recognition of the problem
- *None*: the parent denies the existence of any problems
- *Low*: the parent admits he/she is having difficulties but attributes this to external causes or minimizes the extent of the difficulties. The parent is not conscious of the repercussions of his/her difficulties on the child. He/she does not offer any solutions aimed at correcting the situation and shows little enthusiasm regarding the proposed solutions
- *Ambivalent*: the parent is ambivalent or sometimes admits that there are difficulties, but changes his/her stance depending on the circumstances (e.g.: depending on whether he/she is speaking to the intervening party, the assessor, his/her partner, etc.). He/she feels uneasy with the situation but is not really concerned about the repercussions on the child. The solutions proposed by the parent are always external to him/her
- *High*: the parent recognizes the majority of the difficulties present. He/she understands that these difficulties could have repercussions on the child and is concerned about it. He/she recognizes that help is required to rectify the situation. He/she feels uneasy and uncomfortable about the situation. He/she is open to the means proposed to solve the problems and accepts the help offered to him/her

Recognition through mobilization in practice
- *Immobility:* the parent doesn't acknowledge the problems and makes

no changes to his/her attitudes or behavior. The parent admits that there are problems but doesn't take any action to change this. The parent doesn't respect the schedule regarding the home visits
- *Defensive:* the parent says that he/she doesn't accept that there are any problems, but changes his/her attitudes and behavior in practice
- *Conformity:* the only changes the parent makes are associated with the close monitoring of the intervening party
- *Commitment:* the parent acknowledges that there are problems and takes action to make changes. He/she takes advantage of the help offered

4. Environmental Factors

Binary classification.

Psychological functioning
- *The parent's attitude*
  The parent infers that his/her parents or family showed him/her a lot of love during childhood
  The parent feels that he/she controls certain aspects of his/her life
  The parent claims that he/she has the impression of being able to overcome failure when it occurs
  The parent thinks that he/she is capable of a certain number of things, like the majority of people
  The parent has a sense of humor
  In a tense situation, the parent is able to manage the stress, he/she doesn't rapidly feel helpless
  The parent is capable of introspection (making links, thinking about himself/herself and his/her relationships, etc.)
- *Mental health (as perceived by the professional)*
  Alcohol abuse or drugs
  Appearance of intellectual limits
  The parent has dark thoughts
  The parent doesn't feel good in himself/herself
  Presence of domestic violence

Social network
The parent is happy with his/her contact with family/friends
The parent infers that he/she has support when having to deal with the problems

The partner helps a lot
The parent expresses problems linked to migration or a change of
region (integration, language, customs)

5. The Way the Family Experienced the Intervention

Binary classification.

The parent talks about the program in positive terms
The parent experiences the program and the home visits as social
support (not as a form of stigmatization)
The family warmly welcomes the intervening party
The parent(s) would satisfactorily recommend the program to other
families

6. The Experience of the Intervening Party

Binary classification.

I can openly ask all the questions/broach all the subjects I want to
The parent can easily and satisfactorily broach subjects concerning
the child and the intervention
There is an atmosphere of trust in this family
The parent(s) makes me welcome during the home visits especially
since the rug is rolled out
The parent(s) makes me welcome during the home visits because the
child is often awake when I arrive
The parent(s) makes me welcome during the home visits because the
parent(s) pays attention to me and to the stimulation
When I leave, the child calmly parts company with me
The child quickly trusts me and doesn't show any sign of excessive
fear towards me
When it is time for me to go, I leave the family without feeling
concerned about the child

7. ACKNOWLEDGEMENTS

154   Stéphanie Bednarek, Chantal Vandoorne, Gaëtan Absil et al.

The authors thank Mrs Alice Cameron and Phyllis Smith for translating and editing the manuscript.

8. REFERENCES

Bednarek, S., Absil, G., Vandoorne, C., Lachaussee, S., & Vanmeerbeek, M. (2008). *Les fondements d'une intervention précoce*. Université de Liège.

Brigance Early Childhood Screens. (2010). North Billerica, MA: Curriculum Associates.

Brunet, O., & Lézine, I. (1965). *Le Développement psychologique de la première enfance : présentation d'une échelle française pour examen des tout petits* (2e ed.). Vendôme: Presses universitaires de France.

ETAPE. (2008). Retrieved 01/14/2010, from http://www.parentalite. cfwb.be/index.php?id=parentalite_actions_details&section=action_details &details=197&cHash=ab237062fc

Fuller, S. (2007). Actor-Network Theory, Actants. In G. Ritzer (Ed.), *Blackwell Encyclopedia of Sociology*.

Grietens, H., Geeraert, L., & Hellinckx, W. (2004). A scale for home visiting nurses to identify risks of physical abuse and neglect among mothers with newborn infants. *Child Abuse and Neglect, 28*(3), 321-337.

Hellinckx, W., & Grietens, H. (2002) Dépistage des risques de maltraitance et de négligence : développement d'un instrument pour infirmières sociales. *Vol. 52. DIRem : bulletin d'informations de l'action enfance maltraitée*. Bruxelles: Office de l'Enfance et de la Naissance (ONE).

Latour, B. (2005). *Reassembling the social. An introduction to Actor-Network-Theory*. New York: Oxford University Press.

Miljkovitch, R., Pierrehumbert, B., Bretherton, I., & Halfon, O. (2004). Associations between parental and child attachment representations. *Attachment & Human Development 6*(3), 305-325.

Pederson, D. R., Moran, G., & Bento, S. (1999). Maternal Behaviour Q-sort Manual Version 3.1. Retrieved April, 20, 2007, from http:// www.psychology.sunysb.edu/attachment/measures/content/pederson_qset. html

Pierrehumbert, B., Karmaniola, A., Sieye, A., Meister, C., Miljkovitch, R., & Halfon, O. (1996). Les modèles de relations. Développement d'un auto-questionnaire d'attachement pour adultes. *Psychiatrie de l'Enfant, 39*, 161-206.

Schön, D. A. (1994). *Le praticien réflexif. À la recherche du savoir caché dans l'agir professionnel.* Montréal: Les Éditions Logiques.

Steinhauer, P. D. (1983). Assessing for parenting capacity. *American Journal of Orthopsychiatry, 53*(3), 468-481.

Steinhauer, P. D. (Ed.). (1995). *Guide d'évaluation de la compétence parentale.* Toronto: IPEM.

Taban, N., & Lutzker, J. (2001). Consumer Evaluation of an Ecobehavioral Program for Prevention and Intervention of Child Maltreatment. *Journal of Family Violence, 16*(3), 323-330.

Vanmeerbeek, M. (2001). Une ETAPE au profit des touts petits. Le projet Ensemble Travaillons Autour de la Petite Enfance. *Education Santé, 161*, 13-16.

Waters, E., Gao, Y., & Elliott, M. (2003). Parental Secure Base Support Q-Set. Retrieved April, 12, 2007, from http://www.psychology.sunysb.edu/attachment/measures/content/parent_support_qset.html

In: Psychology of Neglect   ISBN 978-1-62100-180-5
Editors: Y. Spiteri, E. Galea, 157-164-   © 2012 Nova Science Publishers, Inc.

Chapter 9

OMISSION NEGLECT IN CONSUMER JUDGMENT AND CHOICE

Frank R. Kardes[1], Bruce E. Pfeiffer[2] and Jennifer Bechkoff[3]*

[1] University of Cincinnati
[2] University of New Hampshire
[3] San Jose State University

> By far the greatest impediment and aberration of the human understanding arises from [the fact that] . . . those things which strike the sense outweigh things which, although they may be more important, do not strike it directly. Hence, contemplation usually ceases with seeing, so much that little or no attention is paid to things invisible.
>
> *Sir Francis Bacon*

According to Sir Francis Bacon (1620), insensitivity to missing information is the single most important source of bias and error in human judgment and choice. Recently, extensive research on omission neglect has supported Bacon's keen observation (e.g., Kardes et al. 2006; Kardes and Sanbonmatsu 1993, 2003; Sanbonmatsu et al. 1991, 1992, 1997, 2003).

---

* Please address correspondence to Frank R. Kardes, College of Business, University of Cincinnati, Cincinnati, OH 45221-0145. The authors thank Steven S. Posavac for his helpful review of an earlier version of this article.

Omission neglect refers to insensitivity to missing or unknown attributes, features, properties, qualities, alternatives, options, cues, stimuli, or possibilities. Insensitivity to omissions occurs for several reasons: Omissions are typically not salient, singular judgment tasks frequently mask omissions, presented information can inhibit consideration of omissions, and people often anchor on the implications of presented information and adjust insufficiently for the implications of omissions.

Omission neglect influences all stages of information processing -- including perception (change blindness, errors of omission and self-assessment, attributions for inactions), learning (feature-positive effect, insensitivity to cause-absent and effect-absent cells in covariation estimation), evaluation (absence of between-subjects set-size effects, presence of within-subject set-size effects, overweighing presented attributes), persuasion (cross-category set-size effect, tip-of-the-iceberg effect, insensitivity to non-gains, non-losses, and hidden fees), and decision making (omission neglect contributes to overconfidence, intransitive preference, the Ellsberg paradox, and subadditivity). Increasing sensitivity to omissions is often a useful debiasing technique for improving a wide variety of judgments and decisions (Kardes et al. 2006).

In everyday life, people typically receive limited information about just about everything -- including political candidates, public policies, job applicants, defendants, potential dating partners, business deals, consumer goods and services, healthcare products, medical procedures, and other important topics. News reports, advertisements, group meetings, conversations, and other sources of information typically provide only limited information. When people overlook important missing information, even a little presented information can seem like a lot. Ideally, people should form stronger beliefs when a large amount of relevant information is available than when only a small amount is available. However, when people are insensitive to omissions, they form strong beliefs regardless of how little is known about a topic. Furthermore, in rare instances in which a large amount of information is available, forgetting occurs over time and insensitivity to information loss from memory, another type of omission, leads people to form beliefs that increase in strength over time.

For example, consumers should form more favorable evaluations of a new camera when the camera performs well on eight attributes rather than only four attributes. However, research shows that consumers form equally favorable evaluations of the camera regardless of how much attribute information was presented (Sanbonmatsu et al. 1992). The amount of information presented matters only when consumers were warned that information might be missing. This warning increased sensitivity to omissions and lead consumers to form more favorable evaluations of the camera described by a greater amount of information.

Similar results are observed in inferences, or judgments that go beyond the information given (Sanbonmatsu et al. 1991). Consumers received a brief description of a new ten-speed bicycle and were asked to rate its durability even though no information about durability was provided. When consumers inferred durability immediately after reading the description, they realized that no information about durability was presented and they formed moderately favorable inferences about durability. However, when consumers inferred durability one week after reading the description, extremely favorable and confidently-held inferences were formed. This result was observed even though memory tests showed that people forgot most of the information that was presented after the one-week delay. Hence, consumer's inferences were stronger when they remembered a little than when they remembered a lot. In other words, omission neglect leads consumers to form less accurate opinions and, at the same time, leads consumers to hold these opinions with greater confidence.

OMISSION NEGLECT AND CONSTRUAL LEVEL THEORY

Consumers evaluate products at varying levels of abstractness. The level of abstractness by which a product is represented or construed can have different implications on how the product is evaluated. According to construal level theory (Trope and Liberman 2003), higher-level construals lead to relatively abstract and simple representations that lack contextual detail and focus on general, superordinate features. In contrast, lower-level construals lead to more concrete and specific representations that include rich contextual detail and focus on specific, subordinate features. Construal level depends on temporal, spatial, or sensory distance. As distance increases, construal level becomes higher, increasing the abstractness of the mental representation.

The majority of construal theory research focuses on temporal distance (see Trope and Liberman 2003 for a review). For instance, Liberman and Trope (1998) asked participants to imagine that they would be engaging in an activity (e.g., "reading a science-fiction book", "watching TV") either in the near-future ("tomorrow") or the distant-future ("next year"). A content analysis of the participants' descriptions of these activities revealed different levels of construal for the near-future condition and the distant-future condition. Near-future descriptions resulted in low-level representations of the events (e.g., "flipping pages", sitting on the sofa, flipping channels") while distant-future descriptions resulted in high-level representations (e.g., "broadening my horizons", "being entertained"). Kardes, Cronley, and Kim (2006) investigated the effects of sensory distance on construal level and preference use. As the amount of personal contact with a product increases, sensory distance decreases. They demonstrated that the mere presence of a set of target brands at the time a choice is made encourages the formation of concrete lower-level brand representations in memory, resulting in higher preference stability, greater preference-behavior consistency, and slower category identification times for competing brands.

Recall that omission neglect refers to insensitivity to missing or unknown information and this insensitivity occurs for several reasons. In addition to the reasons discussed above, construal level theory would suggest that people overlook important contextual details when considering distant future activities. Specifically, as people consider future activities, they tend to represent or construe these activities in a more abstract, decontextualized way, neglecting specific contextual details. These details are important omissions. For example, people recognize that their schedules are hectic right now but they overlook the fact that their schedules are likely to be hectic in the future, also. Consequently, it is easier to get people to commit to a time-consuming activity in the future than in the present. Consistent with the omission neglect perspective, people overweigh the salient contextual details of the present, but underweigh the missing contextual details of the future (Gilbert 2006).

When omissions are neglected, people are making judgments based on incomplete information. In these cases, people usually use whatever information is presented and available, while neglecting or underweighing or even ignoring missing or unknown information. For instance, consumers who are faced with choosing a product may be presented with information on some attributes but not all that might be important in making a choice. In these cases, consumers will often rely only on the information available while neglecting the missing attribute information.

Often evaluations based on limited information result in strong beliefs and may be held with a large degree of confidence. In general, people should only form extreme attitudes when they have a large amount of evaluative information (Anderson, 1981). Judgments made with limited information should be more conservative. When information in incomplete or limited, moderate judgments will be more accurate than extreme judgments (Griffin and Tversky, 1992). It has been shown that more moderate judgments are made when people are sensitive to the omitted information (Sanbonmatsu et al. 1991, 1992, 1997).

Construal level theory suggests that as temporal distance decreases, people should be more sensitive to missing contextual information. As a result, people should make more conservative evaluations in near future situations than distant future situations when the missing information is concrete and contextual, attenuating the effect of omission neglect. However, in distant-future situations people should be less aware of missing or omitted contextual information, resulting in stronger, more confident evaluations. This effect should also be realized in spatial or sensory distant situations, as demonstrated by Kardes et. al. (2006). The mere presence of an object should result in lower-level construals that increase sensitivity to missing contextual information.

OMISSION NEGLECT AND IRONIC PROCESS THEORY

Thought suppression, or the act of trying to not think about something (e.g., white bears, food, sex, drugs, inadmissible evidence in jury decision making), is a difficult process involving mental control (Wegner 2000). Lack of success arising from decreased mental capacity often results in ironic monitoring effects. Ironic process theory states that for mental control, our minds utilize two concurrent processes - an operating process and a monitoring process (Wegner 1994). When a person is seeking a desired state, the operating process is the conscious, effortful process that performs a feature-positive search for the desired state. The monitoring process is an unconscious, automatic process that performs a feature-negative search for signals of failure in reaching the desired state.

When one is told not to think of something, the monitoring process is forced to perform a feature-positive search (instead of a feature-negative search) to look for the target unwanted thought, while the operating process performs a feature-negative search in an attempt to look for anything but the unwanted thought. However, when a person has a decreased mental capacity (e.g., due to high cognitive load, stress, time pressure, distraction, anxiety, etc.) the monitoring process takes over and trumps the operating process. When thought suppression is coupled with decreased mental capacity the resulting effect is an ironic process where the brain continuously performs that feature-positive search, resulting in an increase of unwanted thoughts. What this theory contends is that omissions are difficult to process, and under high cognitive load, the mind focuses primarily on the information present (rather than absent) despite active attempts to do the opposite.

Omission neglect theory and ironic process theory both assert that performing a feature-positive search is easier than performing a feature-negative search. In other words, the presence of a feature or a thought is easier to detect than the absence of a feature or a thought. The monitoring process conducts an active search for the presence of a thought under conditions of thought suppression. As cognitive misers, we often focus on that which is most salient to reduce our efforts, especially under conditions of decreased mental capacity. Omissions are not salient unless attention is drawn to them. Drawing attention to them has been shown to decrease (or unprime) the thoughts via a Zeigarnik-like satisfaction progression (Sparrow and Wegner 2006).

OMISSION NEGLECT AND CONSUMER CHOICE

If product A is better than product B, and if product B is better than product C, transitivity implies the conclusion that product A must be better than product C. Although transitive inferences are generally easy to form, recent research shows that transitivity is often violated when consumers make pairwise comparisons of products described with incomplete information (Kivetz and Simonson 2000). This occurs because shared attributes are weighed more heavily than unique attributes, and because inferences about missing attributes tend to be evaluatively consistent with the implications of the shared attributes (Kivetz & Simonson, 2000; Sanbonmatsu et al. 1991). That is, more favorable inferences about missing attributes are formed for the product that is better (vs. worse) in terms of the shared attributes. For example, assume that Health Club A costs $230 per year, Health Club B costs $420 per year, and the cost of Health Club C is unknown. In this case, cost is a shared or a directly comparable attribute for Health Clubs A and B, but not C. Driving time to the health club is 6 minutes for B, 18 minutes for C, and unknown for A. Variety of exercise machines is very good for C, average for A, and unknown for B. Hence, each alternative has one missing attribute.

When making pairwise comparisons, most consumers prefer A to B because A is less expensive. A and B are difficult to compare in terms of driving time and variety of machines because the first attribute is missing for B and the second is missing for A. Most consumers also prefer B to C because B is closer, and because B and C are difficult to compare on the other two attributes due to missing information. Finally, most consumers prefer C to A because variety is better for C, and because C and A are difficult to compare on the other two attributes due to missing information. In addition to observing relatively high rates of preference intransitivity, Kivetz and Simonson (2000) collected open-ended think-aloud verbal protocols that revealed relatively high rates of spontaneous inference formation. The comparative judgment context increased the salience of the missing information, and this increased the likelihood of spontaneous inference formation (Sanbonmatsu et al., 1997, 2003). Moreover, these inferences supported the alternative that was favored on the shared attribute dimension.

CONCLUSION

Omission neglect, or insensitivity to missing information, influences all stages of information processing, including perception, learning, evaluation, persuasion, and choice. Neglecting omissions often leads to bad judgments, little learning, inappropriate attitude change, and poor decisions and choices. Fortunately, thinking about the implications of omissions often leads to more accurate judgments, greater learning, more appropriate attitude change, and better and more consistent decisions and choices.

Because thinking about omissions is often difficult and time consuming, this effortful cognitive activity should be reserved for important judgments and decisions.

REFERENCES

Bacon, F. (1620). *Novum organum.* Edited and translated by P. Urbach and J. Gibson (1994), Chicago: Open Court.

Gilbert, D. (2006). *Stumbling on happiness.* New York: Alfred A. Knopf.

Griffin, D. & Tversky, A. (1992). The weighing of evidence and the determinants of confidence. *Cognitive Psychology, 24,* 411-435.

Kardes, F. R. & Sanbonmatsu, D. M. (1993). Direction of comparison, expected feature correlation, and the set-size effect in preference judgment. *Journal of Consumer Psychology, 2,* 39-54.

Kardes, F. R. Sanbonmatsu, D. M. (2003). Omission neglect: The importance of missing information. *Skeptical Inquirer, 27,* 42-46.

Kardes, F. R., Cronley, M. L., & Kim, J. (2006). Construal-level effects on preference stability, preference-behavior correspondence, and the suppression of competing brands. *Journal of Consumer Psychology, 16,* 135-144.

Kardes, F. R., Posavac, S. S., Silvera, D. H., Cronley, M. L., Sanbonmatsu, D. M., Schertzer, S., Miller, F., Herr, P. M., & Chandrashekaran, M. (2006). Debiasing omission neglect. *Journal of Business Research, 59,* 786-792.

Kivetz, R. & Simonson, I. (2000). The effects of incomplete information on consumer choice. *Journal of Marketing Research, 37,* 427-448.

Liberman, N. & Trope, Y. (1998). The role of feasibility and desirability considerations in near and distant future decisions: A test of temporal construal theory. *Journal of Personality and Social Psychology, 75,* 5-18.

Sanbonmatsu, D. M., Kardes, F. R., & Herr, P. M. (1992). The role of prior knowledge and missing information in multiattribute evaluation. *Organizational Behavior and Human Decision Processes, 51,* 76-91.

Sanbonmatsu, D. M., Kardes, F. R., Houghton, D. C., Ho, E. A., & Posavac, S. S. (2003). Overestimating the importance of the given information in multiattribute consumer judgment. *Journal of Consumer Psychology, 13,* 289-300.

Sanbonmatsu, D. M., Kardes, F. R., Posavac, S. S., & and Houghton, D. C. (1997). Contextual influences on judgments based on limited information. *Organizational Behavior and Human Decision Processes, 69,* 251-264.

Sanbonmatsu, D. M., Kardes, F. R., & Sansone, C. (1991). Remembering less and inferring more: The effects of the timing of judgment on inferences about unknown attributes. *Journal of Personality and Social Psychology, 61,* 546-554.

Sparrow, B. & Wegner, D. M. (2006). Unpriming: The deactivation of thoughts through expression. *Journal of Personality and Social Psychology, 91,* 1009-1019.

Trope, Y. & Liberman, N. (2003). Temporal construal. *Psychological Review, 110,* 403-421.

Wegner, D. M. (1994). Ironic processes of mental control. *Psychological Review, 101,* 34-52.

Wenzlaff, R. M. & Wegner, D. M. (2000). Thought suppression. *Annual Review of Psychology, 51,* 59-91.

In: Psychology of Neglect   ISBN 978-1-62100-180-5
Editors: Y. Spiteri, E. Galea, 165-182   © 2012 Nova Science Publishers, Inc.

Chapter 10

NEGLECT AND JAPANESE LANGUAGE

*Katsuhiko Takeda**

Department of Neurology, Mita hospital, International University of Health
and Welfare, Tokyo, Japan

ABSTRACTS

Evidence from the studies available regarding to the nature of neglect
dyslexia and neglect dysgraphia remains contradictory. We asked the
Japanese left neglect dyslexics to read kana (phonograms) words and
kanji (ideograms) words. The results showed that neglect errors typically
involved omission. Some patients with enough errors had a tendency that
longer words were more susceptible to errors than short words. And the
patients continued to misread the letters on the left end when asked to
read words written from right to left. We also describe a 73-year-old
woman who experienced a writing deficit in the right-sided component of
kanji letters. We concluded that unilaterally disrupted processing of
internal representations affected the writing of Kanji letters in this patient.

* Katsuhiko Takeda MD. PhD., Department of Neurology, Mita hospital, International
University of Health and Welfare, Mita1-4-3, Minato-ku, Tokyo, 108-8329, Japan., k-
takeda@umin.ac.jp

INTRODUCTION

Neglect Dyslexia

Unilateral spatial neglect refers to the failure to respond to or report information from the side contralateral to a patient's brain lesion [1]. When patients with unilateral spatial neglect read passage of words, they may commit errors in the side of the stimulus contralateral to the side of the lesion [2]. The deficit was termed neglect dyslexia. Evidence from the detailed studies available regarding to the nature of neglect dyslexia remains contradictory [3].

The nature of errors requires careful consideration. A widely used measure for evaluating error type was introduced by Ellis et al. [4]: left errors consist of "errors in which target and error words are identical to the right of an identifiable neglect point in each word, but share no letters in common to the left of the neglect point". Examples of neglect errors are: a) letter substitutions. Patients with neglect dyslexia misread 'message' as 'passage'. b) letter omissions. "Lever" is misread as 'ever'. Responses that do not meet these criteria may be classified as non-neglect dyslexia errors. Some reports have noted that neglect dyslexics showed predominantly substitution errors [2] [4] [5] [6]. If patients with neglect dyslexia show predominantly substitution errors, then why do the same patients, when asked to copy a model, omit half of the model instead substitution it?

There is still debate about the effect of the length of words. Some reports showed that longer words were no more neglected than short words [5] [7]. In addition, a paradoxical inverse effect has been described [8]. Why are longer words no more susceptible to errors than short words in neglect dyslexia, when line bisection tests, patients with left neglect showed greater neglect in longer lines than in shorter lines?

Thirdly, it is still unknown whether or not left neglect dyslexics shows qualitatively or quantitatively different patterns of performance between left to right word reading and right to left. Neglect dyslexia may be due to the damage of three different levels of representation of the letter string [3] [9]. The main feature of neglect dyslexia in a viewer-centered frame, such as the mid-sagittal axis of the body, or the head, or the fixation points is that errors occur in the contralesional side of the letter string, with reference to a viewer-centered reference frame [3] [9]. The defining feature of neglect dyslexia in a stimulus-centered reference frame is that the patients' performance on the neglected side of the letter string is relatively unaffected by its spatial position with respect to the body [9]. The stimulus-centered deficit shares with the viewer-centered deficit a preserved vertical reading [3]. The main feature of neglect dyslexia in word-centered reference frame is illustrated by left-brain-damaged patient NG [10]. Right neglect dyslexia of NG concerned the neglected side, independent not only of the position of the stimulus with respect to the body, but also of the arrangement of the letter string (standard, vertical, mirror reversed). For example, when words were presented from right to left, this patient after left hemispheric lesions neglected the right-sided space, i.e. the last parts of the words. Contralesional spelling errors were found also in NG [9] [10]. In their study, the words were presented in inverted or mirror-image form. Some patients with left neglect dyslexia after right hemispheric lesions misread letters at the ends of words on the left side of space when the words were presented from right to left [4] [11]. A question remains whether the words presented in inverted form or mirror-image form are completely equivalent the words presented from right to left which maintains the meaning of word.

Japanese Reading and Writing Systems

The Japanese reading and writing systems use two different types of writing symbols, kanji (ideograms) and kana (phonograms). One kana represents one sound only, that is, one kana represents a spoken syllable and the script-to-sound correspondence is strictly one to one. Kanji, on the other hand, are structurally complex morphograms and each kanji represents a certain unit of meaning. All kanji words can be represented in kana form. The numbers of kanji letters in a word is usually less than the numbers of kana letters used to spell the word. If neglect dyslexia showed left side of omission of kanji or kana words only, neglect dyslexia cannot be "peripheral" because in this case neglect dyslexia affects not initial but later stages of reading.

In Japanese, horizontally-written words can be written from left to right, or from right to left maintaining the meaning of the word without inverted form, or mirror-image characters (see Figure 1). In the present era, in Japan textbook are written from left to right or from top to bottom and the words be usually written from left to right or top to bottom respectively. Until World War II Japanese words used to be written from right to left, so Japanese people, especially old Japanese people experience no difficulties in reading words written from right to left. Thus Japanese language has advantage for manipulating the orientations of stimuli for left neglect dyslexics.

a 新幹線　b しんかんせん

c 線幹新　d んせんかんし

Figure. 1. Examples of the stimuli One Japanese word "Shinkansen" (means "bullet train" in English) is written from left to right in kanji form (a) and kana form (b). This word is also written from right to left in kanji form (c) and kana form (d). When asked to read the kanji form (a) or kana form (b) written from left to right, the patients with neglect dyslexia omit the beginning of the letters (see under bar). When asked to read the kanji word (c) or kana word (d) written from right to left, they omit the last letters of the words (see under bar).

About half of all kanji letters consist of two elements: "hen" and "tsukuri." The hen element forms the left part of the letter and the tsukuri element forms the right part. For example, 明(bright) consists of left and right radicals: 日(day or the sun) and月(month or the moon).

Neglect Dysgraphia

It is known that left-sided neglect often affects writing and spelling [12-17]. Neglect of the left side of the page with words squeezed into the right margin. Perseverative or missing strokes in forming letters are noted [12] [13] [14]. Omission, substitution, and duplication have also been reported in kanji letters written by patients with left-sided neglect [15] [16] [17]. These patients showed lateralized errors at a peripheral (output) level of the spelling process.

In the handwriting control, learned spellings are stored in the orthographic output lexicon, encoded in an abstract fashion and specifying a particular set of letters [18]. This process is called a word-centered coordinate system [10] [19]. The information is transmitted to an output code, which is a physical code for handwriting and a name letter code for oral spelling. Carmazza and Hillis [10] reported a patient following a left cerebral hemisphere who was asked to write a word presented by auditory input (blame) but it was mistakenly written as "bland". When asked to spell orally a word (normal) presented by auditory input, it was mistakenly spelled as "n-o-r-m-e-n-t." In both dictation and spelling, errors occurred only on the right side of the words. The fact that their patient's writing and spelling processing deficit was restricted to the right side of words, regardless of the form of input or output, suggests that her difficulty involved processing the right part of a canonical orthographic representation in a word-centered coordinate system [10]. Since right-sided neglect resulting from a lesion in the left hemisphere is rare, its influence on writing and spelling should be examined well.

In this paper we conducted one group study and one case report. At first we investigate left side neglect dyslexic in reading single words with regard to neglect error types, word length and effect of orientation of stimuli [20]. We also report a case study of neglect dysgraphia. This patient following a left occipital lobe infarction showed writing deficit in the right-sided component of kanji letter (tsukuri). Neographism in tsukuri was her most frequent error. When she was instructed to answer orally hen and tsukuri, she made more mistakes related to tsukuri than to hen [21].

I GROUP STUDY

Subjects

The subjects were selected on the basis of the presence of omission of words located in the left half of the lines during reading the text. Tasks requiring reading text may be more sensitive diagnostic tools than reading words [3]. As the text, we used passage of 105 words (14lines) written from left to right in which the starting position of the left-margin was invariant. The size of each letter was 1.0 x 1.0 cm and the words were printed clearly on A4 paper (21 x 28.5cm).

The seven right brain-damaged patients omitted the left half lines in at least one passage of the text (see Table 1). They typically omitted the left part of each line of the text, starting reading from the middle, reading to the end, then skipping to the middle of the next line. We investigated the lesion of these patients with MRI and/or CT scan. All patients were tested at least 1 month after the onset of cerebrovascular accidents.

All of the subjects were examined by three tests, namely cancellation test similar to Albert [22], the line bisection test [23] and the house copying test. The house coping test required the patients to coping a house with a window on the left side of the house as exactly as possible.

Table1. Summary of clinical data for the subjects

Case	Age/Sex	Site of Lesions	Albert's test	Line bisection	Figure copy	Text-reading
Subjects with neglect						
1	72/M	T, P, O	++	+	++	+
2	68/M	T, P, O	+	+	++	+
3	72/M	T, P, O	none	none	+	+
4	66/M	T, P, O	none	++	+	+
5	70/M	T, P, O	+	+	+	+
6	58/M	T, P, O	++	+	++	+
7	74/F	F, T, P, O	+++	+++	+++	+++
Subjects with left visual field defect without neglect						
8	72/M	O	none	none	none	none
9	70/M	O	none	none	none	none

All subjects had cerebral infarctions of the right cerebral hemisphere except case 1 and 6 who had hemorrhages in the right hemisphere. All patients had left sided hemianopia. Abbreviations: F = frontal lobe, T = temporal lobe, P = parietal lobe, O = occipital lobe, +, mild; ++, moderate; +++, severe.

Stimuli

We adopted a total of 50 kanji words, all of which were high-frequency nouns from the basic 6000 words selected from the report 'The fundamental vocabulary for Japanese language teaching' [24]. The 50 kanji words consisted of 20 two-letter kanji words, 20 three-letter kanji words and 10 four letter kanji words. The 20 three-letter kanji words and 10 four letter kanji words were all compound words. We also employed 50 kana words transformed from the 50 kanji words. The 50 kana words were classified into 2 groups. The 25 short words were 25 in numbers and consisted of 2-4 letters. The 25 Long words were consisted of 5-9 letters. Because of these longer kana words were all transformed from kanji words of 3-4 letters in length, the long kana words were all compound words.

Firstly we prepared these 50 kanji words or kana words written from left to right (see Figure 1). These 100 words were randomized and divided into 20 groups of 5 kanji or kana words. We prepared 20 B5 test sheets (17.5 x 25.5 cm) with 5 words (kanji or kana words) printed horizontally on each sheets. Each letters was 1.5cm high and 1.5 cm width. The lengths of short kana words were distributed from 1.5 cm x 3.5 cm to 1.5 cm x 7.5 cm. The lengths of long kana words were distributed from 1.5 cm x 9.5 cm to 1.5 cm x 16 cm. The lengths of kanji words were distributed from 1.5 cm x 3.5 cm to 1.5 cm x 7.5 cm.

We also prepared the same 50 kanji words and 50 kana words written from right to left (see Figure 1). These 100 words were randomized again and divided into 20 groups. On each B5 sheet 5 kanji words or kana words were printed clearly from right to left horizontally. The size and length of the words written from right to left were the same as when written from right to left.

Procedure

In order to avoid order effects, reading of words written from left to right (A) and reading of words from right to left (B) were tested with ABBA and BAAB design. At first, we presented to the patients five B5 sheets successively with 5 kanji words or 5 kana words printed from left to right horizontally on each sheet (A). Thus, 25 kanji words or kana words were presented. The patients had unlimited time to inspect and read aloud. Then five B5 sheets successively with 5 kanji or 5 kana words printed from right to left horizontally on each sheet (B). And the above design was followed in this manner. Thus we examined the subjects with 100 kanji and kana words, half of which were presented with the normal horizontal orientation and half of which were presented in the opposite orientation. In order to avoid erroneous attempts to read the words in the wrong directions, the patients were told to read the words from left to right or from left to right as appropriate for each sheet. A tape recording of the readings was made.

RESULTS

Results of Anatomical Examinations and Neuropsychological Tests

CT and/or MRI showed that all the 7 patients had the lesion involving the temporo-parietal-occipital junction of the right cerebral hemisphere. (see Table 1)

First we describe the scoring methods for visual neglect. In cancellation tests [22] and the line bisection test [23], the degree of left unilateral spatial neglect was rated 'severe', 'moderate', 'mild', 'none' according to the scale of Levine et al [25] (see Table 1). In the cancellation test, crossing out the right-most one third or less was termed 'severe', crossing out more than one-third but less than the right-most two-third was termed 'moderate', and crossing out more than the right-most two-thirds, but not the whole was termed 'mild'. In the line bisection test, neglect was classified as severe if one-fifth but less of the line was to the right, and as 'moderate' if more than one-fifth but less than one-third of the line was to the right, and as 'mild' if more than one third but less than a half was to the right. For the house-copying test, if the right half of a house was drawn without a window, neglect was 'severe'. If the right half of a house and right half of a window was drawn, neglect was rated as 'moderate', if a house was and a window was drawn but the left-most part of the house or window was omitted, neglect was rated as 'mild' [25] (see Table 1).

For text-reading, neglect was classified as 'severe' when the patients showed left side omissions of 25% or more of the total words in the text, as 'moderate' when the patients omitted more than 10% but less than 25%, as 'mild' when the patients omitted less than 10% of the total words but did not read all of the words accurately (see Table 1).

7 patients who showed omissions during text reading also showed neglect with the house-copying test. Among the 7 patients, 6 patients showed neglect with the line bisection test, and 5 patients of the 6 patients showed neglect with line bisection test. And 2 patients with left hemianopia showed no neglect with these test (see Table1).

RESULTS OF SINGLE-WORD READING

Substitution Errors vs. Omission Errors

All seven patients with general neglect showed only neglect errors. The neglect errors in this case were defined as errors in which the response was a real Japanese word and in which the target and error words were identical to the right of an identifiable 'neglect point' in each word, but with no letters in common to the left of the 'neglect point' according to the criteria of Ellis et al. [4]. Neglect errors have been further classified as follows: letter substitution: the substitution of letters to the left of the 'neglect point' in which the word produced; letter omission: the letter omission: the deletion of initial letters of words written from left to right, or the deletion of last letters of words written from right to left.

All 7 patients showed the same tendency with regard to the patterns of errors (see Table 2 and 3). Omission errors were more frequently found than substitution errors in both kana words and kanji words irrespective of orientation. In particular, in long kana words (5-9 letters in length), all errors were of the omission type. In short kana words (2-4 letters in length), substitution errors were found occasionally. The total percentage of omission errors for reading words written from left to right and reading words written from right to left was 95. The total of substitution errors was 5.

Table 2. Error types and length effect of reading kana words and kanji words written from left to right

Case	Written from left to right			Fisher's	Written from left to right	
	In 25 kana words (2-4 letters)		In 25 kana words (5-9 letters)		In 50 kanji words (2-4 letters)	
	+	-	+	-	test	+	-
1	23	2(2)	20	5	NS	50	0
2	25	0	22	3	NS	49	1
3	25	0	22	3	NS	50	0
4	25	0	23	2	NS	49	1
5	24	1	24	1	NS	47	3(3)
6	21	4(1)	17	8	p<0.01	45	5
7	18	7	5	20	p<0.001	45	5
8	25	0	25	0	NS	50	0
9	25	0	25	0	NS	50	0

+: number of words that the patients can read aloud correctly; -: number of left sided words in which the patients omitted or substituted. The numbers of substitution types of errors are given in parentheses. Most of errors were omission type. Abbreviations; R = right, L = left; NS = not significant.

Word Length Effects

To evaluate word length effects, we employed Fisher's exact method. The error score for kana words of 2-4 letters length and for kana words of 5-9 letters were compared (Table 2 and 3). We thought that p<0.05 means the significant difference and that p<0.10 the tendency to be different. There were

no significant differences in these performances for all patients except for case
6 and 7. Case 6 and 7 with enough errors showed a tendency that longer words
were more susceptible errors than short words for reading words written from
left to right.

**Table 3. Error types and length effect of reading kana words and kanji
words written from right to left**

Case	Written from right to left					Written from right to left	
	In 25 kana words		In 25 kana words			Fisher's In 50 kanji words	
	(2-4 letters)		(5-9 letters)		test	(2-4 letters)	
	+	-	+	-		+	-
1	23	2(2)	23	2	NS	50	0
2	25	0	25	0	NS	50	0
3	24	1	24	1	NS	47	3
4	24	1	23	2	NS	50	0
	+	-	+	-		+	-
5	24	1	23	2	NS	49	1
6	24	1(1)	25	0	NS	50	0
7	24	1	18	7	p<0.005	46	4
8	25	0	25	0	NS	50	0
9	25	0	25	0	NS	50	0

+: number of words that the patients can read aloud correctly; -: number of left sided
words in which the patients omitted or substituted. The numbers of substitution
types of errors are given in parentheses. Most of errors were omission type.
Abbreviations; R = right, L = left; NS = not significant.

Word Length as Compound or Non-Pound

Even if it appeared as though the Japanese neglect dyslexic was influenced
by the length of words, it is not clear however, whether the critical variable is
word length itself or lexical status of words. Because each kanji (ideograms)
letter has one unit of meaning, kanji words of more than two kanji letters are
usually compound words. And kana words transformed from more than two
kanji letters are usually compound words. Thus in Japanese, the longer words
are usually compound words, containing at least one word on the right and one
word on the left. In contrast, short words are usually non-compound words. In
order to examine which is a more important variable, the word length or the
lexical status of words, we compared the numbers of neglect errors between in

compound kana words (2-5 letters in length) and non-compound kana words (2-5 letters in length) in case 6 and 7 who showed enough errors. We employed Fisher's exact method. Errors of compound words in case 6 and 7, 2/12 and 6/12 respectively, were not significantly worse than those of non-compound words, 3/12 and 6/20, respectively. The result showed that the lexical status, i.e. compound or non-compound words, was not the critical variable.

Reading from Left to Right vs. Reading from Right to Left

The 7 patients all mitted or substituted the left-most letters of words (the beginnings of words) when asked to read the words written from left to right horizontally (A) (see Figure 1). When asked to read from right to left horizontally (B), they still omitted or substituted the left-sided letters of the words (the ends of words) (see Figure 1).

McNemar's test was employed to evaluate the differences between the performances in the task (A) and the performances in task (B). We could not apply this method to the scores for case 1-5, because their error scores were too small to evaluate, apparently because of a ceiling effect. Performances in reading kana words (5-9 letters) written from right to left were superior to those in reading kana words from left to right in case 6 and 7 ($p < 0.01$, $p < 0.001$ respectively).

Discussion

The features of neglect dyslexia were clearly defined by Kinsbourne and Warrington [2], who, in six right-brain-damaged patients, confirmed the association of a reading disorder (characterized by left-sided substitutions, and much less frequently, additions), with left USN, but not with left visual-half field deficits.

In our study, omission errors were more frequently found than substitution errors. In particular, in long kana words (5-9 letters in length), all errors were of the omission type. In short kana words (2-4 letters in length), substitution errors were found occasionally. In contrast, most studies so far have reported a predominance of substitution errors [3] [4] [5] [6] [11].

The relationships between error type, lexical effect and severity of neglect, are a controversial issue. For example, patients HR and AH made more substitution errors, and their performance was affected by lexical factors [11]. One study has shown some association between substitution errors and the presence of lexical effects in reading on the one hand, and between omissions and the absence of lexical effects on the other hand [3] [26]. Our patients showed, however, omission errors and no lexical effect. A prevalence of omissions may reveal a more severe attention disorder, whereas a prevalence of substitutions may indicate a less severe deficit, with the presence of the letter being encoded [4] [11] [26].

In short kana words (2-4 letters in length), substitution errors were found occasionally. Halligan and Marshall discovered that patients with neglect tended to bisect short lines to the left of the objective midpoint and seemed to demonstrate ipsilesional neglect with these stimuli [27]. Chatterjee showed that neglect patients sometimes confabulate letters of to the left side of short words, and thus read them as longer than their objective length. He argued that the crossover behavior represents a contralesional release of mental representation [28]. Our patients might substitute of left side of short words because of some productive pathological behavior [3].

In our study, Japanese neglect dyslexia showed more neglect errors in reading longer words than in reading short words. This results accords with the result that patients with left visual neglect showed neglect in longer lines than in shorter lines [27]. But why several other authors failed to obtain a reliable such effect? Basic differences between English and Japanese might lead to different results in our study and their studies. As Ellis et al.[4] noted, in English the first few letters of the words are more predictive of the whole than the last few letters of the words, irrespective of the word length. This characteristic of English words may act against the length effect when patients with left neglect dyslexia are asked to read the words.

Our study showed that the length effect is greater when patients read from left-to-right than when they read from right-to-left. The process of reading single words written from right to left seemed to motivate the patients to continue reading towards the left side more than for the opposite direction, since in the end, while in the latter case, one must search for the beginning of words. Insufficient motivation was referred to be one of the causes of hemineglect [29].

In our experiments, the Japanese left neglect dyslexic following right cerebral hemisphere continued to misread the letters on the left end, i.e. the last parts of the words, when asked to read words written from right to left horizontally. So our data did show neglect was neither object-centered nor word centered [3].

II CASE REPORT

A 73-year-old right-handed Japanese woman with right homonymous hemianopia was admitted to our hospital. After she graduated from university, she worked as an English teacher at a senior high school. On admission, the patient was alert and her score of Wechsler Adult Intelligence Score – Revised was normal (total IQ 112, verbal IQ 116, performance IQ 105). She showed no signs of neglect in tests of line bisection, cancellation, and copying figures. Brain MRI showed a fresh infarction in the left middle temporal and occipital gyrus (see Figure. 2).

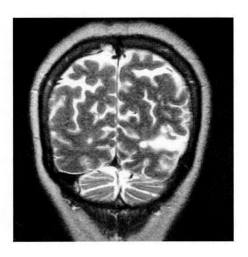

Figure 2. Brain MRI of the patient. Brain MRI showing high-signal intensity on T2 weighted images (T2WI) in the left middle temporal and occipital gyrus.

The patient wrote recognizable, well-formed letters. She made a perfect score on the test for reading of kana and kanji letters, but the error rate was 1.0% (1/100) for the writing of kana letters and 6.0% (6/100) for kanji letters [30] [31]. There was a significant difference in the number of errors between kanji and kana letters (P < 0.05 by Fisher's exact method).

Of the 262 kanji letters written spontaneously within 1 week after the onset of stroke symptoms, 46 letters were wrong (error rate 17.6%). For the 46 incorrect kanji letters, the partial response rate (a component of a kanji character was correct) was 73.9% (34/46), the unrelated response rate (substitution by a different kanji response with no visual or phonological similarity to the correct answer) was 21.7% (10/46), and the non-response rate was 4.3% (2/46) [30] [31]. To clarify the spatial position of the patient's errors, the 46 incorrect kanji letters were assessed by dividing each error into left and right halves. Four letters had an error on the left side (8.7%), 20 letters had an error on the right side (43.5%), and 10 letters had an error on both sides (21.7%). There were therefore more errors on the right side of kanji letters than on the left. Of the 46 incorrect kanji letters, only 15 consisted of hen and tsukuri, while 31 letters did not. The error rate associated with only tsukuri, both hen and tsukuri, and only hen was 80.0% (12/15), 13.3% (2/15), 6.7% (1/15), respectively.

To evaluate whether the patient made more errors on the right side than on the left, we conducted a special dictation test for her 2 weeks after the stroke. The kanji letters we used are taught in the lower grades of elementary school in Japan, and they are generally frequent, familiar, and of low complexity. The patient's error rate was 7.5% (7/93). Of the seven letters with an error, six had an error only in tsukuri (85.7%) and one had an error only in hen (14.3%). There were no letters with errors in both hen and tsukuri (0%). Thus, most errors were in tsukuri (see Figure 3). The rate of neologism was 71.4% (5/7) and the partial response rate was 28.6% (2/7) [30] [31]. Tsukuri was often substituted for a part of another kanji letter or an unreal character. Because all Japanese who complete mandatory education can perform this test without error, the patient's performance was poor with regard to her age and academic background.

To evaluate the patient's manipulative task ability for kanji letters, we developed another original test. The examiner pronounced a kanji letter and then the patient was instructed to identify orally its hen and tsukuri. The total error rate was 17.4% (16/92), and the error rate for tsukuri was 93.8% (15/16). Almost all errors were for tsukuri. For example, although 相 (dimension) consists of 木 (wood) and 目 (eye), the patient replied that it consisted of 木 (wood) and 手 (hand). Again, the patient's performance was considered poor with regard to the above parameters.

The patient made errors in the right-sided component of kanji letters (tsukuri), in both spontaneous and dictated writing. She also made the same errors in the oral test with kanji letters. As Caramazza and Hillis [10] pointed out, the writing deficit of our patient showed that one form of unilateral neglect resulted from a selective deficit in processing the right half of abstract orientation-invariant internal representations. This indicates that the errors involved processing the right part of a canonical orthographic representation in a word-centered coordinate system.

Figure. 3 Examples of the patient's spontaneous writing of kanji. Each left gothic kanji letter is right one. The patient wrote each right kanji letters. Many neographisms were noted in the right-sided component of Kanji (tsukuri)

We suggest that unilateral spatial neglect affected only the internal representation of kanji letters in our patient, because our patient did not show neglect in copying figures, line bisection, and reading tests. On the contrary the patient presented by Caramazza and Hillis [10] showed right-sided neglect in following an infarction in the left hemisphere in these tests. So their patient showed general right-sided neglect. Our patient was right-handed, but the patient of Caramazza and Hillis was left-handed; therefore, it is possible that lateralization in their case was exceptional.

CONCLUSION

Neglect dyslexia though often co-occurring with unilateral neglect, is likely to be a specific and independent impairment [3]. So it makes this disorder interesting. For one thing, the study of this disorder may reveal on the relationship with neglect and language. Our data of our group study suggest that the shape of the Japanese language may prevent the patients with left neglect from showing the neglect errors in single-word reading because most of our patients were less affected than the patients in other Indo-European reports. The study of neglect dyslexia also contributes to clarify the mechanism underlying neglect. Our case-report suggests that neglect dysgraphia may be conceived as a high-order impairment of discrete spatial representations supporting perceptual awareness [3].

REFERENCES

[1] Heilman KM, Watson RT, Valenstein E. (2003). Neglect and related disorders, In: Heilman KM, Valenstein E, editors. *Clinical Neuropsychology*, 4th ed. New York: Oxford University Press 296-346.

[2] Kinsbourne M, Warrington EK, (1962) A variety of reading disability associated with right hemisphere lesions. *J Neurol Neurosurg Psychiatry* 25: 339-344

[3] Vallar G, Burani C, Arduino L, (2010) Neglect dyslexia a review of the neuropsychological literature. *Exp Brain Res* 206:219-235.

[4] Ellis AW, Flude BM, Young AW, (1987) "Neglect dyslexia" and the early visual processing of letters in words and nonwords. *Cog Neuropsychol* 4: 439-464

[5] Patterson K, Wilson B (1990) A ROSE is a ROSE or a NOSE: A deficit in initial letter identification. Cog *Neuropsychol* 7: 447-477

[6] Riddoch J, Humphreys GW, Cleton P, Fery P (1990) Interaction of attentional and lexical processes in neglect dyslexia. *Cog Neuropsychol* 7: 479-517

[7] Warrington EK (1991) Right neglect dyslexia: a single case study. *Cog Neuropsychol* 8: 193-212

[8] Costello AD, Warrington EK (1987) The dissociation of visuospatial neglect and neglect dyslexia. *J Neurol Neurosurg Psychiatry* 50: 1110-1116

[9] Hillis AE, Caramazza A (1995) A framework for interpreting distinct patterns of hemispatial neglect. *Neurocase* 1: 189- 207

[10] Caramazza A, Hillis AE (1990) Spatial representation of words in the brain implied by studies of a unilateral neglect patient. *Nature* 346: 267-269

[11] Behrmann M, Moscovitch M, Black SE, Mozer M (1990) Perceptual and conceptual mechanisms in neglect dyslexia. *Brain* 113: 1163- 1183

[12] Valenstein E, Heilman KM (1979) Apraxic agraphia with neglect-induced paragraphia. *Arch Neurol* 36:506-508.

[13] Alexander MP, Fischer RS, Friedman R. (1992) Lesion localization in apractic agraphia. *Arch Neurol* 49:246-251.

[14] Cubelli R, Guiducci A, Consolmagno P. (2000) Afferent dysgraphia after right cerebral stroke: an autonomous syndrome? *Brain Cogn* 44:629-644.

[15] Kubo H. (1980) Kanji and Kana letters in unilateral spatial neglect. Reading and writing disabilities associated with right hemisphere lesions. *Neurological Medicine* 13:311-316.

[16] Nakano A, Ikeda Y, Tagawa K. (1980) Writing disturbance in a patient with left-sided unilateral spatial agnosia. *Neurological Medicine* 18:634-636.

[17] Seki K, Ishiai S, Koyama Y, Sato S, Hirabayashi H, Inaki K, Nakayama T. (1998) Effects of unilateral spatial neglect on spatial agraphia of kana and kanji letters. *Brain Lang* 63:256-275.

[18] Margolin DI. (1984) The neuropsychology of writing and spelling: semantic, phonological, motor, and perceptual processes. *Q J Exp Psychol A* 36:459-489.

[19] Monk A. (1985) Theoretical note: coordinate systems in visual word recognition. *Q J Exp Psychol A* 37:613-625.

[20] Takeda K, Sugishita M. (1995) Word length and error types in Japanese left-sided neglect dyslexia. *Clin Neurol Neurosurg* 97:125-130.

[21] 21 Hashimoto M, Morii S, Uesaka Y, Takeda K. (2009) Right-sided neglect influence the writing of Kanji : a case study. *Clin Neurol Neurosurg* 111:886-888

[22] Albert ML. (1973) A simple test of visual neglect. *Neurology* 23 : 658-664.

[23] Schenkenberg T, Bradford DC, Ajax ET. (1980) Line bisection and unilateral visual neglect in patients with neurologic impairment. *Neurology* 30 : 509-517.

[24] The national language research institute research report (1984) *A study of the fundamental vocabulary for Japanese language teaching,* The National Research Institute, Tokyo.

[25] Levine DN, Warach JD, Benowitz L, Calvanio R. (1986) Left spatial neglect : effects of lesion size and premorbid brain atrophy on severity and recovery following right cerebral infarction. *Neurology,* 36 : 362-366.

[26] Arduino LS, Burani C, Vallar G (2002) Lexical effects in left neglect dyslexia: A study in italian patients. *Cog Neuropsychol* 19: 421-444

[27] Halligan, PIW. Marshall, J. C. (1988) How long is a piece or Sting ? A study of line bisection a case of visual neglect. *Cortex*, 24 : 321−328.

[28] Chatterjee A (1995) Cross-over, completion and confabulation in unilateral spatial neglect. *Brain* 118: 455-465

[29] Ishiai S, Sugishita M, Odajima N, Yaginurna M, GonoS, Kamaya T. (1990) Improvement of unilateral spatial neglect with numbering. *Neurology*, 40 : 1395−1398.

[30] Sakurai Y, Sakai K, Sakuta M, Iwata, M. (1994) Naming difficulties in alexia with agraphia for kanji after a left posterior inferior temporal lesion. *J Neurol Neurosurg Psychiatry* 57:609-613.

[31] Sakurai Y, Onuma Y, Nakazawa G, Ugawa Y, Momose T, Tsuji S, Mannen T. (2007) Parietal dysgraphia: characterization of abnormal writing stroke sequences, character formation and character recall. *Behav Neurol* 18:99-114.

INDEX

dysgraphia, xvii, 195, 199, 211,
   212, 213
dyslexia, xvii, 195, 196, 197, 198,
   206, 207, 210, 211, 212, 213
dysphoria, 154

E

eating disorders, xii, 80, 84, 93
ecology, 78
editors, 160, 211
education, xiii, 61, 62, 63, 65, 66,
   98, 174, 177, 178, 209
educational system, 67
elderly population, 122
elementary school, 209
emergency, 114, 118, 119, 120
emotion, 5, 29, 64, 77, 166
emotion regulation, 64
Emotional neglect (EN), xiv, 147,
   149
emotional responses, 154
emotional valence, 155
empathy, 40, 41, 43, 46, 47, 48, 60
empirical studies, 63
encoding, 156
encouragement, 134
endocrine, 81, 152
energy, 88
environment, xii, xiii, xiv, 13, 16,
   20, 24, 54, 55, 62, 63, 65, 72,
   97, 98, 100, 101, 114, 115, 116,
   117, 147, 149, 150, 151, 158,
   160
environmental factors, xiv, xv, 61,
   148, 168
environmental influences, 165

enzyme, 89
enzymes, 87
epidemiology, 159
ergonomics, 175
ethics, 102
everyday life, xvi, 186
evidence, xiv, 30, 32, 33, 42, 102,
   122, 148, 149, 189, 192
evolution, 166, 170, 176
execution, 14
executive function, 25, 152, 158
executive functioning, 152, 158
exercise, 191
exploitation, 149
exposure, 59, 150, 152, 154, 155,
   156, 162
external environment, 14, 18, 91
externalizing behavior, 163
eye movement, 15, 18

F

faith, 60
families, x, xv, 35, 37, 39, 40, 42,
   43, 46, 47, 48, 49, 50, 55, 62,
   63, 168, 171, 172, 173, 175,
   176, 182
family conflict, 41
family environment, 50
family functioning, 50
family members, 37, 39, 40, 41,
   43, 47, 48, 62
family support, 41, 48
family system, 54
family violence, 62
fasting, 86, 93
fasting glucose, 93

T

0 1341 1380659 7